Why Do You Need This New Edition?

9 good reasons why you should buy this new edition of *Affecting Change!*

1. A new section, "Your Time Is Now," has been added throughout the chapters to demonstrate the interconnectedness of advocacy and social work values.

2. New vignettes have been added from advocates throughout the field.

3. In Chapter 3, the section on the George W. Bush presidency has been completely revised.

4. Chapter 3 also includes a new section on the Obama campaign and presidency.

5. Chapter 4 has been updated with new information regarding social workers' level of involvement in the policy field.

6. Chapter 8 contains completely revised sections on the roles that technology, newspapers, and radio play in social work.

7. Chapter 10, features a completely revised section on targeting as an essential part of voter contact.

8. Chapter 10 also includes a new section on political action committees.

9. In Chapter 12, the section "Just Say No" has been completely revised.

PEARSON

Affecting Change

Social Workers in the Political Arena

SEVENTH EDITION

Karen S. Haynes

California State University San Marcos

James S. Mickelson

California State University San Marcos

Allyn & Bacon

Boston   Columbus   Indianapolis   New York   San Francisco   Upper Saddle River
Amsterdam   Cape Town   Dubai   London   Madrid   Milan   Munich   Paris   Montreal   Toronto
Delhi   Mexico City   Sao Paulo   Sydney   Hong Kong   Seoul   Singapore   Taipei   Tokyo

Executive Editor: *Ashley Dodge*
Editorial Assistant: *Carly Czech*
Senior Marketing Manager: *Wendy Albert*
Marketing Assistant: *Kyle VanNatter*
Production Editor: *Karen Mason*
Editorial Production Service: *Suganya Karuppasamy/GGS Higher Education Resources,*
  A division of PreMedia Global, Inc.
Manufacturing Buyer: *Debbie Rossi*
Cover Administrator: *Joel Gendron*
Editorial Production and Composition Service: *GGS Higher Education Resources,*
  A division of PreMedia Global, Inc.

Library of Congress Cataloging-in-Publication Data
Haynes, Karen S.
    Affecting change : social workers in the political arena / Karen S. Haynes,
James S. Mickelson. — 7th ed.
        p. cm.
    Includes bibliographical references and index.
    ISBN-13: 978-0-205-76368-9 (alk. paper)
    ISBN-10: 0-205-76368-5 (alk. paper)
  1. Social workers—United States—Political activity.   2. United States—Social policy.
I. Mickelson, James S.   II. Title.
    HV40.8.U6H39 2010
    322.4088'36130973—dc22   2009038223

10 9 8 7 6 5 4 3 2 1—RRD-VA—13 12 11 10 09

Allyn & Bacon
is an imprint of

www.pearsonhighered.com

ISBN-10:   0-205-76368-5
ISBN-13: 978-0-205-76368-9

To those social workers
who dare to enter
the political arena and
translate their ideas and ideals
into actions for the greater good

Contents

Foreword

Affecting Change: Social Workers in the Political Arena, Seventh Edition, is a pragmatic guide that outlines, step by step, how social workers can become agents of change.

This book is just what social workers need to become effective political advocates. This edition of *Affecting Change* offers practical self-help tools to help social workers influence public policy.

The authors, Karen Haynes and Jim Mickelson, look at politics through the eyes of social workers as they offer practical political skills for BSW and MSW students.

But *Affecting Change* is not only for students. This book gives social workers a step-by-step guide to using their professional skills to influence social policy. It shows how the skills of social workers are also the skills of effective lobbyists or elected officials. The examples, assignments, and suggested readings both enhance social workers' skills and demonstrate the importance of social workers' participation in the political arena.

Affecting Change is a practical guidebook to becoming a political advocate. It is as helpful to those who are working with clients on a daily basis as it is to those who wish to seek elected office, including in the United States Senate.

Social workers will return again and again to this book throughout their careers. It provides technical information, such as a glossary of terms. And it provides encouragement and motivation to social workers across the United States who have already stepped forward to make a difference.

In the twenty-first century, we face a time of complex problems. The United States is experiencing a time of great change. There are doomsayers professing the end of an era, but I believe that we are entering a time of great opportunity for every American. I encourage all social workers to join in the political arena to help make this a time of prosperity for our nation.

We must join together to decide what kind of nation we want to be. We must ask ourselves, as a nation: Who are we? Where are we going? How do we get there? I challenge social workers to join in this nation's political debate to help create a shared national vision to make the next century a prosperous time for America. I challenge social workers to help meet the demands of this century—to educate our workforce, to help create an opportunity structure for our future, and to restore character and value in this society.

We need a national vision to create good jobs and give help to those who work hard, play by the rules, and practice self-help. We need to create a new state of mind that—as Americans—we can solve our nation's problems together. These problems all call out for the leadership skills of social workers to help guide us into the future through political activity.

My own experiences as a social worker, as a community activist, as a member of Congress, and as a U.S. senator convince me that it is possible to beat city hall and then help lead it on a better course.

Barbara A. Mikulski, MSW
U.S. Senator, D-Maryland

Preface

We take the request to write a seventh edition of *Affecting Change: Social Workers in the Political Arena* as a positive sign. Throughout this new edition, we note our hope that the relatively recent increase in social work political activity generated during the 2008 presidential campaign and election will continue. In fact, it is that hope that makes us end this edition with the adamant chapter heading, "Your Time Is Now." We do not want advocacy to be left only to the advocates; we want professionals, current and future ones, to see its compatibility to social work values as an impetus to enter the political arena. We hope that advocacy becomes the central mission of our professional association, a mandated standard for all social work education and practice, and a daily part of every social worker's experience. We certainly do not dispute that some social workers have taken an active part in social reform during the previous century, and we know it would be naïve to suggest that individual social workers have not engaged in a variety of political activities. However, throughout more than seventy-five years of formalized social work education in the United States, the curriculum has not consistently included political content, strategies for political intervention, and related skills. Accreditation standards for graduate and undergraduate social work programs have only recently directed such course content and coverage.

Furthermore, many have pointed out that the drive toward specialization and professionalization in social work may be one of the factors responsible for the lack of interest in (or even antagonism to) social action. In either case, lack of knowledge and training in the strategies and techniques fundamental to effective social change intervention must be rectified. A commitment to social change without the means to achieve it is futile. We hope that this book will help to eliminate gaps in student's knowledge and skill.

We are pleased that *Affecting Change* continues to be adopted and read, but we remain somewhat disheartened that more than twenty-five years since we had the idea and thirty years since we individually became angry at the profession for its dispassionate, objective, and apolitical stance, there is still a great need for this kind of message. However, the past three decades have not been positive ones for our clients or for our profession, and so we continue to make *Affecting Change* a call to action. Our intention from the beginning has been to make it a practical guide to developing skills within the political arena, serving as a justification for those activities. We never intended it to be a primary text or a history text; we never intended it to be highly theoretical but rather extremely practical, "starting where the student is." Our intention is not simply to describe political action skills and political processes but also to pave the way for integrating recognized political skills within traditional social work skills, thereby creating an effective and viable advocacy model.

Although it seems evident that social workers are the logical professional group to defend and support human service programs, such support has seldom been forthcoming from either individual social workers or social work organizations. Even today, some practitioners and educators question whether social workers should be politically trained at all. Those who do support political training of social workers are left with the questions of how, by whom, where, and for what particular political positions they should be trained.

There are many more arguments, along with the aforementioned, for including political content in the curriculum of social work schools and departments. There are also distinct advantages to having politically knowledgeable and active graduates. The most obvious advantage is the accumulated potential for creating progressive social policy to deal with unmet needs, to resolve social problems, or to ameliorate unjust or inequitable conditions in society. Another is the ability to amass political strength for promoting and protecting professional standards for human service personnel.

Finally, because the majority of social work programs are publicly funded, a politically effective profession can be a positive influence on human service funding during the budget allocation process. Although this point may appear self-serving, one should remember that unless agencies have sufficient funds to hire professionally trained social workers, human services will be poorly delivered.

There are several ways in which social work education can interject political skills, experiences, and activities into the curriculum without shifting its emphasis. The first prescription for social work education at any level would be to include a political action course in the policy sequence: Rather than teaching the subject descriptively and historically, policy skills for affecting change would be taught. We believe that generalist field placements, at both the BSW and MSW levels, should require inclusion of some political skill development. A logical extension for some graduate programs would be the creation of specializations in political social work.

Once again this edition includes new scenarios and quotes from social workers in the political arena. Once again changing technology and the changed political climate have provided us with areas to update and revise. Throughout the book, we have also updated references and data, as well as incorporating the helpful suggestions of reviewers.

Given that we intended this book to be a secondary text for several different courses, we have decided to continue to suggest where and how it might be used. We envision that it can be used for both BSW and MSW programs, in an introductory course, a history course, a policy course, or a practice course. Therefore, it would be possible (although, we admit, highly unlikely) for a student to purchase this book and read sections of it for several courses.

If used for an introductory course, we suggest that Chapters 2, 3, 4, and 6 would be the most instructive: Students begin with the values of social work versus the values of politics, then continue with a brief history of advocacy, a debate about social reform versus individual treatment, and an explanation of the practitioner's influence on policy. If the textbook is used to complement a history course, Chapters 3, 4, and 12 would frame the historical debate, provide a brief history of advocacy, and suggest ways to begin advocacy efforts.

The text is probably most useful for policy and macro-level courses. For policy courses, Chapters 1 through 7 and 9 would have the greatest applicability. Once again, a brief history of advocacy and framing the debate would be pertinent to a policy course (Chapters 3 and 4). Values and models are also extremely important content in policy courses (Chapters 2 and 5). Chapter 6, which discusses the practitioner's influence on policy, and Chapters 7 and 9, which cover lobbying and monitoring the bureaucracy, present material that is rarely covered in traditional policy textbooks. For practice courses, Chapters 1 through 4 set the stage, and Chapters 6 through 11 discuss the specific roles and skills for political activism.

Chapters are short and user-friendly, with examples and case illustrations. They include assignments and suggested readings for the instructor or student who wants to augment the basics provided here. Given our adamant belief that "all social work is political," in this edition, we have accordingly renamed the "Assignments" sections in each chapter to reflect that they help students build skills for all social work practice.

Content

Chapter 1, "All Social Work Is Political," presents the basic arguments to which the later chapters provide the tools of advocacy. Chapter 2, "Social Work Values versus Politics," illustrates the compatibility of social work values with political action. Chapter 3, "The Emergence of a Social Work Polity," provides a brief history of social work political action so that readers will appreciate the origins of political advocacy. Chapter 4, "The Debate," follows the history and values of social work, including the current debate about the profession's mission and advocacy within that mission. Chapter 5, "Policy Models for Political Advocacy," examines several models that provide guidelines for examining policy and suggest interventive strategies appropriate to each model.

The way in which a practitioner's daily activities can culminate in significant input to the political process is discussed in Chapter 6, "The Practitioner's Influence on Policy." Both traditional and very new methods of lobbying are presented in Chapter 7, "Influence through Lobbying." Additional practical information on the use of technology appears in Chapter 8, "Tools to Influence and Organize Others." Chapter 9, "Monitoring the Bureaucracy," reviews methods for following implementation of and subsequent adherence to legislative intent. Chapter 10, "The Campaign," presents an overview of campaigning to enable the social worker to assist in the election process. Chapter 11, "Social Workers as Politicians," includes the results of a new national survey of social workers who hold elected offices; the chapter also provides reflections and advice on this role. Chapter 12, "Your Time is Now!" provides both a summary and some pointers for getting started.

Suggested assignments of varying degrees of difficulty, complexity, and involvement appear at the end of most chapters to help the student develop political skills. Because this book may be used as a supplementary text, suggested readings are provided for further exploration of a given area. The Glossary of Legislative Terms is included to assist social workers with political jargon.

Acknowledgments

No book is solely the product of its authors, nor is a book, even a seventh edition, the product of single experiences. *Affecting Change* is now the cumulative product of almost three decades of dialogue, interaction with students, collegial challenge, and political observation.

This seventh edition was written because events and changes in the profession and in the political times mandated an update; because it continues to remain, we believe, a unique contribution to our professional literature; and because our belief that social workers must be a positive force for change has not wavered.

We thank Senator Barbara Mikulski for being such a public and positive role model for social workers in the political arena and for writing a foreword of such encouragement to our readers.

We thank the social workers quoted throughout this edition who took time from their already hectic schedules to share their stories and to provide useful advice and challenges. We thank James Reno, student worker extraordinaire, who with technological savvy and excellent organizational skills helped us reach out to social workers for scenarios, tracked down literature resources, and provided a student's perspective to our revisions.

We continue to practice political social work wherever we are, irrespective of the titles and tasks we assume. We continue to support each other to use our social work skills and values to be advocates and social transformers. It is both exhilarating and challenging to be coauthors, executives, spouses, and parents simultaneously, so we thank each other for the necessary good humor, insight, and critical but supportive comments throughout this revision. We finally thank all of you who will read this book and will take away a stronger notion of political social work. The writing of this book fulfills our belief that each of us can truly make a difference.

About the Authors

Karen S. Haynes

Dr. Haynes has been the president of California State University San Marcos since 2004. Prior to arriving in California, she was the president of the University of Houston–Victoria for eight and a half years and served as the dean of the University of Houston Graduate School of Social Work for ten years. She serves on several regional boards and is the Presidential Sponsor for Southern California American Council on Education's Network of Women in Higher Education.

She has authored articles on political social work and published other books, including *A Dream and a Plan: A Woman's Path to Leadership in Human Services* (with Lorrie Greenhouse Gardella, 20ch01), *Women Managers in Human Services* (1989), and *Invitation to Social Work* (with Karen A. Holmes, 1994). She was the first chair of the Indiana Political Action Committee for Human Services (1978) and the cocreator of the first Students Day at the Texas Legislature (1992). As dean, she helped create the only graduate program in the nation with a political social work concentration.

She holds a Ph.D. from the University of Texas at Austin; an MSW from McGill University in Montreal, Quebec, Canada; and an AB from Goucher College in Baltimore, Maryland. Her admonition that "all social work is political" is heartfelt, as is her argument during her tenure in two presidencies that she has not "left social work" but has brought social work values into the presidency.

James S. Mickelson

Mr. Mickelson is Director of ACE Scholars Services at California State University San Marcos, a program that assists former foster youth in obtaining a college degree, where he has been since 2007. Prior to that, he was president and chief executive officer (and founder) of CHILDREN AT RISK, a children's (class) advocacy organization in Houston, Texas, and a member of the faculty of Texas State University – San Marcos school of social work. He has served on many boards and committees that address the needs of children and has served as a political appointee on children welfare commissions.

He has authored many professional articles and contributed the section on advocacy to the *Encyclopedia of Social Work,* 19th edition. Mr. Mickelson has contributed numerous editorials to local newspapers and has written and lectured about "youthism"—the discriminatory treatment of children—which he believes is a major factor contributing to the plight of today's children.

Mr. Mickelson received a BS from Colorado State University – Pueblo and an MSW from Wayne State University. His more than thirty years of social work practice in child welfare has been combined with political action to ensure social justice for children. He has been described by the Houston Chronicle as "the most persistent child advocate in town," which he takes as a supreme compliment.

All Social Work Is Political

In a democracy, where every vote and voice count, doing nothing is a political act.

—Nancy Amidei*

We know what you're thinking: "What does studying policy and political social work have to do with being a social worker? I just want to help people." We have heard that student question for nearly four decades, and this book has been one way to attempt to answer those questions.

Although we do not know you, we will presume to know some of the reasons why you entered a social work program and to anticipate some of your aspirations. We will presume that somehow, somewhere, through personal or professional life experience, you saw injustice and wanted to right it; you saw pain and wanted to heal it; you witnessed discrimination and prejudice, selfishness, and elitism and realized that there were alternatives. We presume that you saw a world with a lot of promise but also with some barriers to attaining that promise. You could see opportunities but also unequal access to them.

If these assumptions are correct, then we further assume that you entered a social work program because you saw the attainment of a professional social work degree as a good method for preparing you to achieve your vision and make changes—to help you to help people. Your social work education should provide the additional skills, knowledge, and experiences you need to enhance your original commitment and passion. In no way, however, can a professional education be a substitute for that original commitment and passion. Skills and knowledge without commitment and without passion are not the makings of a professional social worker.

*Nancy Amidei is project director of the Civic Engagement Project at the University of Washington.

The commitment and passion that we mean include making a contribution that affirms our profession's central values: that acknowledges the "who" in each person, affirms the worth and value of all, celebrates the array of diversity in our society, and enhances social justice for all. If we are mistaken about your interest, your commitment, and your passion, then we suggest you examine your desire to be a social worker. We hope that through this book, you will learn not only to care deeply about these issues but also to connect political action with the roots and history of the social work profession. We hope that this book will help you develop skills to make you a more effective social worker whose repertoire includes political social work skills.

We can almost hear you saying, "I just want to work in a battered women's shelter; I just want to work in a mental health clinic; I'd like to go into private practice. I don't have to understand policy and I surely don't have to *become political*." And you may be wondering what is meant by doing nothing as a political act. Isn't "doing nothing" the same as "staying neutral"? Aren't social workers *expected* to stay neutral? The answer, in short, is *no*.

> "All social work is political" is a strong statement. I would never have agreed with this statement as a young woman working in the human service field, but as time went on and education expanded my thoughts and experiences, I have to say now I totally agree.
>
> At no time is this more evident than right now. After receiving my master's degree in social work, I find myself a single parent with a serious debt-to-income deficit. In looking for solutions to this problem, I have come across the Dorothy I. Height and Whitney Young Jr. Social Work Reinvestment Act. This act recognizes the "insurmountable debt" coupled with "insufficient salaries" that social workers face, and it seeks to create grants to alleviate these issues.
>
> I wrote an email message to Hillary Clinton and Charles Schumer seeking support for this legislation. I am trying to inform my fellow social workers of this act. I am willing to do whatever it takes to see this through. I often advocate for my clients' needs, and today I advocate for them, myself, and the future of social work service. So the statement "all social work is political" takes on a new meaning—one that is both personal and professional.
>
> *Renee Micalizzi, LMSW*
> *Broome Developmental Center and Axia College*
> *Binghamton, New York*

Before describing the pervasiveness of politics in the arena of social work practice, let us take a moment to remind you how policies affect your everyday *personal* life. There are policies that limit your personal choices in voting, marrying, purchasing alcohol or cigarettes, and entering military service. There are policies that mandate certain choices: States mandate that children of certain ages receive education; the federal government mandates that you pay taxes if you earn more than a certain income; state governments obtain much of their revenues through the use of mandatory taxation on personal and corporate incomes and on sales of goods and/or services.

Maybe the best way to explain this statement "All social work is political" is for you to try to think of a social work activity that policy does *not* affect. What about social workers in a private faith based agency, providing family therapy to parishioners? Well, if in the course of that work the social worker discovers any abuse, child or adult, the social worker has to report the abuse. That's the law—that's policy. The church in which you might have your office does not pay taxes—another policy. There are laws (policies) that govern even private, sectarian social work practice.

What about social workers in a corporate setting working in an employee assistance program? Managed care policies will determine where social workers can refer an employee—a policy. Internal corporate regulations will determine how much that employee may have to pay as a deductible or as a copayment. And if you were to learn during your work with this client that the client had misrepresented time taken off as sick leave when it wasn't or had infringed on the rights of another employee, creating a hostile work environment, policies might have been violated, and you might have to inform management of this. Furthermore, if this were an employee with special needs, you would be compelled to treat this employee in a certain way because of the Americans with Disabilities Act—a federal policy. There are policies—federal, state, and internal to the corporation—that govern practice in a private corporate setting.

It is probably more obvious that policies—federal, state, local, and organizational—affect a social worker's practice in a private nonprofit organization as well as in a public agency. Policies in both of these settings likely influence the kinds of clients who can be served, the fees that can be charged, and the alternative solutions that can be offered. For example, social workers employed in public protective services agencies (child or adult) are mandated by state policies following federal guidelines to investigate a potential abuse within a certain number of hours and to keep the informant's identity confidential. Social workers employed in many nonprofit organizations are very likely to have to adhere to multiple policies that the governing board, the state, and/or funding sources require. An example of an extremely important policy is that governing what type(s) of activity can be defined as nonprofit, meeting those requirements, filing those papers, and receiving the nonprofit, tax-exempt status.

Well then, what about a social work practitioner in private practice? Surely, a private practice can set its own policy and function without the intrusion of federal or state interference. Wrong. You can't even call yourself a social worker without a license, and to maintain that license (or certification), you usually have to meet state requirements for continuing education—policies. In private practice, as in all professional social work practice, the licensure (or certification statute) protects social worker–client confidentiality. Without that state policy, all communication with a client can and must be shared with others.

Further, in private practice, a distraught client who is threatening to kill someone must be reported—that's a policy. A client who is having sex with a child must be reported—a policy. All revenues received for treatment must be reported to the Internal Revenue Service—a policy.

The point about making sure that *all* social workers, not only social workers in policy or political settings, know about policy development, implementation, and revision is not only to make them knowledgeable social workers but also to help them understand when policy is impeding or harming a client. Not all policies are well thought through, with input by social work practitioners as to their potential negative impact on clients or of the negative unintended consequences. For example, an old and now outdated policy that allowed only single parents to receive Aid to Families with Dependent Children meant that in two-parent households, one parent had to leave the home. In the quest to help children, laws were passed that had severe negative consequences. Currently, the eligibility standards to receive food stamps require that the recipient own no assets above a very meager amount, thus requiring applicants not to have a car while presumably actively looking for employment.

We can see from these examples that policy *always* affects social workers and social work practice. Consequently, as social workers, we have a choice of either affecting change or allowing policies to affect our ability to help our clients. Policy affects our service to clients—in whatever setting, with whatever client population, in whatever state we reside; therefore, sometimes, to help our clients, we must enter the political arena. Unfortunately, what has happened in the social work profession historically is that we study the history of policy evolution, we analyze how policy is formulated, and we follow policy. What social work has done too little of is to develop policy, determine how to implement policy, or change policy.

What does this mean? It means that it makes no sense for you to spend hundreds of hours to keep a family together, only to watch public policy rip them apart again. It means that it is foolish to work to empower parents to address the issues facing them and then leave them with outdated and punitive policies that may destroy them. It means that if you are willing to devote everything it takes to keep a family, an individual, or a couple functioning and intact, then you must also be willing to turn your efforts to advocacy in the political arena if that's where it leads, because that's what will be required to "help people." Throughout this book, you'll read many stories of the various issues that took social workers into the political arena.

But what does "doing nothing is a political act" really mean? It means that commitment and passion combined with advocacy may suggest that we take private troubles and make them public issues, creating a dialogue and a solution that view societal and structural inequities as the fault needing the fixing, not the people. It means that sitting on the sidelines without providing the knowledge, data, and stories that we have about the impact of policies or their absence is allowing the other side to win. It means that not voting, not sending a letter to your state representative, and not testifying about the potential impact of a new law are political acts.

But you may be saying, "If we do that, we may get in trouble." Yes, with this passion and commitment, we know that there is a risk in swimming against the tide. You may have been told that it is difficult, and perhaps even dangerous, to engage in social change, but dangerous or not, we must engage. You cannot put this off. If we do not do so now, we will be in an indefensible posture in the future.

To a social worker, to not engage in healing pain is unthinkable. To a social worker, to not engage in creating social justice should also be unthinkable.

So do not be daunted by the belief that the struggle is impossible or the problems unsolvable. Just as you work with clients who tell you that it's impossible to change their situations—that there is no hope, that they have no time to fight for themselves, that the problems are insurmountable—and you don't accept that and a good social worker cannot accept that. So, we and our profession will not accept your silence, your pessimism, your excuse that you don't have the time, your notion that the problem is too big, or your assertion that the system can't change and that you can't make a difference.

> Growing up as a member of the Pasqua Yaqui Indian Tribe, I saw the many needs and the social health concerns of American Indians, and I asked myself if I was truly committed to bringing about change in the tribal community. It wasn't until I happened to take a social work class that I realized that social work was more than just taking kids away from their families. I quickly found out that social work focused on how to advocate and bring about change for the individual and for communities. I felt that social work, unlike law or business, was a profession where I could work directly with people and communities.
>
> *Eddie F. Brown, MSW, DSW*
> *Director of American Indian Studies*
> *Arizona State University*

Our vision of good social work practice is that we can make a difference and we must. We also know, because we've experienced it, that when we speak out, we are sometimes confronted by our own colleagues who question our professionalism or who presume that we devalue clinical practice if we value advocacy. We have gotten angry and confused because our vision of good social work practice has always been one of advocacy with and on behalf of clients with the goals of enhancing individual functioning and achieving social justice.

We understand that problems have become more complex, that they are multidimensional, bipartisan, and cross-generational. We understand that we didn't create them. We also understand that we do need to be a significant part of the solution. We honor and support the essential roles that social workers play to heal pain, to support victims, to build on individual strengths, and to advocate for individual clients as an integral part of those roles. We simply want to ensure that when those roles lead to the inevitable strategy of policy change, social workers have the commitment, skills, and knowledge to advocate for their clients in a larger and political arena. We believe that our profession must continue to support positions that connect to what we value, to make us take pride in what we know and in what we do, and to keep us focused on the commitment to achieve social justice (McIntosh, 2004).

You—our students, the future of our profession—must remember, "In a democracy, where every voice and vote counts, doing nothing is a political act." We hope that throughout the remainder of this book, you will see more of the relevance of political social work to whatever it is you want to do in the social work profession. We hope that you will gain insights from the scenarios and case illustrations of real social workers moving from case to cause, from micro to macro, weaving political social work into their work. We hope that you will find these political social work skills absolutely connected to the core skills of social work.

We know that from our profession's inception, two of our foremothers had antithetical approaches toward social work and visions of what it was. Mary Richmond had little use, on the one hand, for what she called the "do-gooders" who cared tenderly for the suffering without any thought to removing the cause and, on the other hand, for the lofty generalizers who loved humanity but could not tolerate human beings. She believed that change could best be produced through the systematic collection of evidence of need about the individual case. Jane Addams was equally committed to the value of facts but used them to look at societal forces and their impact on the individual. Mary Richmond developed a better way of seeing and collecting information about individuals' problems, and Jane Addams saw ways of looking at societal problems and creating policy solutions. But then, as now, they both saw the constant interaction and interplay between private troubles and public issues.

We began this chapter with a quote from Nancy Amidei, a more contemporary and lifelong social work advocate. Because she continued her advocacy, against many odds and even when she was outnumbered and the path was rocky, she was often asked whether she ever became discouraged. Her answer always took this form:

> When I graduated from college in 1963, there was no Medicare, there was no Medicaid, there were hardly any women in sports because there was no Title IX, and there was no Title IX because there was no Civil Rights Act. . . . There was no elementary and secondary education act, there was no Head Start, there were no legal services for low-income people, there was no WIC program, there was no food stamp program.
>
> We would add that in 1963 there also were very few women in Congress, law, and medicine—and even fewer social workers in elected office.
>
> Changes were made not because the guys in Congress decided on their own to change, but because people like us called up, spoke up, wrote up and voted up . . . until the guys in Congress said OK. If enough of us make noise, we can outnumber the people writing the big checks. (Amidei, 2008)

So it isn't a matter of being outnumbered; it's a matter of speaking up, speaking out.

Have we convinced you yet? Perhaps not, but our intent is that by the time you finish reading this book, you will be convinced that to do good social work, to be a professional social worker, you must understand these linkages and enter the political arena when necessary. We trust that you will embrace the notion that the basic and generic social work skills are the same basic and generic political skills: brokering, mediating, negotiating, and influencing, but with one important difference—the unique values that social workers can bring to the political skill set and process.

There has been much for social workers to get involved and excited about during the recent presidential campaign and election. President Obama's commitment to conversation, to inclusivity, and to communication has been not only impressive, but also an embodiment of social work principles. His use of every form of electronic communication has also made his thoughts and speeches accessible to all and has continued to make our democracy participatory.

Social workers were involved in the campaign and as advisors during his transition. Through professional associations, national and state, social workers have provided input into the various initiatives undertaken within President Obama's first 100 days. However, it is our hope that this "reawakening" to political activism is not short-lived. To quote from the end of President Obama's speech at the White House Forum on Health Reform, March 5, 2009:

> But the one thing that I've got to say here: There's been some talk about the notion that maybe we're taking on too much, that we're in the midst of an economic crisis and that the system is overloaded, and so we should put this off for another day. Well, let's just be clear. When times were good, we didn't get it done. When we had mild recessions, we didn't get it done. When we were in peacetime, we did not get it done. When we were at war, we did not get it done.
>
> There is always a reason not to do it. And it strikes me that now is exactly the time for us to deal with this problem. The American people are looking for solutions. Business is looking for solutions. And government—state, federal, and local— needs solutions to this problem.
>
> So for all of you who've been elected to office or those of you who are heading up major associations, I would just say, what better time than now and what better cause for us to take up? Imagine the pride when we go back to our constituencies next year and say, you know what, we finally got something done on health care. That's something that's worth fighting for, and I hope all of you fight for it.

The Time Is Now

We couldn't agree more that "the time is now" to get involved, stay involved, and to raise our voices on behalf of our social work values and our social work clients.

> This is the time for the social work profession to reassert its critical role in championing the needs of those hurting the most in our society. . . . For those of us who have lived through more than a few presidencies, we know just how important the intersection of the government sector, corporate sector and social sector truly is. . . . Given the social work profession's leadership in the social sector, in particular, we are hopeful that social work voices will influence many different halls of power. (Kelly, 2009)

Through this book we provide you with more arguments to get and stay involved; we provide you with techniques to effectively become involved; we share with you the voices of social workers who have become involved and made a difference. We are confident that you will come to agree with us that ALL SOCIAL WORK IS POLITICAL.

References

Amidei, Nancy. 2008. www.uwnews.org/uweek/awards2008/profile

Kelly, James J. 2009. "Time to Reassert Our Critical Role." *NASW News* 54 (2): 3.

McIntosh, D. 2004. "Taking No Action Is an Action." *The New Social Worker* (Spring): 6–8.

Obama, Barack. Speech to the White House Forum on Health Reform, March 5, 2009.

2

Social Work Values versus Politics

A social worker brings to the political process something that's unique: a value system that, if implemented along with the skills, makes the difference. There are people who tell me that the ends justify the means, but this is antithetical to social work values. Social work values involve people in making decisions that affect their own lives. For social workers, the ends and the means must be consistent; that is, if the methods you use to arrive at your ends are dirty, then the end result will be dirty.

—Maryann Mahaffey (late)*

Policy can be defined as the operationalization or the compromise of a set of values, or both. Values are conceptions of what is desirable that influence the choice of action. Policy may begin wherever an individual or group sees the need for a course of action or a change of course. Policy is normally initiated, debated, passed, and codified through legislation, executive order, or the courts. We continue to argue that social workers are uniquely qualified—and, by the standards of their profession, perhaps required—to be catalysts of such change.

The social work profession, though a field resplendent with values, has ironically generally avoided debates over social policy, explaining its apolitical posture by pointing to its "values." The profession has denied that its refusal to intervene politically is, indeed, a political decision. However, just as a clinician, after collecting data, may decide not to treat a client, so may a social worker decide not to take action about a bill or a candidate. Whether "no treatment" or "no political action" occurs through inattention, neglect, or an active and informed decision, the individual or societal consequences can be dramatic and potentially damaging.

*Maryann Mahaffey was a former member and president of the Detroit city council.

The centrality of values to the origins and subsequent development of the social work profession preceded any concern with the development of theory or methodology. In fact, one of the most critical arguments in defense of professionalism in social work practice has been that the development of an independent set of norms, specialized helping skills, and humanitarian values enables social service work to remain autonomous, a power with the potential to offset narrow and repressive sectarian political interests.

Critics have argued that professionalism in social work has reactionary consequences. By supporting present societal values, it may unwittingly strengthen society's repressive characteristics in the long run. The root of social work values may be a set of potentially conservative, system-conserving assumptions about individuals, society, and social change. Thus, it is not that social work values are incompatible in general with politics and the political process but that these values may be less than compatible with the profession's declared goal of public advocacy for societal structural change.

Although social work values appear to be congruent with practice at the individual or small-group level (micro level), often they have been viewed as contradictory to the values and stances necessary at the larger, macro level of practice, particularly in administration. For example, social workers too often have acted as though budgets and fiscal considerations were not only inconsequential to their programs but also as if such considerations were inhumane. They seem to take pride in not understanding the issues. In the 1980s, some social workers moved to the opposite extreme of becoming too "bottom-line" privatization oriented. Social workers must learn to balance caring, competence, and humanitarianism, on the one hand, and fiscal efficiency on the other.

In the 1990s, looking toward the next millennium, social workers faced increasing ethical conflicts as managed care, biomedical and genetic engineering, and technology placed strains on traditional social work values and ethics. Regulatory compliance, fiscal conservatism, and technological capability threatened to take precedence over the best interest of the client. Social workers began to realize that the erosion of confidentiality, informed consent, and privacy would create serious difficulties in client services and that the value of regulatory compliance would define social workers' behavior more than the professional code. Because of these threats, the ethical principle of social workers engaged in political advocacy needs to become more prominent.

This discussion continues in the profession. Indeed, a recent article examines discrepancies between social workers' belief in the National Association of Social Workers (NASW) Code of Ethics and their behaviors. It would be assumed that "if values determine or influence behavior, one would expect a significant positive relationship between belief and behavior" (DiFranks, 2008, p. 170). Supporting our long-standing propositions, this national survey found that social work behaviors most related to values in the code were treating people with care and respect and being aware of difference and diversity; the behaviors causing social workers the most disjuncture from the values in the code were helping people in need and addressing social problems (DiFranks, 2008, p. 172).

This book is devoted to describing and analyzing the politics inherent in social work and the political functions served by social work as a consequence. Some chapters describe the roles that social work does or should play in influencing political events, but this chapter asserts that social work itself contains political theory and plays a political role. Social work practice, at both micro and macro levels, continuously acts either in support of or in opposition to the major institutions, policies, and values of our society. As such, social work is inherently part of the political process in the broadest sense, in that it is concerned with issues of either social conservation or social change.

With the exceptions we discuss later, social workers either have overtly disagreed with this view of the inherently political nature of their work or have been unaware of it. The vast majority believe that social work is and should be apolitical.

Indeed, the argument that the profession's values might be compromised has been used to impede the entrance of social workers into the political sphere. It is the intent of this chapter first to explain the compatibility of social work values with political action and to suggest that these values often have been misinterpreted and second to present arguments illustrating that these values prescribe and mandate intervention by social workers in the political arena.

As a mother and as a social worker, I know the important role families play in a person's life—especially during times of need. Many households have both parents working while at the same time trying to care for their aging parents and young children. All workers deserve extended periods of time off to care for a new child, a seriously ill family member, or their own serious health condition. Most people, however, cannot afford to take this time off without pay.

Over the last seven years, I have worked with a coalition to pass paid family leave in Washington. It has taken patience, dedication, and some tenacity to get this bill passed. Unfortunately, it also took a lot of paring down.

The original bill would have covered time off for parents to care for a new child, a seriously ill family member, or a worker's own serious health condition. Although polls showed that people support this kind of expansive care the most, it was difficult to convince enough legislators. So, we had to stay flexible and decided to focus on parents with a new child. We know that those first few years are critical for bonding with a child. We also know that parents are often forced to choose between staying with their child and keeping their job.

The coalition continued to work together to educate legislators and organize supporters across the state. Many groups, like the Senior Citizens' Lobby, stayed involved and supportive because they knew this program, once in place, could be built upon to include paid time off to care for elderly parents as well as children. When working to pass legislation, it is critical to hold onto your vision while working step by step. We were finally able to pass paid family leave for families with a new child in 2007.

The work wasn't done simply because the bill passed and was signed by the governor. The summer after the bill passed, I cochaired a task force comprised of business, labor, working families, and both parties of the legislature. Together we worked to find ways to make the program more efficient. We ended up recommending efficiencies that saved $5.2 million in one-time start-up costs and $1.7 million annually in ongoing administrative costs.

Mary Lou Dickerson, MSW
Washington State House of Representatives
Seattle, Washington

The Professional Code of Ethics

Any profession has both a formal and an informal code of ethics. In either case, it is the articulation of a set of publicly professed values. The formal code is the written code to which professionals commit themselves on being admitted to practice. Within the social work profession, the formal code is exemplified by the National Association of Social Workers (NASW) Code of Ethics. The coexisting informal, unwritten code carries the weight of the formal code's prescriptions.

Through its ethical code, the social work profession commits itself to certain values as a matter of public record, thereby ensuring the continued confidence of the community and formally obligating itself to client service. This kind of self-regulative code is characteristic of all professions and occupations, both technical and professional, but a professional code usually is more explicit, more systematic, and to some extent more binding than an occupational code. Our Code of Ethics (NASW, 2008) was first ratified in 1960; it was only one page long and included only fourteen broadly framed proclamations. By contrast, the 1996 revision, only the third revision since 1960, constituted a major change in our profession's ethical standards, providing guidance for social workers' conduct, reducing malpractice and liability risks, and providing a basis for adjudication of ethics complaints against NASW members—quite a change from social work's early preoccupation with client morality and values (Reamer, 1998). Indeed, given the profession's placements across education, agency, judicial, and private practices, the revised code has provided a useful guide in framing the special work role in new situations and placements it encounters (Grief, 2004). The NASW Code since this revision now includes this preamble:

> *Preamble*
> The primary mission of the social work profession is to enhance human well-being and help meet the basic human needs of all people, with particular attention to the needs and empowerment of people who are vulnerable, oppressed, and living in poverty. A historic and defining feature of social work is the profession's focus on individual well-being in a social context and the well-being of society. Fundamental to social work is attention to the environmental forces that create, contribute to, and address problems in living.
>
> Social workers promote social justice and social change with and on behalf of clients. "Clients" is used inclusively to refer to individuals, families, groups, organizations, and communities. Social workers are sensitive to cultural and ethnic diversity and strive to end discrimination, oppression, poverty, and other forms of social

injustice. These activities may be in the form of direct practice, community organizing, supervision, consultation, administration, advocacy, social and political action, policy development and implementation, education, and research and evaluation. Social workers seek to enhance the capacity of people to address their own needs. Social workers also seek to promote the responsiveness of organizations, communities, and other social institutions to individuals' needs and social problems.

The mission of the social work profession is rooted in a set of core values. These core values, embraced by social workers throughout the profession's history, are the foundation of social work's unique purpose and perspective:

- service
- social justice
- dignity and worth of the person
- importance of human relationships
- integrity
- competence

This constellation of core values reflects what is unique to the social work profession. Core values, and the principles that flow from them, must be balanced within the context and complexity of the human experience. (NASW, 2008)

Of note is this language: "A historic and defining feature of social work is the profession's focus on individual well-being in a social context. . . . Social workers promote social justice and social change. . . . These activities may be in the form of . . . advocacy, [and] social and political action." Furthermore, another section of the code on the value of social justice states that "social workers challenge social injustice" and continues: "Social workers pursue social change, particularly with and on behalf of vulnerable and oppressed individuals and groups of people. Social workers' social change efforts are focused primarily on issues of poverty, unemployment, discrimination, and other forms of social injustice."

In further defining ethical behaviors within the Code of Ethics, many descriptors of behaviors for ethical social work practice undergird the validity of political practice. The following are examples:

Social workers should monitor and evaluate policies. (5.02a)

Social workers should promote the general welfare of society . . . and should advocate for living conditions conducive to the fulfillment of basic human needs . . . and compatible with the realization of social justice. (6.01)

Social workers should facilitate informed participation by the public in shaping social policies and institutions. (6.02)

Social workers should engage in social and political action that seeks to ensure that all people have equal access. . . . Social workers should be aware of the impact of the political arena on practice and should advocate for changes in policy and legislation to improve social conditions in order to meet basic human needs and promote social justice. (6.04a)

The most recent and full version of the code is available on the NASW website, www.naswdc.org.

Primary Principles: Social Justice and Empowerment

Before we proceed to a specific analysis of social work values, a brief discussion of the principles of social justice and empowerment and their connection to the social work profession is appropriate. We offer this as an additional basis for supporting the notion that all social work is and should be political.

There seems to be little disagreement that the founding principle of social work is related to social justice. To the extent that this is and has been true, it represents a posture that redirects and reallocates resources toward a more "just" distribution. Generally, social work has ascribed to the principle that inequities in power, wealth, income, and other essential resources (e.g., health care) should not exist unless they work for the benefit of all, including, most important, the worse-off members of society. In fact, it is around this basic premise that Specht and Courtney (1994) develop their arguments that Americans of *all* social classes—the poor and the rich alike—have a trained incapacity to see the community of which they are a part, rather than their individual attitudes, training, and motivation, as either the cause or the solution of many social problems. This premise is debated in more detail in Chapter 4.

Because social justice remains a valued principle within the social work profession, it would appear impossible to argue with a politicized practice, for it is within the realm of budget prioritization at the federal and, increasingly, at the state level that these decisions, which are clearly value decisions, become focused. Compatible with this social justice principle is an advocacy-based, social change focus. Many, including the authors, have argued that particularly since the 1970s and into the 1990s, social work has been more concerned with enhancing the profession and less concerned with the issues of racism, sexism, poverty, and access to health care (Haynes, 1996; Haynes, 1998; Mickelson, 1998).

Instead of framing this conflict as conservative and self-serving versus progressive and client focused, the conflict may more likely be the result of the dilemma that social work practice exists within social institutions that, whether public or private, are established and maintained by power groups. However, other practitioners, administrators, policy analysts, and educators might not be as constrained. "There is nothing in the tradition, code of ethics, literature, or curricula that explicitly or implicitly defines social work as inherently conservative. But there is no escaping the fact that social work as an institution in society must always reflect the mainstream culture, or that culture will not support it" (Sarri, 1992, p. 49).

For additional perspectives and arguments, Wagner (1990) sets the debate around ideologies of specialization, elitism, and career structures as part of social work professionalism juxtaposed to ideologies of social justice that are clearly compatible with political (or radical) social work. Perhaps the issue, if framed in this manner, is that to do political social work, the social worker cannot feel loyalty to the profession or to the institution but must feel loyalty to political principles and ideologies (Wagner, 1990, p. 5).

Empowerment-based practice appears to be another fundamental principle to frame this chapter, as associated with a value-based practice. Empowerment-based practice is based on principles that liberate clients, that achieve reasonable control over client destiny. It is associated with and dependent on a strengths perspective, a systems perspective, a social justice value base, and a social change model (Pinderhuges, 1994; Rose, 2000).

Another important aspect of empowerment-based practice, according to Rees (1991), is the connection rather than the separation of policy and practice and the notion that power does not have to mean dominance but should and does mean enabling. Thus, "enabling" power is quite consistent with social work values and most social work methodology and thought, and it is not contradictory to professionalism. In fact, providing both critical understanding of social and political realities—providing students with skills to reduce social injustice—empowers the social work student, thus leading to client empowerment through the use of social justice strategies (VanVoorhis and Hostetter, 2006, p. 117).

In fact, despite their inclusion in the Council on Social Work Education (CSWE) Curriculum Policy Statement since 1994, no research currently exists to determine the degree to which these standards are observed, and no definitive data have been gathered on the scope of political training at the BSW and MSW levels (Wolk, Pray, Weismiller, and Dempsey, 1996, p. 93). One obstacle to political or advocacy placements was the CSWE-mandated requirement for professional supervision, which is often difficult to obtain in these settings. However, in the recent revisions, Standard 2.1.4 allows that "in programs where a field instructor does not hold a CSWE/accredited baccalaureate or master's social work degree, the program assumes responsibility for reinforcing a social work perspective" (CSWE, 2001, p. 14). Furthermore, these new policies and standards appear to remove the critics' concerns that generalist practice and political placements are contradictory. Critics have argued that political placements are contradictory to CSWE's generalist practice definition. Some programs have already found solutions to these problems; excuses must not be -allowed to interfere with preparation of social work students for political intervention. We may answer the social work student complaint, "What does policy have to do with what I'll be practicing when I graduate?" with *"Everything!"*

Specialization versus Systemic Solutions

Among the important elements in any profession are identifying and developing areas of competence within which its members practice; the rights and obligations of the professional's relationship to these stated areas are, thereby, limited. The reason for this is twofold: to protect clients from a professional's involvement in areas that go beyond the professional's technical competence, and to protect the profession from general and undifferentiated demands made by its clients or consumers. Thus specialization in social work has been an important and central component in social work education, even though the type of specialization has been contested, challenged, and changed over time. Specialization has been defined and defended, whether it has been based on method (case work, group work, community organizing, administration), or field of practice (health, mental health, family and children), or target population (the aged, youth).

A problem with specialization of any type has long been apparent to the profession is that it creates a tendency, in fact demands, that the professional focus on and engage in only a piece of a client's life, ignoring other problems the person might have because they are either outside the range of skills (micro versus macro), outside a knowledge base about a field of practice, or outside a targeted client group.

However, as the number of BSW programs has grown, a countervailing trend has emerged in the discipline, namely, a growing concern with the integration and coordination of social services and with the development of generalist practitioners (BSWs) and case managers. Quite clearly, social work has been caught between two competing sets of values: functional specificity versus global or integrated solutions. Given that many clients have multiple problems, sometimes with a single cause, the artificial and narrow focus on one problem that is prompted by specialization may lead to an incomplete resolution. For example, a substance abuser who is also violent in domestic relations may be treated in a residential detoxification program, where the violence may be overlooked or assumed to be the effect of rather than the cause of the substance abuse. Both of these problems also may be the effect of a third untreated problem, such as under-employment.

Inherent in the profession's emphasis on specialization is a more endemic problem: As social problems become the concern of a professional group, a problem-solving arena is created in which both problems and solutions are viewed as technical in nature rather than as structural or political. The resulting dilemma has been that the profession is unlikely to espouse changes on a broader level that could reorder or reprioritize society or societal values. That is to say, professional social work norms may well act as a set of blinders that induce social workers to prescribe easily implementable, technical solutions to problems that could be better addressed by other means. For instance, as social workers came to recognize child abuse as a societal problem, technical solutions based on reporting and investigation systems were most frequently implemented, rather than political alternatives, such as adding the "unemployed parent" option to state Aid to Families with Dependent Children (AFDC) eligibility regulations or increasing public support for day care. Although reporting and investigation systems certainly respond to the problem of unnecessary and critical delays in life-threatening circumstances, they are not solutions to the underlying causes of child abuse: poverty, adult isolation, and lack of adequate child care outside the home.

Another aspect of specialization that seems on the surface to discourage political involvement is the need to identify "turf." Social work increasingly has attempted (via licensing and classification efforts, for example) to define its role in relationship to other "helping professions," such as psychiatry, psychology, community nursing, recreational and occupational therapy, city and regional planning, and public administration. This has contributed to interpersonal rivalry rather than to the building of coalitions for the betterment of society. Perhaps even more debilitating than interprofessional rivalry is the existing intraprofessional rivalry between clinicians and administrators, between clinicians in mental health settings and clinicians in health settings or clinicians in school settings, and the like.

One can argue, therefore, that specialization, although necessary to professional definitions and identifications, may be antithetical to some forms of political action. If it is used as a clinical tool, however, rather than as an all-encompassing value, it will not be a barrier to political activity.

In Pennsylvania, the county where I am one of three commissioners has been controlled by two Republicans for most of the past 100 years. I unseated a 16-year Democratic incumbent Commissioner. The first shock for my colleagues and staff was the difference in my style; the second was that I did not relinquish my credentials as a social worker on Inauguration Day.

In fact, I began by verbally confronting some of the archaic policies and placement practices. Within a few months I received a call from a mother who had turned to the county's Children and Youth Department and asked for help with her bipolar, suicidal, acting-out teen. The Children and Youth Department obliged by placing the child in a residential program for teens with emotional difficulties. When funding ran out, she was transferred to another type of treatment program, where sexual overtures by female peers led her to run away twice in two weeks. At that point, her mother took her home to wait for the fourteen days until the judge could hear the case. Two days before the hearing, the mother received a call that the child was going to be placed in a wilderness camp, as the county guardians and caseworkers feared liability if she continued to run away—the assumption being that a child won't run away or harm themselves once removed to the woods. Upon investigation I learned that neither the assigned guardian nor caseworkers had met with the child or mother over the course of the past five months and that a psychiatrist had actually recommended partial hospital and family treatment. I advocated by meeting with the assigned workers, the director of human services and related officials. I was not mild in my criticism of the handling of this case.

Although the child was placed in the wilderness program despite my efforts, two things resulted: First, the Republican judges and my Republican colleagues began a full-force campaign to attack my actions by insisting I was inappropriate and had judicially interfered. Of course, I knew the boundaries from my social work training and had done nothing inappropriate with the case. The second thing to happen was an absolute outcry of support for me and my actions by both the press and the public. In fact, this episode served to remind people who had grown accustomed to an inactive board of commissioners that advocacy could occur and protection of children was possible. It also forced the county to begin addressing the questionable way in which it had been evaluating and reacting to the needs of youth.

Diane Marseglia, LCSW
Bucks County Supervisor, Pennsylvania

Self-Determination versus Compromise

Self-determination, frequently touted in the profession as the "king" of social work values, is certainly a cornerstone of social work practice. In its ideal form, self-determination gives the client the right and the responsibility to be involved in life choices and, of course, in treatment choices. This value derives from a belief system that imparts to all clients equal human worth and dignity, equal ability to enter into the decision process, and equal rights to determine for themselves the best choice of treatment.

Nonetheless, a number of inherent problems arise in the operationalization of this value. On the clinical level, it assumes that the social work practitioner has the knowledge and agency sanction to adequately and comprehensively present all treatment alternatives. In fact, we know that quite often this is not possible. Particularly among specialists in social work practice, knowledge of treatment alternatives may be limited.

Unfortunately, social work education does not consistently and comprehensively provide information about community resources, eligibility requirements, or accessibility issues. Thus, the array of alternatives suggested by the social worker may be artificially and even arbitrarily constrained by lack of knowledge, geographical limitations, or, as earlier noted, problem definition or even agency policy. Social workers also may find themselves in personal conflict with the professed policies of their agencies. An obvious example would be a case in which a pregnant teenager is a client of an agency whose restrictions and policies prohibit the discussion of abortion as an alternative. Additionally, referral to an appropriate agency might be prohibited because of any one of a number of eligibility requirements, such as income, gender, age, residence, ability to provide payment for service, or language restrictions.

Equally important to the operationalization of this value in social work practice is its inherent assumption that all clients can actively engage in self-determination, when in fact many social work clients are unable to choose the best options because they have been unable to negotiate the larger system in an adequate manner. For example, a parent who has a child with behavior problems might inappropriately be referred to an agency for counseling because the parent is unaware of the possibility of testing the child for learning disabilities. One must also be suspicious of rules that merely appear to foster client self-determination. For example, under the Temporary Assistance for Needy Families (TANF) legislation, all applicants must be asked, "Are you ready to enroll now and have the clock start on your benefits?" Although this question appears to allow client self-determination, in many instances it has operated as a threat and has kept needy clients and their families from receiving the available support.

Whether we view this failure to be knowledgeable about all treatment options as a personal or a structural deficiency, it clearly diminishes the possibility of client self-determination. Whatever the cause—be it the client's age, gender, or emotional or intellectual dysfunctioning—the result is an inability to choose rationally among alternatives that would be in the client's best interest. Young children, the aged, those who are emotionally disturbed, and those who are developmentally disabled are the most obvious examples of client groups for whom self-determination may be a meaningless notion. Social work practitioners, therefore, must see that it is well within their professional creed to assume an active responsibility for deciding the best treatment alternative for a particular client or client group and that the creed cannot cover every ethical issue found in community organizations (Hardina, 2004). Many practitioners, however, even community organizers and administrators, feel that to make such decisions contradicts social work values by taking away rights from clients and putting social workers in the position of being paternalistic and manipulative.

At the macro level, some social work administrators, researchers, and program evaluators have interpreted self-determination in operational terms that may speak against the long-term interests of clients and the profession. By committing themselves to an unbiased interpretation of data and the presentation of the full array of either funding or programmatic prescriptions, or both, they assume in others—funders, policymakers, and program designers—the same ability to be all-knowing and unbiased that practitioners have assumed in their clients. Unfortunately, administrative and evaluative decisions are not often made solely on the basis of the objective data presented; they are made on the basis of a set of values or operational norms that may be unstated or unconscious but nonetheless are persuasive.

Social workers entering the political process tend to reveal their inexperience with the political process. They want political candidates, elected officials, and administrative executives to have all available information, rather than a biased and limited perspective, and the freedom to make informed and self-determined decisions. In a political process that has been built on competing political ideologies and values, this approach to macro-level intervention is naïve, unrealistic, and too often supportive of the status quo. The problem is not the incompatibility of self-determination and political intervention but the perceived misfit. Although practitioners cannot implement self-determination in a pure fashion at either the micro or macro level, at both levels this value can contribute in important and useful ways to promoting informed and humane decision making.

When victims of sexual predators came forward in 2002 with accusations against Catholic priests in Kentucky, many of them said they felt victimized all over again when the crimes were covered up for years, sometimes decades. After the scandal finally broke into public view, 242 plaintiffs sued the Archdiocese of Louisville over sexual abuse by priests in a case that resulted in a $25.7 million settlement in 2003.

As a social worker, I've seen the ways trauma caused by sexual abuse can have long-standing effects throughout a person's life. I also knew that the systemic failure to prevent these crimes required a systemic response.

When victims approached me with requests that I sponsor legislation to strengthen the fight against sexual predators, I listened to their stories and found it painfully obvious that our state's laws had not provided the victims with the protections they deserved. Their suffering was compounded in many cases by the fact that they were abused by an authority figure, someone they thought they could trust, as well as the efforts to cover up the crimes.

As a result of my meetings with victims, I began working with them to come up with legislation that would address their concerns and give them an opportunity to channel their hurt and anger into efforts to better protect children from sexual predators.

Once we knew which statutory changes we wanted to achieve, I worked to empower the victims. Many were not familiar with the steps needed to change state law. But they were eager to throw their hearts and minds into the effort as I began coaching them on ways to effectively lobby state lawmakers, testify before legislative committees, and round up support from citizens and groups across the state.

With the backing of victims, youth advocates, and Catholic bishops, the bill I successfully sponsored in the Kentucky General Assembly strengthened penalties for sexual abusers, as well as for those who fail to report the crimes. The legislation also contained provisions that represented victims' wishes for a longer statute of limitations on sexual abuse, since it often takes children many years to open up about the abuse.

Thanks to the organized efforts of victims that resulted in hundreds of people across the state contacting legislators in support of the legislation, the measure was passed by the legislature and signed into law in April 2008.

After the new law was signed by the governor, more than one victim noted that the efforts to affect public policy not only would help protect children in the future from sexual abuse, but also gave past victims a voice and an opportunity for healing.

Jim Wayne, MSW
Kentucky House of Representatives
Louisville, Kentucky

Emotional Neutrality versus Client Self-Interest

Another major premise of social work professionalism is objectivity or emotional neutrality. Social workers are strongly encouraged to become aware of and to control the degree of their emotional involvement with clients. The development and operationalization of this value has been said to represent the essence of the "professional self." Particularly in a profession such as social work, in which the primary tool is the social workers themselves, emotional neutrality is required to differentiate professional exchanges from other kinds of person-to-person encounters. Without neutrality, the expertise of the social worker would not be publicly or legitimately identifiable and sanctioned.

One potentially negative consequence of emotional neutrality is that it may induce social workers to deny or repress emotional experiences or emotional reactions. The isolation and suppression of emotions, however, may only serve to thwart justifiable anger and frustration at the social inequities that clearly are at the root of many client problems. Thus, it may be possible for social workers to intervene with a low-income, multiproblem client and find short-term, ameliorating solutions and at the same time to ignore the anger they feel toward the societal injustices that created the client's problems. If social workers were to become aware of and to express their feelings of anger at systemic and institutional barriers and inequities, a consensus might emerge that subsequently could lead to cooperative efforts at societal reform.

On a positive note, emotional neutrality may help the worker to continue practicing without experiencing despair or "burnout" in the face of enormous, overwhelming, and depressing social problems. At the macro level, many decision makers (both administrators and legislators) encourage a posture of neutrality because it supports the objective collection, analysis, and presentation by social workers of "hard data." Although collection and presentation of data are functions the professional must perform, restricting one's efforts to these functions may reduce one's effectiveness in being politically persuasive.

In providing legislative testimony, social workers too often have used indices of need, reported gaps in human services, and projected dysfunctions to support their argument for improved service delivery to clients. Although these can be useful elements in a political strategy, what often has been missing is the descriptive, emotionally charged illustration. Torn between a history of breast-beating, at one extreme, and scientific argumentation, at the other, it may be that social work has swung too far in the direction of objectivity.

Social worker/advocates, for example, might prefer to present aggregate statistics about the probability that a proportion of the elderly in a midwestern state are unable to pay their heating bills rather than to vividly describe the deaths of two elderly people as a result of exposure. The presentation of statistics not only might be less persuasive but also might mask real human suffering and pain caused by a particular inequity. Thus, emotional neutrality serves a useful function in a helping profession, but it should not be interpreted in a way that prevents the expression of justifiable and effective emotions, such as anger at social injustice.

> In general I think that social workers do not like to get their "hands dirty" by participating in the political process. I have heard many social workers say that the legislature should "just do the right thing." Unfortunately, if social workers are not active participants, their concerns and interests will be ignored.
>
> *David Knutson, Senior Research Analyst, House of Representatives*
> *Children and Family Services Committee*
> *Washington State Legislature (Influencing State Policy, 1999)*

Impartiality versus Partisan Politics

Impartiality, as a professional norm, means serving clients without regard to race, religion, personal traits, gender, sexual preference, or political ideology. It suggests that professionals should stand above and apart from these differences and be available to provide service equally to all clients. For micro-level practice, it requires social workers to identify in themselves personal values and prejudices that may deter, influence, or mitigate against equal and impartial service to all clients. Impartiality is an essential professional value. However, like the values previously mentioned, it has a potential bias, particularly when applied to macro-level interventions. Predicated on a limited definition of injustice, impartiality can lead to unthinking support of the status quo, especially if equality and social justice are held to be synonymous with equality of opportunity. As we emphasized in our opening chapter, doing "nothing"—which can frequently be the result of a commitment to impartiality—is, in itself, a political act that usually sides with the status quo. For example, although social workers supported the civil rights movement and the equal opportunity legislation of the 1960s, many of these measures assumed that people start off equally. These laws and the programs they created attempted to guarantee equality of opportunity or of access without necessarily taking into account that people start life in unequal positions. In fact, measures to guarantee equal opportunity, however laudable, do not automatically guarantee equal outcomes for all.

In all societies, ours included, there is a scarcity of valued resources. As a political concept, impartiality, which has given rise to certain guarantees of equality of opportunity, may influence a more equitable distribution or redistribution of resources by randomizing distribution across racial, gender, income, or geographic lines. This may promote equality of opportunity, but it does not alter the total available amount of a given resource.

The Reagan and Bush administrations repeatedly argued that the federal government and federal budget should not be involved in any form of income redistribution, yet, in reality, income redistribution is precisely what budget and tax programs do. The issue, therefore, is the direction and extent of that redistribution. An impartial stance on income transfer programs may, in some administrations, be tantamount to support of redistribution of wealth to the upper class, which is what resulted from many of the tax changes in highly publicized tax cut programs, beginning with Reagan's 1981 Economic Recovery Act and extending and escalating through George W. Bush's two terms in office.

The multiple debacles of the last year of the Bush administration (2008) gave repeated examples that "doing nothing is a political act" and that limited government intervention does not necessarily protect the people. Reducing fiscal regulation, although touted as reducing governmental intervention, left the American public completely unprotected from the excesses and unethical behaviors of the financial systems. Bailouts to multiple, private corporate entities with public taxpayer monies is, in fact, income redistribution and, we would certainly argue, public welfare by another name.

Conclusion

Although the values discussed in this chapter are central values in social work, by no means do they comprise an exhaustive list. Other important values include confidentiality, service, human worth, and dignity. As noted earlier, these values will likely encounter additional conflict in the future.

We have attempted to stress the importance and indeed the nobility of social work values. However, two important considerations remain: (1) an inability to operationalize these values into programmatic or legislative objectives and (2) the leaning of many of these values toward preservation of the status quo rather than social change. It is difficult to imagine that these values are inimical to political strategies or ideologies. However, they are commonly misconstrued as being barriers to political intervention by social workers.

Interestingly, value conflicts can become the center of a political debate within the NASW. Consequently, it is important for social workers in all arenas to make social work values an integral part of any issue or controversy.

As expressed earlier, the intraprofessional debate about whether social workers should be actively engaged in political action committees and legislative lobbying issues in large part arises from the perceived conflict between political ideology and professional impartiality. It may also be the result of the profession's belief that knowledge and theory are more important to the profession's development. Additionally, the code itself has functioned increasingly to define misconduct, rather than "inspiring the profession to a higher ethical level of practice" (Walz and Ritchie, 2000, p. 213). Finally, although our professional code may help social workers make practice decisions (Lowenberg and Dolgoff, 1996), as the editor of *Social Work* noted,

> I am concerned, for example, that our ethics discourse are more reactive than proactive, more about acts of commission than omission, more about individual conduct than collective responsibility, more about right or wrong than issues of power, more about sexual improprieties than draconian economic policies, more about poor people than rich people, more about individuals who suffer from physical and emotional pain than those who restrict and profit from their care. (Witkin, 2000, p. 199)

An Experience with Advocacy-Based Ethics

Knowing the standards and then applying our obligation to the broader society as social workers presents a professional challenge in a changing world of overtime, family, privatization of services, layoffs, consolidation, and funding cutbacks. These issues, which affect not only our professional lives but also our individual selves, all too often place macro advocacy practice at the bottom of our priorities. Sometimes in our hectic lives, it is easier to ignore or forget these infrequently cited ethical obligations. We, as copresenters of advocacy ethics training, have lived this as well, experiencing the contradiction that not having enough time to be an advocate often results in silence that subsequently has neglected, maybe even hurt, the broader society we are obligated to. From this concern came the passion and catalyst to educate others about social workers' ethical obligation to broader society.

Our Beginnings

After being asked to develop an ethics workshop by the Houston branch of NASW-TX in January 2006, the copresenters wanted to design a unique ethics workshop to engage participants beyond the usual grumbling about continuing education and licensure requirements. We know—we have done some of that grumbling ourselves. Therefore, as copresenters we saw this as an opportunity to exert our passions for macro-level practice and advocacy. It was clear that this topic would be different from most ethics workshops in that it would both fit within our interests and also, we hoped, inspire other social workers to engage in the ethical obligations of macro practice and advocacy.

We were naturally drawn to this topic because of our professional and political leanings and hoped that others would be interested, or at least willing, to consider the ideas inherent in such a presentation. As licensed social workers who had worked with individuals but been drawn by necessity or passion to advocacy for vulnerable populations, we are clearly macro-level practitioners and educators. Having served on political action committees, in community coalitions, in roles as public policy analysts, and more, we felt that professional social workers could benefit from a renewed exposure to our ethical obligations to engage in political action. We also knew that if nothing else, there would be participants needing continuing education units credits to renew their state licensure!

About Us
We believe that a part of the success from our advocacy ethics workshop has its origins in our political leanings, bias toward advocacy, personalities, combined and differing knowledge, use of self, and established friendship—both collegially and socially. It seems to help that we have different reasons for entering the macro practice arena: Amy, having worked in the mental health field for years and experiencing the dramatic impact of state budget cuts, was driven into advocacy to save her job and the jobs of other social workers; Heather was initiated into the world of political social work during her master's training and completed the first policy analysis dissertation at the Graduate College of Social Work at the University of Houston, and she has never looked back.

It was also of benefit that we had different experiences and expertise in the macro practice arena but are similar in our sense of humor and expectation that all social workers engage in advocacy to promote social justice (even in the simplest of ways). Amy was drawn to the philosophical suppositions around ethics and ethical practice, and Heather was drawn to the applied arena of ethical practice; this combination resulted in a relatively comprehensive review of ethics for focusing on advocacy and macro practice. During our presentations, we trust that if one presenter misses something, the other will catch it and expand on the topic. Also, we have expertise in different areas; when one of us cannot answer a question, the other more than likely can. Most important, we share the value that it is negligent not to engage in advocacy practice to the broader society, and we have made it our charge to convey this responsibility to others through our advocacy ethics workshop. We are determined to inspire this in others, because in our ever-changing social welfare environment, not doing so can, and has, resulted in harm not only to our clients, but also to our livelihood and profession.

Professional, Personal, and Political Environments
It seemed that at this time in our profession's history and in our state and nation's political trajectory, it was imperative that social workers engage in the discourse and debate of working to promote social justice, thus necessitating that we engage

in advocacy. Whether operating within a micro, mezzo, or macro professional environment, social workers in the past several years have experienced a feeling of imposition—that things were happening *to* us and our clients—and perhaps we felt helpless as our working world morphed into something different, styled by political powers beyond our reach. Although these reactions were natural and hence kept professional social workers in their micro worlds, we were both often frustrated by some colleagues who continued to focus on this realm of intervention and who failed to share their insights and understanding of social problems and social need with larger decision-making bodies. Who better to advocate for the vulnerable and oppressed than the professionals who work with those in need each and every day, particularly given our ethical obligation to do so?

In addition, while the first iteration of this presentation was being developed in January 2006, the 2006 election cycle was approaching: a historic time when helping professionals, as well as ordinary citizens, were beginning to assert their voices and gain momentum in political action. This momentum was more evident in the 2008 election cycle, when professionals and citizens alike engaged in civics and volunteerism for campaigns, followed the primaries, considered candidate's platforms, and ultimately cast their votes—one of the most fundamental acts of advocacy and political action. Over these past two election cycles, both state and federal, social workers have transitioned from the helpless feelings of disempowerment to reclaiming that power, professionally, personally, and politically, through a renewed awareness of the broader society, macro-level practice, and political advocacy. Perhaps we can even assert this cultural shift within our profession, which we have seen in a fresh response to our advocacy ethics presentation.

The Presentation and Response

We've conducted this ethics of advocacy training on several occasions now, and, fortunately, we find that social workers and helping professionals are interested and enthusiastic about the content. We find that audience reactions have been different from the normal expectations of conventional ethics workshops; the grumbling is not as loud! We work hard to ensure that the training is interesting; it is difficult to sit still for three hours, no matter what you're listening to.

Our title was Advocacy Ethics: Connecting the Code to Macro Practice, and our goals were as follows:

- facilitate the connection between the code of ethics and our responsibility to broader society through advocacy and macro practice;
- demonstrate ethical principles by utilizing ethical dilemma screens as tools to resolve macro-level conflicts;
- apply learning in discussion of implications of macro-level practice and advocacy in current trends and environments; and
- advance social work professionals' knowledge of specific methods and vehicles available for engaging in macro practice and advocacy.

Having offered this training on four occasions thus far, we have found that the social workers and helping professionals who have attended have been open to the content and acknowledge their responsibilities to the broader society, outlined in the NASW Code of Ethics. Participants have openly and passionately shared their advocacy and social action experiences during the course of the presentations, including their own ethical dilemmas in social action as well as their frustrations with professional and political environments from which they are operating.

It has become clear that the vast majority of people in their professional or personal lives engage in advocacy to promote social justice on some level in their community or other communities around the world. We validate and emphasize the importance of any social action, regardless of preconceived judgments of its efficacy, during the training. This is crucial because we assume our social actions must have some immediate result, when in reality they rarely do and are instead the stepping stones to social change. The social workers in the sessions have shared an appreciation for reenergizing their commitment to social justice. We find additional gratitude for offering alternative language and constructs for use in defining their activities. Additionally, social workers who are less involved in these areas appreciated the specific tools, websites, and ideas of local groups involved in advocacy as vehicles, affording them the opportunity to begin their involvement in macro practice and advocacy. Our best measure thus far of responses, in addition to the venue and number of attendees, has been the scenario experiential learning piece within the training.

Scenarios
We put attendees in groups to apply ethical screens, previously delivered in the training content, to various controversial and challenging scenarios, using this interaction to gauge reaction to the ethics workshops through the exchanges during the scenario problem-solving process. We change these scenarios to meet a particular audience's specific needs. For example, we pose funding and cut-back issues to administrative professionals. This is not a deliberate attempt to make attendees uncomfortable, but rather to help them think about macro issues and the advocacy implications embedded in the scenarios.

A scenario example:

> You are the director of the state department of social services. The governor tells you and all other state agencies to cut 10 percent of the budget for the next biennial fiscal year. You have to revise your budget immediately. You meet with your senior staff to discuss ways to cut programs, with all programs being affected. You realize that to comply with the governor's mandate, you have to reduce the number of people eligible for public emergency assistance by 43,000, who will mostly be persons who are unable to work, single, and in need of health care and welfare benefits from the state.

The issues that are addressed by groups attempting to solve the macro-level ethical dilemmas are relevant to their professional setting, namely, administrative concerns, differing professional arenas, and funding issues that are macro reflections of how social welfare is valued, or not, within our state and federal governments.

While the scenarios serve as a measure of the increase in receptivity to macro-level advocacy and participation, they also convey some primary issues inherent in our obligation to the broader society. First, macro practice is uncomfortable, so we tend not to engage in it or avoid it altogether; it touches our deepest concerns about society and ourselves through learning and experience. Second, it is daunting, and we assume that it must be so; therefore, we feel it is beyond our grasp or influence. And last, it is a collaborative effort that entails the coming together of many differing values but with the same ethical purpose in social action. Our purpose as copresenters in the scenario exercises is to dispel advocacy myths and reveal that macro-level advocacy is not only crucial, but also feasible and rewarding.

Implications

Considering our passion and purpose in delivering this advocacy ethics training, we have noticed some professional implications as we continue to present this topic. The first implication is that this type of content must be disseminated to beginning social workers. If this ethical code and value are instilled in new social workers and individuals new to the profession—made a part of their fundamental work ethic—then their ability and success at macro-level advocacy will become second nature.

We are social workers, and what makes us unique is our obligation to the broader society and our passion for fulfilling this obligation. If we reach newly developed social workers with this primary value quickly, we will not have to undo their potential fear of it. A second implication is that social workers in different roles do respond differently to advocacy ethics. We think in terms of our working world, which is natural, and ethics trainings on macro-level practice should integrate and be flexible with content to address the specific macro issues of various social workers. We have attempted to do this by modifying training content to be work site–specific, predominantly in the scenarios. A third implication is the level of stress a social worker may be experiencing when participating in this type of workshop. For example, we Texas social workers have experienced much trauma over the past several years engaging in social activism for hurricane evacuees and then becoming hurricane evacuees ourselves. We have also dealt with privatization and funding cuts, consolidation and job loss, restructuring, and systemic changes. As advocacy ethics trainers, we must attend to these needs and validate our audience's difficulty in engaging in macro-level action while sometimes barely making it financially, personally, and even professionally. A final implication is whether delivering the content or receiving the content, we must convey a context of comfort, be it through humor, the interplay or expertise of the presenters, or relaxed interaction with the audience. Requiring the critical thinking involved in advocacy and macro practice easily conjures discomfort; therefore, what we do as copresenters to make the process engaging, inspiring, and composed will increase learning and decrease anxiety about the topic. Again, just as with beginning social workers, those of us who have been around for a while are called to recreate this second nature within ourselves: that nature that makes us unique and effective as macro-level practitioners and political advocates.

What Next

As we have seen during our short tenure as advocacy ethics trainers, evidenced in the attendees' evolving responses to macro-level political advocacy, we are encouraged that this trend will continue and that we can reach more diverse audiences to spread our passion for the political. Especially since the election of President Obama and significant changes in the Texas legislature, there may be a consensus of renewed hope to increase social work advocacy with a new-found and powerful

voice. Cultural paradigms are shifting, and for social workers this is a great opportunity to instill inspiration and create a "second nature" of public agency and political action, taking the lead in the ethical obligation to our broader society.

Heather Kanenberg, Ph.D., LMSW
University of Houston–Clear Lake
Amy Russell, Ph.D., LMSW
Texas State University–San Marcos

All Social Work Is Political, So . . .

1. Read the new NASW Code of Ethics, and highlight all areas that reference political action.

2. If your colleague did not take the necessary advocacy effort to address a client's problem, do you think your colleague should be reported? State your reasons.

3. Read the editorial page of a newspaper for five days in a row. How much was written on social issues? Did the editorials take a position that is consistent with social work values?

4. Interview three practicing social workers involved in political activity, and discuss why their political activities are consistent with their social work role.

5. At your school, organize and conduct a panel of policy players (local legislators, lobbyists, providers, clients) to discuss a policy that is currently being proposed or revised. Frame questions from the described value perspectives.

Suggested Readings

Edelman, Murray. 1974. "The Political Language of the Helping Professions." *Politics and Society* 4 (May): 295–310.
Gordon, William. 1965. "Knowledge and Value: Their Distinction and Relationship in Clarifying Social Work Practice." *Social Work* 10: 32–39.
Levy, Charles S. 1976. "Personal versus Professional Values: The Practitioner's Dilemmas." *Clinical Social Work Journal* 4 (Summer): 110–120.

References

Council on Social Work Education. 2001. *Educational Policy and Accreditation Standards.* Alexandria, VA: CSWE.
DiFranks, Nikki Nelson. 2008. "Social Workers and the NASW Code of Ethics: Belief, Behavior, Disjuncture." *NASW News,* 53 (2): 167–176.
Gallagher, L. Jerome, Megan Gallagher, Kevin Perese, Susan Schreiber, and Keith Watson. 1998. "Welfare Reform and Children: Potential Implications." *The Urban Institute,* No. A-23.
Grief, Geoffrey L. 2004. "When a Social Worker Becomes a Voluntary Commissions and Calls on the Code of Ethics." *Social Work* 49 (2): 277–280.
Hardina, Donna. 2004. "Guidelines for Ethical Practice in Community Organization." *Social Work* 49 (4): 595–604.

Haynes, K. 1996. "The Future of Political Social Work." In *Future Issues for Social Work Practice*, Paul R. Raffoul and C. Aaron McNeece (eds.), pp. 266–276. Boston: Allyn & Bacon.

Haynes, K. 1998. "The One Hundred Year Debate." *Social Work* 48 (6): 501–509.

Influencing State Policy. Fall 1999. "Student Projects." *Influence* 3.2: 10.

Lowenberg, F., and R. Dolgoff. 1996. *Ethical Decisions for Social Work Practice*. Itasca, IL: F. E. Peacock.

Mickelson, J. 1998. "Advocacy." In *Encyclopedia of Social Work*, 19th ed. Washington, DC: NASW Press.

National Association of Social Workers. 2008. Code of Ethics. Washington, DC: NASW Press.

Pinderhuges, Elaine. 1994. "Empowerment as an Intervention Goal: Early Ideas." In *Education and Research for Empowerment Practice*, Lorraine Gutierrez and Paula Nurius (eds.), pp. 17–30. Seattle: Center for Policy and Practice Research.

Reamer, F. G. 1998. *Ethical Standards in Social Work: A Critical Review of the NASW Code of Ethics*. Washington, DC: NASW Press.

Rees, Stuart. 1991. *Achieving Power: Practice and Policy in Social Welfare*. North Sydney, Australia: Allen and Unwin.

Rose, Stephen M. 2000. "Reflections on Empowerment-Based Practice. *Social Work* 45 (5): 403–412.

Sarri, Rosemary C. 1992. "Is Social Work Inherently Conservative—Designed to Protect Vested Interests of Dominant Power Groups?" In *Controversial Issues in Social Work*, Eileen Gambrill and Robert Pruger (eds.), pp. 39–51. Boston: Allyn & Bacon.

Specht, Harry, and Mark Courtney. 1994. *Unfaithful Angels: How Social Work Has Abandoned Its Mission*. New York: Free Press.

VanVoorhis, Rebecca morrison, and Carol Hostetter. 2006. *Journal of Social Work Education* 42 (1): 105–122.

Wagner, David. 1990. *The Quest for a Radical Profession: Social Service Careers and Political Ideology*. Lanham, MD: University Press of America.

Walz, Tom, and Heather Ritchie. 2000. "Gandhian Principles in Social Work Practice: Ethics Revisited." *Social Work* 45 (3): 213–222.

Witkin, Stanley L. 2000. "Ethics-R-Us." *Social Work* 45 (3): 197–200.

Wolk, James, Jackie E. Pray, Toby Weismiller, and David Dempsey. 1996. "Political Practica: Educating Social Work Students for Policymaking." *Journal of Social Work Education* 32 (1): 91–100.

The Emergence of a Social Work Polity

You take people as far as they will go, not as far as you would like them to go.

—Jeannette Rankin*

Jeannette felt the cool fall winds of Montana on her face as she walked through the park, thinking about her past and about what the immediate future would bring. In just a few moments, the course of her professional life could alter dramatically.

She had known she was in the right profession when she received her degree in social work from a New York university. Yet, after practicing in various agencies, she had begun to develop mixed feelings about her work. She liked children and found meaning working with orphans and abused children, but more and more she felt empty and confused. Some difficult questions were on her mind: Why are children abandoned? Why are orphans treated poorly in institutions? Why are so many women beaten and left homeless by their husbands? Could one social worker really make a difference?

Jeannette understood that people have problems in the course of their lives, but it perplexed her that society didn't seem to care. Why did the government spend so much money on the military and so little on what she considered to be the country's greatest asset—the welfare of its children?

Jeannette knew she was good at her profession, but now she wasn't sure whether the new direction in which her career was heading would bring about help for the children. She was taking a hard road, yet she was convinced that it was necessary. She recently had spent many months traveling around the state discussing the problems that she encountered.

She knew that she could not continue working at the Children's Home Society. She found the job of locating homes for orphans intolerable. Seeing her clients traded like cattle or living under the deplorable conditions that existed in institutions, she became increasingly frustrated with the necessarily slow and

*Hannah Josephson, *First Lady in congress: Jeannette Rankin* (Indianapolis: Bobbs-Merrill, 1974), p. xii.

singular efforts she made on behalf of these children. As an advocate for these defenseless and unloved children, she could not help but realize that many of the institutions' policies negated the positive changes she could make. She had come to know that the greatest possibility for reform was through influencing the laws that govern social institutions.

It seemed like only yesterday she had filed with the election commission to run for Congress, yet here she was today on her way to learn the election results. Competing with seven men had definitely been an uphill battle, but her background and knowledge of social problems had made a difference. If she were elected, her hard work in campaigning would pay off.

It took several days to tally all the votes, and in the end the Democrats swept the election except for one instance: Jeannette won her congressional seat by only 7,567 votes. On April 2, 1917, at the age of 36, Jeannette Rankin was installed as the first woman and the first social worker in the U.S. Congress (Lavassaur, 1984).

For Rankin, case advocacy for children led to a career in class and legislative advocacy. She lost her bid for reelection in 1919 because of her controversial vote opposing the United States' entry into World War I. Hers was the only opposing vote. The defeat did not stop her political activities, however, and she continued to work hard for women's suffrage and for reform of government policies toward children. She was reelected in 1941, only to vote again against American entry into another war, this time against Japan. She left her imprint on this country and its policies, on the peace movement, and on women's rights.

Jeannette Rankin portrays the transition and movement from individual to political reform today. Embodied in her, and in many of the early social workers of this period, is the simultaneous growth of social conscience, "scientific methodology," and macro-level reform that logically emanate from individual problem solving. Her career exemplifies the fact that involvement in social action to meet human needs and improve social functioning is a logical outgrowth of social work practice. Clearly, today's social workers are the heirs of a powerful tradition of social action.

Although social action is not synonymous with political intervention, social action strategies, when used to intervene in the affairs of government, are political strategies. Furthermore, although social workers have been influential in the political arena, politics has not consistently been a central arena for social work practice. Consequently, a historic and ongoing dynamic tension exists between the two institutions.

During the decades of professional development following World War I, the main body of social work may have turned away from its tradition of reform, but social workers never totally abandoned this tradition. In fact, the intensity of the debate over social reform changes with the general social climate. A lessening of disagreements among social workers on this issue not only will contribute to the unification of the profession but also could produce a multitude of interventions aimed at the formation and renovation of public policy.

No profession is in a better position to judge the impact of social policy than is social work. Although other professions direct their services toward specific problems, social work as a profession is involved with the overall impact on both the individual and the community of unemployment, inadequate health care, lack of education, poor housing, and insufficient income. Nonetheless, the social work profession has not systematically and consistently sought, nor has it been asked to take, a significant role in the planning of social programs or the formulation of social policy. Currently, there is increasing emphasis on professionalism within the field. Social workers should not be criticized for their efforts to attain professional standing because acceptance of social work as a profession is basic to achieving the respect and authority necessary to effectively meet its obligations to those it serves. But the drive toward professionalism seems to have paralleled the profession's weakening concern with social reform.

> The coalescing and maturation of the trends in social work, in terms of the performance of a function rather than a cause, in emphasizing methods and techniques rather than goals, and in grasping for higher professional status . . . appear to be commitments of the process of professionalization itself in the United States, but if this complex of trends continues, where are we headed? Three consequences are likely to follow. First, a continuing de-emphasis on the controversial social action which has broad social implications; second, a related lessening of attempts to influence social policy and the acceptance of the role of technician implementor, and third, change in the ideology of social work that will lessen the gap between its system of ideas and that of the dominant groups in society. (Bisno, 1969)

Indeed, at times, social action has been de-emphasized to the point that many question whether it really is the business of social work. For example, in a 1972 study of fifty-one schools of social work, the majority of social work graduate students and educators did not consider social action or the initiation of social change to be a primary function of the profession (Carlton and Jung, 1972). A mid-1980s survey of undergraduate and graduate bulletins of schools of social work found there was minimal inclusion of course titles or descriptions that reflect political content or terminology (Haynes and Mickelson, 1985). A review of MSW program concentrations indicated that five had community organization concentrations, two had community or social development concentrations, one had social strategies, one had social justice, and one had political social work. Therefore, fewer than 10 percent of the accredited MSW programs self-describe anything resembling a "politicized" social work concentration. Add to this the data that approximately only 5 percent of MSW students in these ten programs are likely enrolled in these political concentrations, and it is clear that we are not, in the early twenty-first century, preparing many political social workers (Haynes, 1996).

These findings may reflect the professional MSW program's traditional bias toward the direct-service method of intervention. The arguments suggest that the passionate but uninformed quest for relevance in activism may be a factor that is responsible for deprofessionalizing social work. Others have suggested that activism in social work downgrades professional practice.

We have noted in previous editions of this book a professional educational trend for MSW programs to include political content and/or specializations;

however, that trend seemingly has been reversed. That reversal and the "generalist" focus of many MSW programs may provide diminished visibility for the role of political advocacy and the specific skills it entails. However, strengthened language within the profession's code of ethics and accreditation standards (Chapter 2) seems to support an optimistic prediction that political awareness will increase. Change continues to be slow, but there may be a gradual shift to a renewed focus on advocacy, empowerment, and political social work.

In fact, it was not until the mid 1990s, nearly a decade after the first edition of this book was published, that we were able to include a significant number of contributions to the literature in this area. It is a great satisfaction for us that each subsequent edition has included new authors or more recent updates and revisions to earlier work, thus suggesting a readership for this focus. However, we continue to contend that despite this continuing literature, political social work or politicized social work practice is still viewed as atypical, aberrant, temporary, or nonprofessional even in today's professional and political realities.

We understand that historic tensions between specialization and generalist practice, between macro and micro methods of intervention, and between enhanced professionalism and increased politicalization—as well as the perceived conflict with our professional ethics and the real and mistaken limitations with social workers' participation in political activity—have been deterrents to including political advocacy in social work curricula.

According to a 2008 NASW work force study, 68 percent of social workers indicated that they worked at the micro level (NASW, 2008). Unfortunately, this is an increase since the mid-1990s study indicating that 57 percent of social workers functioned as direct service providers. In both studies, most social workers practicing at a mezzo or macro level do so as managers, administrators, planners, or program evaluators. Indeed, there is little provision for operating at a level beyond or outside direct-service treatment and management. Only community organization work includes taking action to improve social conditions as a primary area of responsibility. Yet unfortunately, as noted earlier, training in this orientation is no longer provided in most social work graduate programs. Although advocacy may be an underpinning for BSW programs, the reality is still that content, placements, and curriculum space are devoted more to direct practice, which is where the majority of BSW-level jobs will be (Wolk et al., 1996).

Generally, professional schools do not furnish training in the strategies and techniques fundamental to effective implementation of social reform. The option of social action simply is not offered to most social work students, although without the means to achieve these ends, a commitment to social change and reform is useless (Reeser and Leighninger, 1990). In the survey by Wolk and others (1996), among the reporting programs, fewer than 20 percent of BSW and 50 percent of MSW programs offered practica in government relations; fewer than 15 percent of BSW and 33 percent of MSW offered practica in policy advocacy and development; and only two BSW and no MSW programs offered practica in electoral politics. Studies have suggested that holders of BSWs and MSWs ranked social policy and social legislation as among the least important areas of knowledge and skill

(Bigger staff and Kolevzon, 1980; Figuera-McDonough, 1993). Balancing these bleaker realities are some reasons to be optimistic about consistent attention to, if not growth in, the curriculum focus on political social work practice and, therefore, students' readiness to embrace it. One reason for this optimism is the report from a survey about social workers' political participation (Hamilton and Fauri, 2001). Four categories of predictor variables were used: resources for participation, networks of recruitment to participation, political engagement, and political socialization. Of importance to the authors' premise was the fact that the strongest predictor of political participation was political engagement, or the sense of the effectiveness of their political skills.

More validation for this finding came from a 2008 study, which concluded that "study results support previous suggestions that social work students are more adequately prepared for clinical or direct services work but do not receive sufficient preparation for policy practice" (Ritter, 2008, p. 355). The implications for social work education, according to this author, are as follows:

> Instead of students being passive learners, policy courses should enable students to develop advocacy skills through a variety of experiential activities such as lobbying legislators, testifying at in-class mock congressional hearings, developing media campaigns, field organizing, working with coalitions and grass-roots movements, volunteering for political campaigns, attending political meetings and debates, and writing op-eds, letters to the editor, position papers, and policy briefs. Social work educators should provide opportunities for students to get involved with local politics or advocacy organizations in their community as part of their preparation for policy practice. This could be accomplished in policy or community courses, or as part of a field practicum or service learning experience. (Ritter, 2008, p. 355).

Beyond social work education, organizations are generally endorsing the inclusion of civic engagement into higher education curricula and experiences. Indeed, as these authors have been arguing for more than two decades, "courses and programs do succeed in increasing students' political understanding, participation, skills, and action. This is so both for students who enter the courses and programs with little interest in politics and those who enter already very interested and engaged" (Carnegie Foundation for the Advancement of Teaching, 2007). This initiative is working with the American Democracy Project of the American Association of State Colleges and Universities (AASCU). While it seems remarkable that others are generating greater interest in and advocacy for advocacy, policy practice, or civic engagement than is the profession of social work, their acknowledgment and legitimacy may well be harbingers of a more progressive time in social work education and practice.

As earlier noted, both the revised code and accreditation standards, the latter of which go into effect for all programs with the October 2010 CSWE Commission on Accreditation meeting, show visible progress. Additionally the initiation and growth of Influencing State Policy (ISP) (www.statepolicy.org) continues to be heartening. This national organization was established in 1997 to assist social work faculty and students to gain awareness of and skills in the means to influence state policy. As an important by-product, ISP has collected base count data to set goals that measure the political participation of social work faculty and students, such as number of faculty liaisons to ISP, number of students who visit their state legislature, and number of students in political placements. To further these goals, ISP has initiated a national competition for MSW and BSW students called State Policy Plus, and in 2001 the organization raised funds to help support a doctoral dissertation in state policy research (Schneider and Netting, 1999).

 Another important element of ISP is an annual contest for MSW and BSW students to submit examples of their attempts to influence state policy. There are cash awards for this competition. Although we assume that it has been effective in raising visibility and legitimacy, for 2007 there were only fourteen BSW submissions and twelve MSW submissions, and in both categories some educational programs produced more than one submission. So, given that as of 2009 there are 465 accredited BSW programs and 191 accredited MSW programs, submissions came from fewer than 4% of these programs.

However, there is optimism that standards will provide more direction and support for this content in curriculum, that national organizations within and outside social work will bring continued visibility to its efficacy, and that the more it is included and the more proficient students become in the skills areas, the more these new professionals will connect political advocacy to their practice. And as optimism in the country builds, we view the increased interest and efforts in political advocacy by both NASW and CSWE to be positive, if not yet as strong and dramatic as we would like. The NASW document *Turning Priorities into Action: How the Social Work Profession Will Help* (2009) and the fall 2009 CSWE Annual Program Meeting theme "Bridging Rights, Cultures and Justice: Social Work as a Change Agent" are flashpoints that bear watching.

Despite these harbingers of optimism for the future, the failure of the social work profession to assume a position of leadership in the movement for social reform is inconsistent with its historical and philosophical background. The relatively nonactivist professional even in this first decade of the new millennium stands in stark contrast with reformers from the turn of the previous century. A major characteristic of social workers of yesteryear was their efforts to direct the attention of the public toward social injustice (Meyer, 1970, p. 20), whereas a frequently noted characteristic of social work since the 1970s is its failure to speak out about the inadequacies of welfare and other programs in urban communities as well as in the rest of the United States (Ginsberg, 1970, p. 19; Thompson, 1994). Clearly, the profession's apparent reticence to address social problems that undermine the self-respect and morale of the individual is incongruent with its belief in the dignity and worth of human beings. How can a profession that regards the welfare of the individual or group as its primary obligation fail to speak out for social change?

It is our contention that professional social workers must oppose social injustice and, more important, intervene to right social wrongs. However, we repeat: It is insufficient and futile to promulgate moral imperatives without sensitizing professionals to these issues and providing them with techniques for successful intervention.

In 1969, I was a struggling social worker with a social conscience. I had a master's degree from the University of Maryland School of Social Work (1965) in community organizing and social planning. I was busy trying to decentralize the local welfare department. Then I got a call that started me on the "road" to the U.S. Senate.

A community group had learned that a highway project was going to destroy the East Baltimore neighborhood where my family settled when they first came to this country. I also knew that there was an expressway coming through the west side of Baltimore that was going to take out the first black home ownership neighborhood in Baltimore City. The road was going to take the homes of a lot of people in Baltimore's proud neighborhoods—Polish, Italian, Greek, and Black—and give them almost nothing in return. And it threatened the most historic neighborhood in Baltimore, Fells Point, where good and solid citizens had lived and worked since before the Revolutionary War.

I got fired up. "We didn't let the British take Fells Point, we didn't let the termites take Fells Point, and we're not going to let the state roads commission take Fells Point," was what I said when I found out that their idea of community input and community participation was choosing the color of the planning grid and the kind of stone we wanted the guardrail made of.

We talked to the planners, the architects, and the politicians. We organized the neighborhoods and we challenged the cost–benefit analysis. We ran bake sales so that we could rent buses to take us to City Hall, the State House, and Washington, DC. We put our mimeograph machine borrowed from the Holy Rosary Society up against their $5,000 audiovisual equipment, and our coalition up against their design concept team.

And today, when people talk about the wonderful, new downtown Baltimore, they are seeing a "revitalization" that began with a citizen protest movement and an organized community. Because we won the fight against the road commission, we won the fight for Baltimore's neighborhoods.

And I decided it was time to quit knocking on City Hall's doors, move inside, open them up, and let the people in. I announced my candidacy for the Baltimore city council. Running against an established political machine, I did what I know best: grassroots organizing. Through the summer of 1971, my team and I went door to door. I knocked on 15,000 doors that summer, wore out five pairs of shoes, I got mugged by fourteen Chihuahuas, and I won my seat on the city council.

In City Hall, I took my social worker's skills and made the personal political. From potholes to public education, I worked to save neighborhoods one person and one problem at a time. And at every step, I was trying to do more good for more people.

In 1976, I ran for the U.S. House of Representatives. Going back to my training, I went back to the community and that grassroots organization. And I carried the same skills and values to Washington when I won.

After ten years in the House, I ran for the U.S. Senate. After a tough primary against another sitting congressman and the sitting governor, I had a general election campaign for the history books. For the first time, both parties nominated women candidates for the U.S. Senate. Expanding my grassroots organization statewide, I ran a people-based campaign and won decisively.

In the Senate, I have achieved a number of firsts: the first Democratic woman to hold a seat not previously held by her husband, the first Polish American to serve in both houses of Congress, the first woman to chair a subcommittee on the powerful Appropriations Committee.

Being the first, however, is not the most important thing. Although I am honored, I know there will be many more who follow in my footsteps. I worked hard to get seats on important committees, committees where I can make a real difference for people's day-to-day lives and needs.

There is one first, though, that has meant a real difference: I am the first social worker in the U.S. Senate. Now I have a caseload of four million Marylanders! And though I am practicing in a different forum, those skills and values I learned as a community organizer on the streets of Baltimore are what make me an effective leader in the corridors of Congress.

Barbara Mikulski, MSW
U.S. Senator (Maryland)

Although it was almost ninety years from Jeannette Rankin's election to Congress to the election of Barbara Mikulski to the U.S. Senate, there is no clearer indication that social workers are achieving a greater political influence than to see them elected and accepted to one of the nation's highest representative offices.

The Reform Period

The Progressive Era (1895–1915) often is hailed as a proud moment in social work history. Early figures in social work have been lauded for their efforts on behalf of social action, and Jane Addams frequently is chosen as a model of the "involved" social worker. Caseworkers from charity organizations and settlement houses that existed in that era are heralded for having been in the vanguard of social reform. However, even though advocacy once occupied a prominent place in social work practice and this function was highly visible early in the history of social casework, in examining the actions and interventive styles of this era in more detail, one notes that many social workers honored advocacy more with rhetoric than with practice.

Not only was the Progressive Era a prominent time for social work advocacy but these also were the years during which social work became established as an identifiable vocation. This era probably was the liveliest period of social reform and political advocacy in the history of the social work profession, as well as in the history of the United States. Thus, it is not coincidental that the social work profession began with a focus on social reform. This was a direct result of the larger societal political climate at the time.

Social work during this period emerged from two separate interacting movements, both of English origin: the Charity Organization Society movement, which began in this country in the late 1870s and spread rapidly, so that by 1900 it had made its way into virtually every major American city and many smaller ones as well; and the settlement movement, which took root in the United States in the 1880s and spread just as quickly.

By 1900 both of these movements were solidly established. Although their overall goals were essentially the same (protecting individual initiative and freedom), their short-range goals and methods were quite different and frequently in conflict. The Charity Organization Society movement sought to reform on an individual level the character of those who were "losers" in society, whereas the settlement movement worked to reform the social environment that made people "losers." The Charity Organization Society movement was not as oblivious to reform as this oversimplification might suggest, but social reform was never its dominant theme, nor was the idea of reforming an individual's character totally absent in the settlement movement.

Furthermore, a gap apparently existed between what was said by the Charity Organization Society's leadership and what was done by its staff and volunteers. The principles of scientific charity were never uniformly diffused or implemented. Although articles and agency records from this period contain some statements by social workers impatient to see the day when charitable relief, with all its humiliations and harrowing uncertainties, would be replaced by a fairer distribution of income and a complete system of social hygiene, education, and insurance, the -society's handbook seems insidiously pervaded by nineteenth-century social Darwinism. It suggests, for example, that only two possible reasons could explain why a family with a father present would be in need of assistance: either the father is physically or mentally incapacitated, or he is handicapped by some defect of character or temperament (Lloyd, 1970; Sears, 1918).

Even during this period the social worker seemed to play more the role of facilitator or broker than that of advocate. Although references to professionalization abounded in publications of the era, settlement workers were indifferent or even antagonistic to proposals for formalizing methods for helping. For this reason, their activities notwithstanding, settlement house workers did not significantly contribute to the development of social work methodology but were more engaged in activities such as promoting factory legislation, better housing, adequate wages and working hours, arbitration of labor disputes, and providing free employment services. A passage from Jane Addams's *Twenty Years at Hull House* notes:

> We found ourselves spending many hours and efforts to secure support for deserted women, insurance for bewildered widows, damages for injured operators, furniture from the clutches of the installment store, constantly acting between the various institutions of the city and the people for whose benefits these institutions were erected. (Addams, 1940, p. 167)

Case-level advocacy was prevalent within the settlement movement. Particularly in view of its espoused objective of improving living conditions, the settlement movement epitomized the idea that a social agency should serve as an arena for the conversion of private troubles into public issues.

In summary, even during the Progressive Era reform period, case rather than class advocacy was the primary strategy of social workers. Furthermore, the translation of these skills into more formalized methodology did not materialize. Consequently, the decade of the 1920s left social work open to psychoanalytic theory and technique.

The New Deal and Beyond

With the New Deal era of the 1930s came another wave of political involvement by social workers. Although social action strategies were not necessarily well developed or formalized, the widespread recognition of social problems and the simultaneous identification of the public's responsibility for them provided broad opportunities for public policy intervention.

The massive social problems created by the Depression encouraged the development of a coalition of spokespersons for the poor, many of whom had been apathetic or even hostile to the idea of public welfare. Consequently, during this era the social work profession became enmeshed in the national swing toward radicalism that was evident at the time in political parties.

By the 1930s, professional schools of social work provided a forum and a focus for critical thought about social service administration and the broader vistas of social welfare. However, their curricula were still somewhat disorganized, and their primary emphasis was still on casework. The social work profession was not the leading faction in the nation's political–social reform movements but a participant. Political activity was viewed by the profession as a short-term requirement for achieving its reform goals but not as a legitimate social work method.

It was, however, during this period that Harry Hopkins, a social worker and political adviser, attained recognition as the controversial administrator of the first federal relief program in the history of the United States. His ascent from an administrator of a temporary state emergency relief fund in New York (at the time the largest state relief fund ever created) to head of the Federal Emergency Relief Administration and then of the Works Progress Administration was unprecedented.

Although unfortunately he came to symbolize the lavish use of federal funds, Hopkins contended that these thousands of projects not only had fed the hungry, clothed the needy, and sheltered the homeless but also had enriched the economy, ultimately affecting the lives of 15 million Americans. Because of his policies and programs devoted to mobilization of human labor power, he often has been hailed as the first national conservator of human resources in the United States. There were also other social workers during this period, such as Frances Perkins and those in the Children's Bureau and the Women's Bureau, who furthered important social causes.

The War on Poverty

From the time of the New Deal through the 1950s, social work matured as a profession. During these years, the social casework method was refined, and ego psychology became its dominant approach. United community charities and councils were developed to provide an organized method of meeting community needs. World War II and economic resurgence reemphasized individual dysfunctioning and, consequently, micro-level interventions. Social action was not a major emphasis during this period. Its absence set the stage for the subsequent renewal of professional interest in social action, which began to increase in the 1950s as professional social workers saw that many of the issues that concerned them could not be dealt with through individual therapeutic methods. Social workers issued calls to undertake social action against the erosion of civil liberties under McCarthyism, against the arms race, and in support of the developing fight for civil rights. Demonstration projects sponsored by the federal government and by foundations in the 1950s and early 1960s, such as the Grey Areas Project and Mobilization for Youth, provided a testing ground for new directions in community programs and new social work roles.

The mid-1950s were a landmark time for social work activity. The National Association of Social Workers was formed from the merger of several professional organizations, including the Association for the Study of Community Organization. The 1954 amendments to the Housing Act of 1949 required citizen participation in the formation of urban renewal plans, a requirement that set the stage for citizen participation clauses in other federal legislation. At the same time, a militant phase of the civil rights movement in the South introduced freedom rides, sit-ins, strikes, and protest marches.

Nonetheless, social action still was not emphasized in social work education, despite its use and partial legitimization in social work practice. Only a few practitioners and educators expected social action to become a major theme in social work education. As interest in social change spread, community organization became the focal point for students, practitioners, and educators oriented toward social change. Although community organization became a recognized methodological specialization built on a social action and class advocacy model, the general social worker's role was further removed from political involvement and intervention.

In the early to mid-1950s, fewer than 2 percent of all students enrolled in social work programs specialized in community organization. Community organization training was concerned with social welfare organization as a method of bringing about and maintaining adjustments between social welfare needs and social welfare resources. Preparation was primarily for practice in community welfare councils.

In 1955, Murray Ross presented community organization as a process in which community cooperation and collaboration could be built around problem solving. His formulation added new dimensions to community organization theory and practice. To the role of resource coordinator, popular in community welfare organizations, was added the enabler role. This practice method stressed helping communities to establish cooperation and reach goals by providing them with information and services in an objective manner (Ross, 1955).

Social Action Models

Attempts to respond to social changes gave rise during the 1950s to three models of social action in social work: citizen social worker, agent of social change, and actionist. The first model of social action, that of citizen social worker, is the oldest of the three. It calls for the professional social worker to use the information and knowledge gained through work with individuals and groups to inform the larger society of needed programs and policies. The citizen social worker confronts the problems of civil rights, international peace, equality of opportunity, expansion of social programs, automation and mechanization, suburbanization, and the need for preventive services as a concerned citizen, not as a professional obligation.

Many social workers came to embrace this model. Noting the professional social worker's responsibility for social action, Youngdahl (1966, p. 132) states:

> First, we must have knowledge and fact, then we must derive our convictions based on these facts, this is followed by zeal to do something about them. It is not one or the other, that is, case work or social action; rather, it is taking advantage of every opportunity to be helpful to people as individuals, groups, or in society as a whole.

He goes on to say that social work, in trying to understand the individual, has made efforts to get at the causes of situations and that our experience in dealing with numerous individuals has brought us to advocate certain social policies that will remove these causes and prevent the same thing from happening to others. This accounts for social work's broad interest in social legislation pertaining to housing, nutrition, recreation, and migrant workers, among other issues. However, according to this model, the primary reason social action is taken is because the social worker is an informed citizen.

The second model—agent of social change—developed in the late 1950s. Within this model, social action is defined as efforts toward purposeful change. The goal is to achieve desirable social goals using well-developed and well-formulated theoretical systems as guides to action.

This model developed new roles for the professional practitioner that emphasized active participation in an organization's political process. It suggested that social workers should be directly involved in political action and social policy formulation. These new roles were intended to produce change in institutional relations and policies via nondisruptive tactics.

Calls for more aggressive professional stances in policy formulation were extended during this period. Many theories suggested that social workers should enter the political arena and learn to deal more effectively with the community power structure.

In this model, the importance of working within agency or community structures is emphasized. The use of disruptive tactics, such as protests or strikes, is viewed as action that prevents the target system from continuing to operate as usual and, thus, is counterproductive.

The third social action model is that of the actionist. Actionists share the traditional social work concern for client groups but reject detachment, insistence on societal sanction for the profession, and the belief that rational planning and cooperation are possible. They believe that social change, particularly for disaffiliated people or groups, can be achieved only by developing and using political, economic, or social pressure.

The actionist role is one of involvement with the client group the actionist seeks to help. The goal is to bring about desired changes based on what the client group identifies as its needs. The selection of tactics or strategies is determined by whether they will be effective in achieving the desired goal.

The social actionist operates to a great extent on the basis of general principles, value considerations, and some operational instructions deduced from practice. The social actionist role is epitomized by the work in Chicago of Saul Alinsky (not a social worker by professional training) and the People's Organization in the 1960s. The primary ideology of that organization was that "all groups are moved by self-interest, the poor and the nonpoor alike; as soon as the poor and the victimized learn to see it that way, they'll be able to get power and control their destiny" (Alinsky, 1971, p. 41).

The actionist, although not opposed to using cooperation and collaboration as strategies, has more often been identified with attempts to develop power strategies. Actionists reject as confining the professional's identification with organizations and with social sanctions, and they tend to view conflict and bargaining as the best methods to bring about desired change.

What is important to actionists is the sanction of the group with which they are identified rather than the social sanction of their profession. The actionist model stresses ideological identification of social work with society's victims: the poor, the mentally ill, the unfortunate. Central to this method is the need for social work to support the attempts of the disaffiliated to develop power and fulfill their needs.

Although the preceding three models provided direction and sanction for an array of social action strategies for social workers, the first and last models are not based on a social action orientation for the social work profession as a whole. Rather, they focus on the social worker as an informed and politically active private citizen and as a member of a temporary coalition.

With the national rediscovery of poverty in the late 1950s and the packaging of an array of federal programmatic responses to "cultural deprivation" and "pockets of poverty" growing out of the 1964 Economic Opportunity Act, social work once again had the methods and social sanction to engage in social reform. Community organizing, local community needs assessments, welfare rights advocacy groups, and "maximum citizen participation" clauses in federal legislation gave increased impetus to macro-level interventive techniques. Schools of social work developed a community organizing curriculum; social workers were active in antiwar, civil rights, and welfare rights organizations; and African American social workers such as Whitney Young were active in the political arena.

Federalism

During the early 1970s, some of the reform ideologies and movements of the 1960s continued. Unfortunately, however, as the decade progressed and the War on Poverty programs became increasingly bureaucratized, social work practice and social work education began to focus on management and administrative theories and techniques, losing sight of advocacy and reform goals. As federal monies dwindled, competition for funds increased and skills in grant writing, planning, and financial accountability took on more importance.

Despite some shifts away from social action, in a 1970–71 report titled "Social Work Education in a Period of Change," Arnulf Pins, executive director of the Council on Social Work Education, made the following comments:

> Our nation, along with the rest of the world, is facing major social problems. Large segments of our population suffer from neglect, physical and mental illness, poverty, discrimination, and racism. Government leaders, citizen groups, and all professions must give immediate attention to the solution of these social and human problems. Social work has a unique role and opportunity. Consequently, social work education has a special responsibility and challenge, for it must prepare social work personnel with the commitment, knowledge, and skills needed: (1) to recognize and call attention to social needs, human injustices, and dysfunctional systems for service delivery; (2) to plan and bring about needed changes; and (3) to provide and administer social services in a more humane and effective way.

Additionally, the leadership of the Council on Social Work Education testified in the early 1970s before the Senate Finance Committee, highlighting deficiencies in existing family assistance plans and seeking the inclusion of funds for labor power development in a proposed companion social services bill.

Furthermore, Daniel Thursz exhorted fellow social workers to consider one of a number of social action strategies. He debunked the common myths that have kept social workers from participating in many common social action strategies: the limits set forth by federal and state Hatch Acts and false notions related to the profession's expertise, status, or dignity. In addition to the social action models of the previous decades, Thursz added civil disobedience, disruption, and "watchdogging" (Thursz, 1975).

The term *civil disobedience* refers to "any act or process of public defiance of a law or policy enforced by established government authorities, insofar as the action is premeditated, understood to be illegal or of contested legality and carried out for limited public ends through carefully chosen and limited means" (Thursz, 1975). The important aspect of this definition is that civil disobedience is a method of social action to be used by persons unwilling to accept the rules of the system as a whole. Consequently, the social worker who participates in civil disobedience, regardless of the motive, must be ready to pay the price imposed by society.

Most professional social workers do not condone violence. Disruption, however, is a social action technique that should not be confused with violence. Disruption may serve to call public attention to a cause and may serve as a prelude to new negotiations and advances in the relationship between an institution and the population it is expected to serve. The emergence of the National Welfare Rights Organization is a good illustration of this.

The watchdog role that Thursz describes, also called *monitoring,* is a social action strategy aimed at keeping institutions and their administrators faithful to a mission or policy objective. Administrators making complex determinations to establish criteria, determine eligibility, assess capability, evaluate past performance, or set a range of permissible experimentation have the power to advance or to thwart policy goals that will benefit or not benefit the intended service recipient and to realize or to subvert democratic will. According to Thursz (1975), social workers should be watchdogs of administrative regulations to ensure their consistent adherence to policy goals.

During the 1970s social work practice and education changed in three important ways. First, with the increased emphasis on program and financial accountability, training in macro-level skills, particularly at the graduate level, was directed toward management, budgeting, and program evaluation. Second, a baccalaureate-level, professionally trained social workforce emerged with the accreditation of BSW programs nationally. Third, doctoral education in social work experienced unparalleled growth.

These changes forced consideration of the differential use of social work labor power, as well as reconsideration of the core skills taught at all educational levels. The BSW core skills included linking, advocating, and brokering; master's-level specializations were either clinically or managerially oriented; and doctoral education focused on research and education. Consequently, as the profession entered the 1980s, social workers continued to play a minimal role in the political arena and to view political activity as the result of individual, idiosyncratic preferences rather than as a clearly stated objective of social work education and training.

However, some professional developments did occur during the 1970s that signaled the profession's reemerging awareness of political activities and processes. These included the National Association of Social Workers' (NASW) development of the Education Legislation Action Network (ELAN) and Political Action for Candidate Election (PACE). These subdivisions of NASW were created to affect legislative processes. ELAN was to do this through lobbying and PACE through the election of pro–human service candidates.

The primary strategies of these two organizations were to educate social workers through the dissemination of information about both legislation and candidates and to encourage social workers to support pro–human service issues and candidates and to oppose anti–human service issues and candidates. These efforts slowly filtered down to the state level, with parallel functions being performed by autonomous state organizations. Although both of these organizations have matured during the past decade, in 1990 they were still in the early stages of development. In fact, in some states neither of these organizations exists.

The New Federalism

The 1980s and the election of President Reagan began the era that, once again, shifted societal and, consequently, social service concerns toward fiscal conservatism and privatization. The expansion of public and federal programs evidenced throughout the decades of the 1960s and 1970s was blamed for increasing the federal deficit, was harkened as the harbinger of encroaching socialism, and did not "cure" poverty or social problems in this country.

Probably the most significant, long-lasting, and symbolic effect of this retrenchment was the Gramm-Rudman Balanced Budget and Emergency Deficit Control Act of 1985. This legislation was enacted to enforce substantial reductions in the amount of the annual deficit permitted in each of the ensuing five years, declining to zero in 1991.

Although the figures clearly indicated that the deficit had risen in less than five years by $130 billion, the reason for this increase was not expenditures on social services but rather enormous increases in military spending coupled with substantial reductions in federal taxes. Placing the burden of deficit reduction on domestic programs, primarily social services, was not only unreasonable, but inhumane and shortsighted.

The shortsightedness is marked by the fact that poverty, by any measure, increased by more than 27 percent in the 1980s, disproportionately affecting women, minorities, children, and the elderly. Moreover, the ranks of the working poor were considerably larger in the 1990s than in the late 1970s. Because these policies also simultaneously cut educational funds, these two forms of budget reduction together increased the problems of illiteracy, unemployment, family dissolution, homelessness, hunger, and domestic violence.

These policies have returned the focus to moving public assistance recipients off welfare rolls and into employment. However, they have largely ignored another major segment of the poverty population—the working poor—and have ignored the social supports necessary to effectively move people into productive, and not marginal, employment.

Further, the expectation that the private philanthropic arena would replace these federal and state dollars was not achieved. Greater unemployment left fewer individuals to contribute, and more problems strained the private sector as well.

However, these issues helped to spur the establishment of Human Serve, a national organization created in 1984 that employs a grassroots empowerment strategy. It targets increased voter registration and reduction in barriers to voter registration, as well as educational outreach on selected issues. As social workers nationally became engaged in strategies to enfranchise their clients, an important, if unintended, consequence was the finding that many social workers themselves were not registered voters.

Perhaps another consequence of this reduction of federal dollars and the return of decision making to local entities was the increased incentive within the social work profession to examine accountability strategies and to describe outcome effectiveness along with humane solutions. Further, toward the end of the decade, with the pendulum swing back to greater interest in social problems, more students enrolled in social work programs and became more politically active.

Unfortunately, the 1980s caught the profession short of social workers trained or even interested in some form of political activity, either as a professional career choice or as an adjunct activity to clinical practice (Witherspoon and Phillips, 1987; Wolk, 1981). It continues to be true that legislators do not have an accurate perception of who social workers are and what they do, indicating the continued necessity to educate legislators in order to increase social work's potential influence and impact in the future (Mathews, 1982). Social work education needs to continue its role in fostering political activism and related skills (Hull, 1987).

When President Reagan's second term ended, the same popular platforms of reduced taxation and antiwelfarist attitudes swept George Bush into office with a mandate to continue the reforms of the previous eight years. As noted earlier, these were (1) to decrease social spending, (2) to build up the military, and (3) to reduce taxes. Although many authors concluded that the decade ended with the welfare state intact, the damage done to the New Deal legacy may be permanent (Midgeley, 1992).

The 1990s

Although President George Heabert Walker Bush lost his bid for reelection and the Democrats won the presidency with Bill Clinton, the Republicans took the leadership in both houses of Congress for the first time in decades and thus could attempt to continue the Reagan priorities. This continuous campaign against the "welfare state" was, in large part, prompted by the fact that welfare spending had increased, yet problems and poverty remained. However, the opposing voices were few or were silent. No one made the argument that costs had increased over time not because people had gotten lazier but for several other reasons: The U.S. population had increased; competition in our industrialized and urbanized nation had become more intense; social problems had changed; and, perhaps most importantly, public responsibility has always been seen as a remedial, last-minute gap filling, whereas prevention was never publicly funded (Haynes and Mickelson, 1992).

What was important about the Republicans' contract with America was that it contained provisions that ensured that social progress would not be made; instead, it protected and further supported the widening gap between the classes, making the individual, not the society or its structure, the target for change. We contend that the Republican campaign will continue to be implemented and effective unless social workers increase their political action.

Not every element of Republican policy was counterproductive. For example, the provision to balance the federal budget may not have been a bad idea, though some economists argued that it was a fiscally poor idea and impossible to achieve by limiting spending cuts to domestic social services. The policy of increasing military spending during peacetime and past the end of the Cold War should have been questioned. The anticrime package to strengthen penalties, fund additional prison construction, and cut social spending contained in the Crime Control Act is yet another example of blaming individuals for social problems; it is an expensive choice given that institutional care is always more costly than prevention or outpatient care.

The Personal Responsibility and Work Opportunity Reconciliation Act of 1996 changed the nation's welfare system from an entitlement program to one requiring work for time-limited assistance. This comprehensive legislation made drastic changes to child care, the Food Stamp Program, Supplemental Security Income (SSI) for children, benefits for legal immigrants, and the Child Support Enforcement program. Child nutrition programs were modified, and the Social Services Block Grant was reduced. It has been estimated that this legislation will save $54.5 billion over six years.

This legislation denied benefits to poor children born to unmarried mothers younger than 18, as well as to poor children whose paternity has not been established; it eliminated benefits for almost all legal immigrants and significantly reduced assistance for low-income children and their families. In other words, this legislation continued to "blame the victims" and further impoverished women and children. The system did not teach women employable skills, did not provide affordable good-quality day care for young children, and continued to regard unemployed single mothers as lazy and immoral.

Congress specifically limited the authority of the federal government to regulate the new Temporary Assistance for Needy Families (TANF) program. States receive a block grant allocation that allows them the flexibility to design their TANF programs to promote work, responsibility, and self-sufficiency and to strengthen families. There is a five-year total benefit limit (or less, at state option) on eligibility for cash aid, with an exemption available for 20 percent of cases. However, additional funding is available as a performance bonus to reward states that achieve reductions in out-of-wedlock births, move welfare recipients into jobs, and reduce the number of abortions.

The law also allows states to take money that now goes to welfare checks and use it to create community service jobs or to provide income subsidies or hiring incentives for potential employers. The funds can be used for services related to job readiness, job placement, post-employment support, on-the-job training, community service or work experience, short-term wage subsidies, job retention, and supportive services such as child care and transportation. The target population includes long-term recipients of TANF who face barriers to employment, individuals who may lose their TANF benefits within twelve months, and non-custodial parents of children in TANF households. The Urban Institute has initiated a multi-year project, "Assessing the New Federalism," with a website at www.urban.org.

The decade of the 1990s saw the erosion of some significant human rights. With arguments and appeals to turn back affirmative action legislation, state referendums to deny benefits to illegal aliens, "new education initiatives" that sought to provide vouchers to parents of schoolchildren, taking public funds away from public schools, basic human rights and basic human dignity are in jeopardy. The very values that social work has always supported, which undergirded the Social Security Act, the Medicare and Medicaid bills, the integration of neighborhoods and public schools, and expanded opportunities and access for women and persons of color, will be lost if social workers' voices are not raised.

The George "Dubya" Bush Era

The presidential election of 2000 and his subsequent reelection in 2004 helped continue the "mandate" of George W. Bush and underscored the additional concerns for social welfare policies and services. The role that the Electoral College played in the 2000 election—and subsequent reminder that one-person, one-vote does not necessarily result in electing the popular choice for president—created a larger disparity between the composition of the electorate and the population, as well as a loss of faith in the power of the vote itself. The 2000 election seemed to display, according to many political analysts, an overall distrust in government as a problem solver, as well as a desire to maintain existing service without increasing the overall tax burden (Reisch and Jarman-Rohde, 2000). What was also obvious in that election was the increased role of the media and the hurried, and ultimately incorrect, use of polling information in media coverage.

Of the 2004 election, the attention of the candidates, the media, and therefore the electorate was focused primarily on the war on terror, the war in Iraq, and the emotional climate of a post–9/11 nation. This resulted in less attention to or interest in domestic needs and programs to meet those needs, along with the continued interest in maintaining existing services, funding for war and terrorism protection services, drug benefits for seniors, and a series of tax cuts. Meanwhile, the number of individuals, families, and communities that relied on human services was rising. As our society became increasingly more diverse, the disproportionately high needs and vulnerabilities of ethnic groups were becoming more apparent. The terrorist attacks of September 11, 2001, necessitated a shift in national policy. The increased security measures and the war on terror depleted the national budget surplus dramatically. The hopes of many social workers that past surplus would be directed toward, or at least limit the decline in, social services funding were lost.

During his second term, President George W. Bush continued the policy of moving power from the federal government to the states, giving both state and local officials great latitude to shape a full range of federal social, regulatory, and public works programs. Debates over faith-based programs, stem cell research, social security, and reform and privatization prevailed. Once again in our country's recent history we watched the consequences of ideologies that government, particularly federal government, is bad; that returning decision making to the most local of levels is the American way; that reducing taxes will inherently feed the economy and make it stronger.

In the final two years of our forty-third president's term he and his policies remained focused on eliminating the "axis of evil." Increased efforts, and thus expenditures, for military operations primarily in Iraq but also in Afghanistan and elsewhere continued to build federal budget deficits again while holding or reducing expenditures to social services. Domestic issues related to immigration began to fuel racial and ethnic policy issues not only federally but also in local communities.

Amid this smoldering storm of the continuation of an ongoing conflict in Iraq and its costs, fiscal and humanitarian, came Hurricane Katrina. The federal government's response to that "real" storm illustrated another layer of incompetence and uncaring of the national leadership. In quick succession came heightened polarization of opinions about immigration, the beginning of the global economic meltdown beginning with the "bubble" of the U.S. domestic housing market, the crumbling of Wall Street giant corporations, congressional bailouts, and an escalating unemployment rate. Never before had the world seen such dramatic evidence of the extent of the interconnectedness of global markets as we watched similar issues play out worldwide.

Amid these divisive national arguments and unprecedented global problems, the U.S. presidential primaries were being played out. The primaries were the longest in our history and drew a more diverse group of candidates—women, people of color. They offered the American people a greater diversity of styles, beliefs, experiences, and backgrounds than ever before. By the summer of 2008, when both national parties would choose their presidential candidates, the issues noted above were accompanied by increased debate and emotion over domestic issues related to health care, social security, taxes, and ethics reform, to name a few.

The issues and the candidates compelled us to be involved; to get involved; to return the U.S. presidency and our place in the world to one of credibility, ethics, and leadership. A more energized electorate, a country more ready and in need of change, resulted in an historic outcome in the 2008 presidential elections, the election of Barack Obama. The popular mantra, "Yes, We Can" translated to so many different demographics in so many different ways—all necessary to his successful bid for the presidency. More people voted; he won across multiple demographic groups; he raised more money (three-quarters of a billion dollars) than any previous candidate; and he overcame the odds against our country electing a black, biracial, young, intelligent person. As *Time* magazine noted when they named him Person of the Year in December 2008, "He [Obama] hit the American scene like a thunderclap, upended our politics, shattered decades of conventional wisdom, and overcame centuries of the social pecking order. . . . for infusing our democracy with a new intensity of participation, for showing the world and ourselves that our most cherished myth—the one about boundless opportunity—has plenty of juice in it" (Von Drehle, 2008).

Era of Government Activism: The Obama Presidency Begins

The election of our 44th President, Barack Obama, in November 2008 and his inauguration in January 2009 was both a response to the growing lack of credibility of President George W. Bush and the Republican Party more generally, and also an outcome of the American spirit to have hope in the future, to believe in the American democracy that peoples' voices count.

> It is that American spirit—that American promise—that pushes us forward even when the path is uncertain; that binds us together in spite of our differences; that makes us fix our eye not on what is seen, but what is unseen, that better place around the bend. (www.change.gov, January 6, 2009).

In the first two months following President Obama's inauguration, the country witnessed not only quick and decisive actions and plans to begin solving the nation's many problems—housing, health care, international relations—but also the continued commitment of this new administration to communicate and to listen. The website change.gov obviously transitioned to whitehouse.gov and became a website destination of constantly updated information, speeches, quotes, and commentary.

While the partisan political wars are still waging, the electorate is more engaged and continues to have confidence in this new administration. We are heartened that the values of a leader concerned with "Main Street and Wall Street" and the continued commitment to being accountable and to providing transparency in budget and other areas strengthen the belief that "in a democracy, every voice and vote count."

Conclusion

The examination of a century of social work history reveals that over the years the profession has used a variety of political action strategies and activities. Playing roles that range from social worker as informed citizen to active lobbyist to federal or state administrator to politician, social workers have been engaged in political activity. Regardless of whether it is part of their formal role or training, political action for social workers has been part of social work history and will be part of its future.

Just as Jeannette Rankin made history as the first social worker elected to Congress, there are social workers today who are making history and are part of the continuing efforts of the profession to affect change in the political arena.

In this past 2008 election, the social work profession was involved in many ways and with multiple strategies from candidate endorsements, state to federal, to fund raising, to creating social work platforms. In fact, for the first time NASW created and delivered a document, *Turning Priorities into Action: How the Social Work Profession Will Help* (2008 to President-elect Obama's transition team). Within that document NASW addresses the major challenges of the new administration and connects social work historic interest and skills to helping this agenda move forward.

Perhaps NASW leadership, like the authors, were moved by a presidential candidate who both acted like a "good social worker" and cared about issues of deep and abiding interest to social workers. President Obama was a community organizer in Chicago born to a single mother and of biracial parents. He showed he was a listener; believed in inclusivity; believed in people. More than any president in the profession of social work's history, he connected with social work values and social work actions.

The change we need isn't just about new programs and policies. It's about a new politics—a politics that calls on our better angels instead of encouraging our worst instincts; one that reminds us of the obligations we have to ourselves and one another. (www.change.gov, January 6, 2009.)

All Social Work Is Political, So . . .

1. Choose a contemporary social problem, describe the policy solutions enacted (federal or state), and indicate, as a result of the solution, which social policy model was utilized. If you would have chosen a different model, indicate which one, and why.

2. Choose a period in U.S. history in which a major piece of social work legislation was passed. Identify the role of the profession or of individual social workers, or both, in its introduction or passage.

3. Choose one notable social work activist, and trace his or her educational and experiential background.

4. How can you take historical knowledge and make advocacy more effective within the social work profession in the future?

Suggested Readings

Cohen, Wilbur. 1966. "What Every Social Worker Should Know about Political Action." *Social Work* II (July): 3–11.

Davis, Allen F. 1982. "Settlement Workers in Politics, 1890–1914." In *Practical Politics: Social Work and Political Responsibility*, M. Mahaffey and J. W. Hanks (eds.), pp. 32–45. Washington, DC: National Association of Social Workers.

Gilbert, Neil, and Harry Specht. 1976. "Advocacy and Professional Ethics." *Social Work* 21 (July): 288–293.

Jansson, B. S. 1990. "Why Study Social Policy and the Practice of Policy Anyway?" In *Social Welfare Policy: From Theory to Practice*, pp. 2–39. Belmont, CA: Wadsworth.

References

Addams, Jane. 1940. *Twenty Years at Hull House with Autobiographical Notes.* New York: Macmillan.

Alinsky, Saul. 1971. *Rules for Radicals.* New York: Random House.

Biggerstaff, Marilyn A., and Michael S. Kolevzon. 1980. "Differential Use of Social Work Knowledge, Skills, and Techniques by MSW, BSW, and BA Level Practitioners." *Journal of Education for Social Work* 16 (3): 67–74.

Bisno, Herbert. 1969. "How Social Will Social Work Be?" in *Perspectives on Social Welfare*, Paul E. Weinberger (ed.), pp. 304–318. Toronto: Macmillan.

Carlton, T. O., and M. Jung. 1972. "Adjustment or Change: Attitudes among Social Workers." *Social Work* 17 (6): 64–71.

Carnegie Foundation for the Advancement of Teaching. Project Summary: The Political Engagement Project. 2007.

Council on Social Work Education. 2001. *Educational Policy and Accreditation Standards.* Alexandria, VA: CSWE.

Figuera McDonough, J. 1993. "Policy Practice: The Neglected Side of Social Work Interventions." *Social Work* 38: 179–188.

Ginsberg, Mitchell. 1970. "Changing Values in Social Work." In *Social Work Values in an Age of Discontent*, Katherine S. Kendall (ed.), pp. 13–34. New York: Council on Social Work Education.

Hamilton, David, and David Fauri. 2001. "Social Workers' Political Participation: Strengthening the Political Confidence of Social Work Students." *Journal of Social Work Education* 37 (2): 321–332.

Haynes, Karen S. 1996. "The Future of Political Social Work." In *Future Issues for Social Work Practice*, Paul R. Raffoul and C. Aaron McNeece (eds.), pp. 266–276. Boston: Allyn & Bacon.

Haynes, Karen S., and James S. Mickelson. 1985. "Social Policy: The Hidden Power Base." Presentation at the Council of Social Work Education Annual Program Meeting, Washington, DC.

———. 1992. "Social Work and the Reagan Era: Challenges to the Profession." *Sociology and Social Welfare* 19 (1): 169–183.

Hull, Grafton. 1987. "Joining Together: A Faculty–Student Experience in Political Campaigning." *Journal of Social Work Education* 3 (23): 37–43.

Jansson, Bruce S. 2002. *Becoming an Effective Policy Advocate: From Policy Practice to Social Justice*, 4th ed. Pacific Grove, CA: Brooks/Cole.

Lavassaur, Jean M. 1984. "Jeannette Rankin: Political Social Worker." Paper presented at Political Institute, Michigan State University.

Lloyd, Gary. 1970. *Charities, Settlements, and Social Work: An Inquiry into Philosophy and Method, 1890–1915*. New Orleans: Tulane University School of Social Work.

Mathews, Gary. 1982. "Social Workers and Political Influence." *Social Service Review* 56 (4): 616–628.

Meyer, Carol. 1970. *Social Work Practice—A Response to the Urban Crisis*. New York: Free Press.

Midgeley, James. 1992. "Society, Social Policy and the Ideology of Reaganism." *The Reagan Legacy and the American Welfare State, Special Issue of the Journal of Sociology and Social Welfare* 19: 13–29.

National Association of Social Workers. 2009. *Turning Priorities into Action: How the Social Work Profession Will Help*. Washington, DC: NASW Press.

Pins, Arnulf. 1971. *Social Work Education in a Period of Change*. New York: Council on Social Work Education.

Reeser, L. C., and L. Leighninger. 1990. "Back to Our Roots: Towards a Specialization in Social Justice." *Journal of Sociology and Social Welfare* 17: 69–87.

Reisch, Michael, and Lily Jarman-Rohde. 2000. "The Future of Social Work in the United States: Implications for Field Education." *Journal of Social Work Education* 36 (2): 201–214.

Ritter, Jessica. 2008. "A National Study Predicting Licensed Social Workers' Levels of Political Participation: The Role of Resources, Psychological Engagement, and Recruitment Networks." *Social Work* 53(4): 347–357.

Ross, Murray. 1955. *Community Organization*. New York: Harper & Row.

Schneider, Robert L., and F. E. Netting. 1999. "Influencing Social Policy in a Time of Devolution: Upholding Social Work's Great Tradition." *Social Work* 44 (4): 349–357.

Schneider, Robert L., and Lori Lester. 2001. *Social Work Advocacy: A New Framework for Action*. Pacific Grove, CA: Brooks/Cole.

Sears, Amelia. 1918. *The Charity Visitor: A Handbook for Beginners*. Chicago: Chicago School of Civics and Philanthropy.

Thompson, J. 1994. "Social Workers and Politics: Beyond the Hatch Act." *Social Work* 39: 457–465.

Thursz, Daniel. 1975. "Social Action as a Professional Responsibility and Political Participation." In *Participation in Politics*, T. R. Pennock and John W. Chapman (eds.), pp. 13–232. New York: Leibor Atherton.

Von Drehle, David. 2008. "Person of the Year Barack Obama: Why History Can't Wait." *Time*. December 29, 2008/January 5, 2009.

Witherspoon, Roger, and Norma Kolko Phillips. 1987. "Heightening Political Awareness in Social Work Students in the 1980s." *Journal of Social Work Education* 23 (3): 44–49.

Wolk, James. 1981. "Are Social Workers Politically Active?" *Social Work* 26 (July): 284–288.

Wolk, James, Jackie E. Pray, Toby Weismiller, and David Dempsey. 1996. "Political Practice: Educating Social Work Students for Policymaking." *Journal of Social Work Education* 32 (1): 91–100.

Youngdahl, Benjamin E. 1966. *Social Action and Social Work*. New York: Association Press.

4

The Debate

While most of the leaders of the Charity movement deplore the fact that politics should enter our field, I cannot agree with them. I believe that if our people would get out and help elect friends of our measures and defeat our enemies, we should accomplish a great deal more than we can do by getting women's clubs, churches, etc. to pass resolutions and look wise.

—Kate Barnard*

After more than 100 years, one would think that professional social workers would agree about the basic goal of the profession, yet any social work conference, journal, or even professional dialogue is still filled with disagreements about that goal. We still hear "Social work's basic treatment modality is clinical practice, and its primary goal is individual treatment" versus "Social work's historical roots and major goal is social reform." These debates flare up and then quiet down, and professional consensus has never been achieved. This debate is still current and extremely critical to our profession in the beginning of the twenty first century.

> The quest for status and identity has occupied center stage within social work since its inception. Its efforts in this regard have been hampered by the breadth of the profession, its relationship to the external sociopolitical and economic environment, and divisions within the profession itself. Examples include the historical divide between macro- and micro-practice and between agency based and independent practice. (Gibelman, 1999, p. 298)

The presidential campaign of 2008 brought a great deal of this historical rhetoric front and center. Anti-human services and anti-government forces charged that the solutions to our global economic crisis could not and should not be solved

*Kate Barnard, a social worker, was Oklahoma's first Commissioner of Charities and Corrections, elected in 1907 (Peavy and Smith, 1983).

with government intervention, while many campaigns and, ultimately, the voting public, agreed that the "free market" not only was not the solution, but also had created the problems.

In fact, the social work profession became more engaged both in the electoral process and the policymaking process than ever before. The National Association of Social Workers (NASW) endorsed many candidates from local elections to the presidential campaign. According to workforce projections based on demographic and economic projections, social work as a profession is projected to grow at a much faster than average rate through 2016. In response, NASW began an early initiative to create understanding and support for increasing and retaining the social work labor force.

"Memorandum to the Next Presidential Administration: A Vision for Social Work Education" was published, and the two social workers who are U.S. sena-tors, Barbara Mikulski (Maryland) and Debbie Stabenow (Michigan) were enlisted as cosponsors for the Dorothy L. Height and Whitney M. Young, Jr. Social Work Reinvestment Act. Supporting our contention that "all social work is political," Dorothy Height said about this bill: "We need the people who have the skills and commitment to help us deal with the problems and move us forward" (*NASW News*, 2008). Ed Towns, a social worker in the U.S. House of Representatives, noted, "As a social worker, I know of the significant contributions that social workers have made to the socioeconomic fabric of our nation."

Although the attributes of professionalism that we ascribed to nearly 100 years ago may, to some, support an apolitical posture, the very elements of our pro-fession compel us to enter the political arena. Flexner (1915) originally described five elements as essential attributes of a profession, and social work has directed its attention to them for decades: (1) a scientific knowledge base, (2) autonomous practice, (3) a code of ethics, (4) a professional association, and (5) public sanction. Yet these attributes do not necessarily prescribe an apolitical posture. In fact, it is possible to interpret each as mandating political action.

Both the CSWE and the NASW have strengthened their support of these concepts since our previous edition. Two of the six purposes of social work, as listed in the 2001 Educational Policy and Accreditation Standards, are directed at the formulation and implementation of policies that meet human needs and achieve social and economic justice (CSWE, 2001). Further, in the section "Achievement of Purposes," there are additional, supportive statements, and in the foundation program objectives, objective 8 specifies: "Analyze, formulate, and influence social policies." Also as was previously mentioned, language within both the Social Welfare Policy and Services section and the Social Work Practice section strengthen this focus.

Similarly, the NASW Code of Ethics has undergone several significant revi-sions since it was originally adopted in 1960. The most recent code describes the goal of the profession of social work as follows:

> To enhance human well-being and help meet the basic human needs of all people, with particular attention to the needs and empowerment of people who are

vulnerable, oppressed and living in poverty. A historic and defining feature of social work is the profession's focus on individual well-being in a social context and the well-being of society. (NASW Code of Ethics preamble, 1999)

Thus, NASW provides an inclusive goal with a statement of focus on the disadvantaged. This code includes even stronger prescriptive language regarding political action:

Social workers should engage in social and political action that seeks to ensure that all persons have equal access to the resources, employment, services and opportunities that they require in order to meet their basic human needs and to develop fully. Social workers should be aware of the impact of the political arena on practice and should advocate for changes in policy and legislation to improve social conditions in order to meet basic human needs and promote social justice. (NASW Code of Ethics, sec. 6.04, 1999)

These goals seem clear, comprehensive, and noncontroversial. Even given these professionally sanctioned goals, debate continues within the profession: What skills do social workers need? What target client group should be served? What is the goal of "treatment"? The debate continues even though both CSWE and NASW have strengthened their support for the concepts and methods of advocacy and empowerment, thus providing greater legitimation for social work educational programs to strengthen these elements, not to replace or diminish the focus on individual treatment through clinical methods.

Perhaps because of our quest to be like other professions, such as the medical field, we lost track of those attributes of social work that distinguish it from other professions. Some of these distinguishing elements are (1) a systems approach that includes examination of the environment as a critical factor both in causing and in solving individual and social problems; (2) the importance of history in shaping the lives of people and of communities; (3) a respect for people, their strengths, and their problem-solving capacities; and (4) a belief in the inevitability and desirability of change (Reisch, 1995). Why has our profession focused on our similarities with other professions rather than on our uniqueness, thus perhaps minimizing these unique characteristics?

Part of the problem of "who we are" is the continued change in the social work labor force. Thirty-plus years ago, the largest proportion of social workers worked for the government; employment in the for-profit sector was virtually nonexistent, and private practice was limited by the ineligibility of social workers to receive third-party (insurance) payments for services. Social workers held leadership roles in public welfare and in nonprofits. Today, there is increasing specialization in social work education and in practice; private practice and for-profit practice are increasingly significant alternatives for service delivery (Gibelman and Schervish, 1997).

In a 2008 NASW labor force study, 68 percent of social workers indicated that they worked at the micro level, whereas only 14 percent indicated that they worked at the macro level. Additionally, and in support of the statement above, only 30 percent of social workers reported working in the public sector, 42 percent work in private nonprofit organizations, and 28 percent work in private for-profit organizations (NASW, 2008). Such labor force data surely inform, if not direct, the nature of the continuing debate and the companion questions that were raised during the previous CSWE review of accrediting standards.

Some Perspectives

As it does today, social work historically depended on heuristic frameworks that included interventions ranging from consciousness raising to reallocation of resources, that were concerned with the attainment of basic needs as well as self-actualization, and that directed strategies toward individual as well as community and societal needs. Given the breadth of these targets of intervention that are derived from the goals of our profession, the authors have contended that political social work practice legitimizes social work's role in policy formulation as well as in the policy implementation stage (Haynes, 1996).

Probably nowhere is this debate as well articulated as in the Abramovitz/Bardill debate (Abramovitz and Bardill, 1993). Although both agree that the profession's mission is to train students to become experts in individual and social change, both agree that the internal arguments between personal treatment versus social reform (micro/macro) are debilitating and divisive and that the systems perspective is a unique and useful one to maintain. However, they remain opponents because they appear to hold that there is a dichotomization and mutual exclusivity of direction and purpose of these two perspectives, that it is essential to accomplish only one of these, but not both, because in attempting both, both will be diminished. And the argument is waged that there is an ideological schism because social change ideology might mean a radical and partisan political basis.

It seems to be increasingly difficult to retain a professional posture of political neutrality and objectivity when the political agenda is to wage war with the profession of social work and with our clients. The choices, and they are the political choices, are choices central to the lives of our clients, and, as such, are choices about which the profession of social work ought to have a stake.

It is somewhat heartening that a recent study of MSW students showed that more students at graduation held a strong desire to work in core social work areas and more felt social work should emphasize societal/institutional change over individual change (Limb and Organista, 2006, p. 286). But whatever measures of progress we might optimistically discover, there is as yet no professional consensus. Given that we had to argue that there would be any demand for the first edition of this book in 1986, the request for a seventh edition is testimony to the increased attention to this important component of the profession.

However, others must keep the debate alive until political social work, by whatever terminology, is firmly entrenched in social work education and in social work practice. Until that time, we welcome the debate and even the controversy because it is what will ensure a socially relevant and credible profession.

The controversial position explicated by Harry Specht and Mark Courtney in *Unfaithful Angels* (1994) raised the level of the debate within the profession several notches as it continued this dialogue. Although we did not concur with all their points, we agreed with their basic premise that social work may have lost sight of the public social services and the public arena as a legitimate place for social work intervention. In fact, we have noted in previous editions and in public places that it has been almost thirty years since we became angry at the profession for its dispassionate, objective, and apolitical stance.

Like Specht and Courtney, we have disliked the profession's silence in the political arena, its distance from its historical roots and from its commitment to public service. And we disliked being labeled "anticlinical" or "antiprofessional" for these views. Despite what appears to be a reawakening and a more sophisticated involvement in both electoral politics and policymaking, we have witnessed almost simultaneously the dimunition of politcal social work content and concentrations. Therefore, we want to continue to ensure that advocacy, empowerment, and public social services are included and are valued in social work.

When Karen Met Harry: Unfaithful Angels *Disputed*

The following is the text from a speech given by Karen Haynes.* It was to have been the keynote speech given by Dr. Harry Specht at the Texas National Association of Social Workers Conference in November 1994. However, Dr. Specht became ill. Dr. Karen Haynes, coauthor of this book, was asked to step in. Although she agreed to present Dr. Specht's remarks, she did so only with the notion that she could debate them. All of Dr. Specht's words are those written by him for the intended speech. Permission to publish this speech was obtained from Dr. Neil Gilbert after Harry's death.

Dr. Harry Specht may need no introduction to many in the profession; he was the author of numerous books and articles on social welfare policy and was the dean of the School of Social Welfare at the University of California, Berkeley, from 1977 to 1995. However, since Harry died in 1997, perhaps a few more words about his place in our profession are appropriate. Indeed, Harry was a scholar, having authored more than a dozen books and over fifty papers. But they weren't just some books, for example, the book he wrote with George Brager, *Community Organizing* (1973), was a landmark in the field; another book, written with his colleague Neil Gilbert, *Dimensions of Social Welfare*, represents a milestone in the literature on social policy. His final book, *Unfaithful Angels: How Social Work Has Abandoned Its Mission*, with Mark Courtney, (1994) was undoubtedly his most

*A variation of this chapter is found in the centennial issue of *Social Work* in an article by Karen Haynes title "The One Hundred Year Debate: Social Reform versus Individual Treatment"(Haynes, 1998).

controversial and most immediately influential—and the one that delighted him most. Harry's list of scholarly works is long; it is not the number or scholarship of his works, however, but their passion and cogency that account for the pervasive influence of his writings on the practice of the profession and the nature of social welfare education. His ideas were often unsettling, but they were always stimulating and influential, and in the end the persuasiveness of his argument usually prevailed. When Karen Haynes made this presentation, she was the dean of the Graduate School of Social Work at the University of Houston (1985–1995), the only graduate program in social work that had at the time a political social work concentration.

Karen Frames the Debate

"Well, if you think that you're disappointed, so am I. Not only did I want to listen to Harry, with his acerbic humor, thought-provoking message, and lengthy perspective on our history, but I had hoped to ask provocative questions. When I received the call asking if I could replace Harry, I knew that no one could replace Harry, be Harry, or dare to speak for Harry. But, I thought, maybe I could still have the conversation with Harry that I had wanted to have.

"Perhaps like many of you in the audience, I met Harry more than two decades ago through his written communications—articles, the initial edition of the infamous Gilbert and Specht *Dimensions of Social Welfare Policy* (Gilbert and Specht, 1974). Perhaps he was a bit less controversial twenty-five years ago, but I found his work interesting, as I was also concerned about the big picture and the long view.

"It was probably ten years later before I heard Harry give a speech at the Council on Social Work Education meeting, and I was intrigued by his quick wit and his enjoyment of controversy. You couldn't not react to what Harry said. Then I met him in closer proximity when I became a new dean. And in 1985 when I became a new dean, Harry was a senior dean, and not just any senior dean, but Berkeley's dean. And he was saying outrageous things in deans' meetings.

"And then he and Mark Courtney published *Unfaithful Angels*, and I was not surprised that it raised considerable controversy within the profession. I knew that was Harry's intent . . . to keep the debate alive. I read *Unfaithful Angels* and, not surprisingly, there was much in his perspective with which I heartily agreed. There were, however, a number of points of departure. Someday, I thought, I shall share these thoughts with Harry.

"So today, I have constructed a conversation with Harry about *Unfaithful Angels*. Harry's remarks are his own."

Harry Begins

"The profession of social work is somewhat more than 100 years old. In the 1920s it took a wrong turn in the direction of modern psychiatry and psychoanalysis. In the seventy-plus intervening years, it has not veered from that path. Today, the profession is about to be engulfed by the psychotherapy industry. In 1991, 57 percent of the members of the National Association of Social Workers were engaged in for-profit practice doing psychotherapy at least part of their work week. That does not include another large proportion of social workers employed by public and non-profit social agencies who use psychotherapy as their major mode of intervention. I am not alone in perceiving that our profession is fast being converted to a major battalion in the psychotherapeutic armies. In August 1993, the Associated Press released a story about the NASW Delegate Assembly, referring to NASW as 'a professional association of psychotherapists.' The group, they said, 'is made up of professional psychotherapists who work in a broad range of social work jobs. . . . Social workers provide psychotherapy and counseling. . . . Some 145,000 social workers are members of the group.' "

Karen Interrupts

"Harry, my version of history, not to mention causality, differs from yours. First, and this is my women's thing, Harry, is that if our profession significantly veered from its historical path in the 1920s it was because men convinced us what the tenets of professionalism were. We have, since our profession's beginning, allowed and even encouraged men to determine whether we are a profession at all. First Flexner in 1915, Greenwood, and Etzioni later, determined that social work wasn't and maybe never would be a profession, and we have continued to believe that and have allowed it to push our national education and practice agendas for almost eighty years.

"Secondly, Harry, you seem to ignore the waves and cycles of social reform—the 1930s, 1960s, and perhaps, the 1990s? You seem to overlook the entrance of a significant group of professionals—the BSWs—who represent almost as large a cadre of students and practitioners as MSWs.

"And, thirdly, if we're looking at the same data set, only 11 percent of NASW members were engaged full time in private practice, and 32 percent are not in direct practice at all. And, finally, I don't equate direct practice with psychotherapy."

Harry

"May I continue, Karen?

"Now before I go on, I want to emphasize that there is no single set of people responsible for the profession's drift into psychotherapy and private practice. The organized profession has endorsed it, the schools of social work have taught it, many social agencies have taken psychotherapy as their major intervention mode of practice, and the community has always given only unwilling support to social work and public services, in contrast to the great love Americans have for psychotherapy of all shades and varieties. It is for that reason that I addressed my book to a broad audience. The current state of social work and the social services is a community problem. One part of the problem is social work's abandonment of its mission; the other part is the deep and sincere belief the Americans have in the utility and efficacy of psychotherapy. Let me speak to the latter problem first.

"Psychotherapy is a big enterprise. According to a study by the National Institute of Mental Health, 1990 spending on mental health care in the United States was $67 billion, approximately 10 percent of all spending on health care. Approximately $27 billion (40 percent) of these expenditures was for care of the hospitalized mentally ill. The remaining $40 billion was spent on outpatient care for a wide range of disorders, including depression, mania, panic attack, codependency, addictions, and dysthymia.

"A significant proportion of outpatient care is for people with mild kinds of mental health problems. This group can be characterized as 'the worried well': 20- to 40-year-old professionals, primarily Caucasians, who are unfulfilled and searching for meaning in their lives and for ways to increase their self-esteem. . . .

"Findings of the National Institute of Mental Health's Epidemiologic Catchment Area (ECA) program indicate that 44.7 million people (28 percent of the U.S. adult population) have some sort of mental/addictive disorder. (The ECA program is the largest and most comprehensive study ever done on the state of Americans' mental health.) The ECA figures are modest compared to some others. For example, Melody Beattie, a national authority on the problem of 'codependency,' says that 96 percent of all Americans suffer from it. But even the conservative ECA figures should cause us to wonder whether or not the mental health experts have created, at least in part, a phantom epidemic that society is attempting to eliminate at great cost and with decreasing success.

"The evidence for the efficacy of psychotherapeutic interventions to deal with these problems is not persuasive. Study after study indicates that there is little difference in the success rates achieved by one or another of many forms of psychotherapy ranging from psychoanalysis to humanistic psychology, gestalt therapy, rolfing, channeling, and primal screaming, to name only a few. And there appears to be little difference between success rates attained from treatments given by professionals compared to those given by nonprofessionals."

Karen

"But Harry, do we have valid and reliable measures of any kind of social work intervention, even today? Our 'welfare' programs have been repeatedly criticized for their ineffectiveness in eliminating poverty. Our public child welfare programs have measured increases in reported child abuse and neglect since the initiation of state legislation in the 1970s, a finding which might be contradictory to a measure of success."

Harry, a Bit More Firmly, Continues

"But, the public doesn't enjoy welfare benefits or parenting classes.

"There is, though, clear evidence that patients like and enjoy psychotherapy, and that they like and enjoy their psychotherapists. . . . If you're feeling bad, they can help you recognize that this is because you have been abused, maltreated, misunderstood—generally victimized in any number of ways—by parents, spouse, boss, or teacher. The therapists are on your side for a very good reason: You or your insurance companies are paying them a lot. They can persuade people that they have psychological problems because the psychotherapeutic process is designed to make the patient emotionally dependent on and eager to please the psychotherapist.

"Worst of all, psychotherapy is an essentially individualistic means of problem solving that has become the choice intervention for dealing with such social problems as alienation, loneliness, child abuse, economic dependency, and violence. But these are community problems, and it is time to devote resources to enlisting the community in solving them. The fact that many people like and enjoy psychotherapy is no more of a reason to cover these treatments by public funds or insurance benefits than to cover massages or attending the symphony in order to relax. If the resources we now spend on radical individualistic treatments were devoted to development of social care, society would benefit enormously. Healthy people grow and develop in healthy communities, not in psychotherapists' offices. I believe, therefore, that it is time for Americans to consider a new approach in delivering social services to communities."

Karen

"Well, I certainly can't disagree with your basic premise—the growth in incidence, severity, and criticality of societal problems is frightening, and social problems can't entirely be solved by treating individuals. And on this point we certainly agree that our profession is at least partly at fault.

"Given how dramatic these changes have been and how desperate the troubles have become, it is amazing that it has taken us so long to speak out. I believe our silence during much of the last decade may have been viewed as consent. Our de-emphasizing of cause and focusing on function; our fixation on methods and techniques rather than on social goals; and our 'buy in' to the privatization model, which has created higher caseloads, volunteers functioning in professional roles, and marketplace models for low-income and marginalized families—all have helped contribute to the societal malaise. As for those of us who have not always kept silent, we have sometimes been rebuffed by our own colleagues. When I have spoken out repeatedly in the past for macro-level advocacy, I have been questioned about my political interests, I have been confronted about my professionalism, and it has been presumed that I devalue clinical skills and clinical practice. I not only get angry, I get confused. My vision of good social work practice has always been, and, I don't doubt, will always be, one of advocacy with, and on behalf of, our clients toward the enhancement of individual social functioning and community empowerment. Isn't that your vision, Harry? I have believed, for as long as I can remember, that direct interpersonal involvement with people, families, and small groups who are in pain is essential. I equally strongly believe that political intervention and macro solutions might effectively achieve permanent goals that will also alleviate that pain and suffering.

"Yes, I still hear from some students and from some community practitioners the question, 'What does policy and political action have to do with what I'll be practicing?' In other words, 'What do private troubles have to do with public issues?'

"We must define private troubles as public issues right now. And you and I would agree, Harry, that it must be we, not they, who define those public issues.

"Does it make any sense for clinicians to spend hundreds of hours to keep a family together, only to watch public policy rip them apart again? Is it reasonable to work to empower parents to address the issues facing them, and then leave them with outdated and punitive policies that may destroy them? If we are willing to devote everything it takes to keep a family functioning and intact, then we must also be willing to turn our efforts to advocacy in the political arena.

"We must simultaneously pull our clients out of the destructive river *and* go upstream to prevent their being pushed in.

"And, before you remind me, yes, it is true that I have been dismayed that two-thirds of the legislative priorities of state chapters involved licensure or third-party payments.

"But I balance that anger with a great deal of pride that there are so many of us who devote professional lifetimes to HIV-infected persons, to victims of violence, to securing basic services for people—not the 'worried, well, or wealthy,' but the stigmatized, forgotten, and oppressed—that there are many who remained 'faithful' to our mission and who are uplifting spokespersons for us all.

"But, are we doing enough? Have we veered a bit from that mission? Yes!"

Harry

"Here we most assuredly agree, Karen. So, how did this happen? I believe it has to do with our mission. In truth, the mission of the profession has never been very clear in this country. Also in truth, the profession and social work education have never embraced the publicly supported social services as the major institutional area of social work as is the case, for example, in the United Kingdom, Canada, and Australia. To the extent that public services are an area for social work jobs in the United States, it has been largely relegated to BSWs. This is unfortunate for many reasons: The public social services meet the needs of the poorest and most oppressed people in society; the public social services represent the most refined expression of the community's desire to help those in need, and, equally important, the public social services represent a much needed, powerful, significant, and natural constituency for our profession. There are not many powerful and significant people around who are ready to speak up for social work, and I believe the profession missed the boat on public social services. (I'll come back to this point later on.)

"Both Jane Addams and Mary Richmond began their careers in social work (in 1888 and 1889) with a much higher degree of clarity about their objectives than that which pertains in the profession thirty years later. They both began their work with a kind of missionary zeal. Their goal was to uplift the downtrodden. They were both guided by a Victorian morality and a desire for social justice. When you read their earliest works—Jane Addams's *Democracy and Social Ethics* (1905) and Mary Richmond's *The Good Neighbor in the Modern City* (1907)—you can hardly tell them apart. Here is an excerpt from one of them:

> Certain it is that no sufficient study has been made of the child who enters into industrial life early and stays there permanently, to give him some offset to its monotony and dullness, some historic significance of the part he is taking in the life of the community.

And here is an excerpt from the other:

> I have said that the city might be made a much safer and more attractive place for children to grow up in. What might each one do to bring this about?
> In the first place, we might, instead of talking so persistently about the importance of keeping them off the streets, talk much more about the importance of making the streets cleaner places, in every sense, for the children to run about it. City children must be out of doors often if they are to be kept healthy, and the city's out-of-doors should be well enough policed, lighted, cleaned, and protected from illicit traffics of all sorts to be a fit place for children to spend part of each day.

"The first example is from Jane Addams, and the second is from Mary Richmond. You can see in these brief quotations the altruism and concern for the community betterment and social reform that they shared.

"Two great institutions grew up around these women in a relatively short period of time: the Charity Organization Societies (COS) around Mary Richmond and the settlement houses around Jane Addams. In that short period Richmond developed the idea of a 'social investigation' of the supplicants who came to the COS, and she described the procedure for a social investigation in great detail in her famous book *Social Diagnosis*. She called what she did 'social treatment,' and it later came to be called 'social casework.' Richmond had a deeply held belief that if you got all of the information about a person, the solution to his/her problem would become evident.

"Later on, Richmond came to be disappointed with the results of 'social diagnosis.' There didn't seem to be anywhere to go after the investigation. This was especially disappointing to Richmond and her colleagues because of Dr. Abraham Flexner's famous 1915 paper, 'Is Social Work a Profession?' Flexner answered his question with a resounding no; his primary reason for saying nay was that social work lacked a theoretical base. Well, in short order a set of theories arrived: first, theories of modern psychiatry in the 1920s and, second, psychoanalytic theory in the 1930s. These theories were interesting, compelling, gripping, and available for adoption. They were the wrong theories for social work, but, to put it simply, there was nothing better available. Mary Richmond was not happy about that. She was reaching for a different, more socially oriented set of theories. But the kind of theory she would have liked didn't start developing until the

1940s. These are the theories of social psychology. There is in social psychology a powerful set of theories for working with persons in the social environment: Examples are social exchange theory, symbolic interaction, attribution theory, and social network analysis. Social psychology's body of knowledge has been developing for over 50 years. It is quite substantial and it has been, for the most part, ignored by social work practitioners and educators.

"And what became of Jane Addams's perspective? Her view of social services was very close to the notion of community-based social care that I discuss in great detail in my book [*Unfaithful Angels*]. But the settlements are largely out of business. Why did the form not become institutionalized in the United States? There are several reasons. First, Jane Addams, like Mary Richmond, did not believe in programs financed by governments. She largely ignored the New Deal programs. But the kinds of programs we need to serve American communities require public support along with volunteerism.

"Second, Jane Addams's views about professionalism differed considerably from Mary Richmond's. She was very cool toward professional education. The failure to build a professionalized workforce reduced the possibility of institutionalizing the social function of the settlements.

"Third, the settlement house arrangement of Jane Addams's day was based on very strong social class distinctions: middle-class settlement workers ministering to poor and working-class people. As the settlement house users assimilated, they moved up the social class scale and began to perceive of the settlement workers as patronizing and the settlement as a place for poor people.

"Fourth, the settlements had their greatest successes with immigrant communities that had a strong communal orientation and that were upwardly mobile. That was the Jews, Greeks, and Italians. The settlements had less success with the immigrant and in-migrant populations that replaced the groups originally served by the settlements, such as the Puerto Ricans and African Americans.

"Finally, there is the powerful force of American individualism. We are the most individualistic people on earth. We are a young nation and the sense of 'us' and 'them' pervades our thinking about our neighbors. (And, as we all know, the Reagan/Bush administrations served to undermine considerably whatever fragile and small sense of community Americans have.)"

Karen

"Well, Harry, I've been quiet for a while now, but I must interrupt. Let me see if I can keep my points straight.

"First, relative to public social services being 'relegated to BSWs'—one can look at that from a different perspective—that BSWs are educated to do generalist social work practice, which is congruent, in my view, to roles within many public social services. Also, still on this point, your language that 'public social services represent the most refined expression of the community's desire to help those in need' if true is a terrible indictment of community caring given the per capita expenditures for public social services in many states.

"Secondly, what happened to Mary Richmond's and Jane Addams's influence on our profession? Well, another take is that it's a women's issue again. You know (because you wrote it in your book) that it took the National Conference of Charities and Corrections thirty-seven years to elect a female president—Jane Addams, who had won the Nobel Peace Prize by then. Both Addams and Richmond lost their bids for the election in 1923.

"I'm not laying blame on any single group either, but a theoretical base was not the only criteria that Flexner described—autonomous practice was another. Why did we allow a predominantly female profession to be so directed by a male medical model of practice?"

Harry

"I probably shouldn't respond to that, so let me turn now to our part of this century. I believe we must be concerned about the profession's drift toward psychotherapy, and especially about the increasing number of social workers engaging in the private practice of psychotherapy. Increasingly, over the last twenty years, both schools and the profession have become disengaged from those agencies serving the poorest and neediest members of society: the publicly supported social services. Under Presidents Reagan and Bush, federal social welfare programs suffered budget freezes and cuts. As jobs in government disappeared and working conditions worsened, even more social workers left public service for private practice."

Karen

"Harry, it's really never been clear to me that professionally educated social workers were ever in the public sector in large numbers, so I've always been a bit perplexed by the notion that we've abandoned that practice setting.

"But I'm willing to concede that those settings have not been appealing to many professionals—but let's not blame the victims. Caseloads are unconscionable, liability and public scrutiny are high, rewards are low, and the congruence with our mission of change and prevention is almost nonexistent.

"But have we focused our collective efforts to change these institutions and their practices? Only lately; and you, Harry, and your California colleagues have been a national exemplar."

Harry

"Thanks, Karen, but I see that the social work profession and social work education over these last fifty years have become increasingly engaged in a triple misalliance, the elements of which are science and empiricism in professional education, psychotherapy, and private practice. Correspondingly, we have failed to embrace our most natural constituency, which consists of the professionals, administrators, and users of publicly supported social services."

Karen

"I agree, Harry, that social work education bears some of the blame. The recent debate by Abramovitz and Bardill (1993) in the *Journal of Social Work Education* about the place of social change in social work curriculums clearly indicates that we remain divided."

Harry

"Karen, can I get back to my point?

"The twentieth century has given rise to a great new institution—the welfare state. It is a significant institution in modern society. However, social work has never perceived the welfare state as its major institutional arena. Instead, the profession and social work education have responded to any and all demands made upon it for casework, group work, psychotherapy, group therapy, behavior modification, advocacy, planning, management, and other functions, fads, and fancies under public, voluntary, and for-profit auspices. At times, the profession must appear to outsiders to be a gigantic fuddle factory without a core. Frequently, social workers appear to be in competition with flocks of other professionals (for example, psychologists, MFCCs [marriage, family, child counselors], and physicians) to provide psychotherapeutic services that are of dubious social value to a population that is affluent. In that respect, social work as a profession does not have the integrity of some other professions because it lacks a clear institutional mission."

Karen

"Oh, Harry, I can't keep still any longer. I am baffled by the use of the word *integrity* with respect to other professions, implying that they have not followed leads and funding streams. Perhaps life is different in Berkeley, but I am hard-pressed to see more of a central mission, or more integrity, in the professions of law and medicine than in social work today. In fact, I would vehemently argue that we in social work may have remained more steadfast than others about how we can help those in pain.

"Enough said ."

Harry

"Well, Karen, I am also concerned that social work's hard-won legitimacy in the university and the community will erode as the profession is less and less able to demonstrate that it has a significant service mission because universities are becoming more and more concerned with demonstrating their social relevance, and the community will give even less support than it does now to a social work profession that does not carry out a significant social function. This was pointed up very sharply to me in a review of my book by Jan S. Efrau (1994) in *Networker*. Efrau writes as follows:

> What may be needed is a new profession or calling that fills the void social work has left behind. It need not be connected with mental health, and its methods might have to be invented from scratch, the way Mary Richmond and Jane Addams carved out a model for social work 100 years ago. A number of years back, community psychology took a stab at such a project, but it failed miserably. This was partly due to a rapid change in the political climate, but it was also because of unclear goals, inadequate theory, and divided loyalties—it tried to be an amalgam of psychology, sociology, and political action, and it wasn't very good in any of those departments. Perhaps the next social reform attempt will be more successful. However, one thing seems painfully clear: the vitality needed for such a venture will not come from recruiting contemporary social workers to return to the fold.

"That is a rather harsh assessment of our profession's prospects for restoring a significant mission for ourselves. I hope Efrau is wrong."

Karen

"Harry, I believe he is wrong. I, too, have despaired that our profession may not always appear to see the big picture, to intervene in the public debates, to sit at the policy table.

"I was furious a decade ago when publisher after publisher refused *Affecting Change* because there were no social work courses in which political advocacy existed. I was dismayed fifteen years ago in Indiana when the Moral Majority chose Dan Quayle to defeat Birch Bayh, Indiana's eighteen-year democratic pro–human service senator, and social workers weren't already positioned to fight this.

"I was dumbfounded in 1984 when NASW nationally refused to help me collect data about social workers in state and federally elected and appointed positions. I was surprised to hear, given that I began Indiana's PAC [political action committee] in 1979, that Connecticut was just now beginning one.

"But, Harry, times are changing."

Harry

"Karen, that's what I'd like to talk about now, before we're out of time.

"It is now time for social work to move on to the next phase of its connection to the community. The direction of the move must be outward to the systems of service that are directed at meeting the needs of the poor.

"A move in that direction is not a bad idea politically. As I said earlier, there is not, today, any significant constituency to speak in support of social work. The psychotherapy lobbies will not carry us over the long haul. Insurance companies and government are increasingly becoming disenchanted with the results of these interventions, and the competition from psychologists, physicians, MFCCs, and others is fierce. But there is no other profession that can match social work's capacity to be the major workforce in a welfare state that is committed to the provision of social care. The public services are huge agencies that manage enormous resources. The administrators of these agencies are well connected to legislators and other elected and appointed officials. The opportunities to do, and to fund, significant, relevant, and interesting practices, programs, and research on social programs are enormous if one tries to imagine an ideal kind of political, organizational, and economic support system for social services.

"If we, as a country, are to solve our major social problems, we must focus our efforts on the primary source of those problems—on the community, or perhaps more correctly, on the absence of community in American lives. To develop healthy communities we must build community systems of social care that will eradicate highly fragmented social services, education, child care, public health, recreation, job training and development, and criminal justice arrangements. The major objective of such a system will be to help Americans learn to live with, care for, and love one another. That is a very tall order. But it is a mission worthy of and appropriate for our profession."

Karen

"See, Harry, we do agree. The mission of this profession is, and always has been, to heal individual pain and to create or maintain a just society. Jeannette Rankin, the first woman and the first social worker installed in Congress, in 1917, saw that vision and that connection.

"Today Senator Barbara Mikulski and Representatives Ed Towns and Ron Dellums share and operationalize that vision. And at least 165 social workers in elected office nationally do, too.

"And, Harry, one of the most privatized and entrepreneurial cities in the United States—Houston, Texas—has a political social work concentration; the School of Social Work does not teach 'psychotherapy' as mainstream practice, but 'empowerment,' and that city has a multitude of community practitioners who engage in change efforts as part of their paid employment or in their volunteer time, and many of them are in direct practice."

Harry

"Well Karen, that's part of what I was going to say.

"Fortunately, we have a new national administration that does believe in building community. Whether they will find the resources to fund it and can muster the political support for it remains to be seen. But there is the potential and the hope for a new day. Maybe we can build a twenty-first-century system of community-based social care.

"In the meantime, I have three recommendations we can work on:

1. The profession and social work education must make a major commitment to build the professionalism of the public social services.

2. We must abandon clinical psychotherapeutic practice and begin to replace it with adult education, community work, and group work.
3. We must reform social work education. Education for psychotherapy must be replaced by education in law, community work, group work, and adult education.

"So, you see, we have a great deal to do."

Karen

"Well, Harry, I agree with professionalizing the public social services and reforming parts of social work education. I would not suggest the abandonment of clinical practice, nor do I see it as synonymous with psychotherapy.

"But, Harry, before we end our conversation, I'd like to just say thanks.

"Thanks for not backing away from controversy, for it is necessary to our professional growth and integrity. Thanks for feeling so strongly about our mission regarding society's most difficult problems and about our profession's commitment to offer solutions. And thanks for being so angry that we may be veering too far off, that we may become too complacent, that we may forget our historical roots."

Conclusion

This debate was included because our profession's future depends on social workers celebrating and publicizing our multiple skills and our diverse interests. We must strengthen our commitment both to clinically help individuals and to intervene for or advocate more expansive and humane social welfare policies. While we broaden our client base and our fields of practice, we must not lessen our attention to disadvantaged clients and the public social services. We must not lose sight of or reduce the value of those attributes of our profession that distinguish it from other professions; the systems perspective, for example, includes the examination of the environment as a critical factor in both causing and solving individual problems (Haynes, 1998).

This chapter is intended to present the argument that the strength of our profession lies in the breadth of its interventive techniques and in its historical commitment to both case and class advocacy. Although it is clear that we agree with much of the Specht/Courtney framework, the authors are unconvinced that the profession must choose between the mutually exclusive paradigms of individual treatment and social reform.

We are certain, we will become stronger if we truly believe that to do social work and to be a social worker requires commitment both to the goal of social justice and to the goal of healing individual pain. As we embrace the notion that the goal of social work is to act to right social wrongs, to work to increase diversity and reduce discrimination, and to expand choice and opportunity, we will come to understand that these ideals might equally and legitimately lead us either to individual treatment or to social reform strategies, and we as professionals must follow them there. If, in the future, we forget or become distracted by these broad and noble goals, then we hope that someone will raise his or her voice and pique our conscience as Harry and other social workers have.

All Social Work Is Political, So . . .

1. Review the recent social work literature, and provide two illustrations of this continuing debate.

2. Given this debate and the current political climate, make three recommendations to the professional association for policy endorsement.

3. Interview a social worker who works for an elected official or has some kind of policy position to see whether this kind of work would be of interest to you. Find out how this person obtained his or her position and whether the person's background was in micro or macro practice or generalist practice.

4. What do you think the difference is between case advocacy and cause advocacy?

Suggested Readings

Abramovitz, Mimi, and D. Ray Bardill. 1993. "Should All Social Work Students Be Educated for Social Change?" *Journal of Social Work Education* 29 (1): 6–18.

Specht, Harry, and Mark Courtney. 1994. *Unfaithful Angels: How Social Work Has Abandoned Its Mission*. New York: Free Press.

References

Abramovitz, Mimi, and D. Ray Bardill. 1993. "Should All Social Work Students Be Educated for Social Change?" *Journal of Social Work Education* 29 (1): 6–18.

Addams, Jane. 1905. *Democracy and Social Ethics*. New York: Macmillan.

Council on Social Work Education. 2001. *Council on Social Work Education Educational Policy and Accreditation Standards*. Alexandria, VA: CSWE.

Efrau, Jan S. 1994. *Networker*.

Flexner, Abraham. 1915. "Is Social Work a Profession?" In *Proceedings of the National Conference of Charities and Corrections*, pp. 576–590. Chicago, IL: National Conference of Charities and Corrections.

Gibelman, Margaret. 1999. "The Search for Identity: Defining Social Work—Past, Present, Future." *Social Work: Special Centennial Issue* 44 (4): 298–310.

Gibelman, Margaret, and P. Schervish. 1997. *Who We Are: A Second Look*. Washington, DC: NASW Press.

Gilbert, Neil, and Harry Specht. 1974. *Dimensions of Social Welfare Policy*, 2nd ed. Englewood Cliffs, NJ: Prentice Hall.

Haynes, Karen. 1996. "The Future of Political Social Work." In *Future Issues for Social Work Practice*, Paul R. Raffoul and C. Aaron McNeece (eds.), pp. 266–275. Boston: Allyn & Bacon.

———. 1998. "The One Hundred Year Debate: Social Reform versus Individual Treatment." *Social Work* 43 (6): 501–509.

Limb, Gordon E., and Kurt C. Organista. 2006. "Change between Entry and Graduation in MSW Student Views of Social Work's Traditional Mission, Career Motivations, and Practice Preferences: Caucasian, Student of Color, and American Indian Group Comparisons." *Journal of Social Work Education* 42 (2): 269–290.

National Association of Social Workers. 1999. *Code of Ethics.* Washington, DC: NASW Press.

———.2008. *NASW Membership Workforce Study: Social Workers at Work.* Washington, DC: NASW Press.

NASW News. 2008. "Reinvestment Act Introduced in Congress." *NASW News* 53 (4): 1.

Peavy, Linda, and Ursula Smith. 1983. *Women Who Changed Things: Nine Lives That Made a Difference.* New York: Scribner.

Reisch, Michael. 1995. "It's Time to Step Up to the Plate: Political Action and the Right-Wing Agenda." *Social Work Education Reporter* 43 (2): 6–9.

Richmond, Mary. 1907. *The Good Neighbor in the Modern City.* Philadelphia: J. B. Lippincott.

Specht, Harry, and Mark Courtney. 1994. *Unfaithful Angels: How Social Work Has Abandoned Its Mission.* New York: Free Press.

5

Policy Models for Political Advocacy

Social workers have a passion and an understanding of the needs and problems of parts of society that the legislative process, left to its own, will do little for. Understanding the process is key. Don't work at odds with it. Figure out how it works, embrace it—it can be made to work for the very people for whom I believe it was designed—those who have the least.

—Sandy Ingraham*

One can view, affect, and evaluate the policymaking process in a number of ways. The choice of an appropriate political interventive action should be based on one's evaluation of the policy. Just as a clinician must examine the personal, situational, and environmental elements of a client's problem before reaching an appropriate diagnosis and intervention, the political strategist must holistically examine a problem and then specifically focus in order to determine the appropriate intervention.

The similarity between determining a client's diagnosis and analyzing social policy can prove quite useful. In the same way that a client's presenting problem may initially be incomprehensible, social policy formation can appear complex and mysterious. To gain a clearer understanding of its various components, the client's problem or the social policy must be subdivided. This helps the clinician or the political strategist to identify the various components of the problem, determine the most important aspect thereof, and develop a plan of attack.

Within this clinical model of a generic problem-solving process that cuts across all levels of client intervention are all the steps and processes involved in political advocacy. For the clinician, the first step in the process is to get the client's view of the presenting problem. Intervention then requires a systematic collection of data either to substantiate the client's definition of the problem or to revise it. This data-gathering process, often called the *psychosocial history*, includes

*Sandy Ingraham is a social services consultant in Harrah, Oklahoma.

collecting information about the client's problems and significant relationships, understanding perceptions of these problems and relationships, and encouraging interaction with the community and environment.

Likewise, the political advocate first must come to understand society's definition of the social problem. A needs assessment or social indicators analysis must then be conducted. This includes collecting data about the size and scope of the problem, identifying the primary population at risk, and outlining current policies and procedures that already influence or are influenced by current or new policy goals and administrative regulations.

After the collection of data, a clinician must assess or diagnose the client's problem. This step involves decisions about the scope of the intervention, as well as whether it is change or maintenance that is required. The clinician must decide whether to provide treatment to the individual, to a dyad, or to a group.

On the political level, assessment involves identifying whether the appropriate intervention is administrative, legislative, or judicial and whether it should take place at the policy formulation, implementation, or evaluation stage. The decisions involved in such an assessment move the social worker, whether clinician or political advocate, to develop the treatment plan or political strategy that seems most appropriate.

Ideally, at this stage each social worker should have an array of interventive models from which to choose. Clinicians can choose from a continuum of models ranging from the psychoanalytic to the behavioral to the client-centered approach. Likewise, political advocates can choose from interventive approaches that view policy from various perspectives: institutional, process, group, elite, rational, or incremental. These perspectives are explained later in this chapter.

Obviously, the next step in both the clinical and political processes is execution of the treatment plan or political intervention, followed by an evaluation of the chosen treatment or intervention. This evaluation will result either in a termination of the process or in a repetition of certain steps in the process, so that a new or revised treatment plan or model for political intervention can be chosen.

Knowledge of policy models, assessment techniques, and evaluative tools is essential for all social work practitioners not only for political social work practice. Policies may address any and all levels of social work practice, and indeed, policy intervention at one level will undoubtedly affect and be affected by other levels. So just as with the clinical generic model, the parts or steps in the model may not always and only be addressed in one order. One may need to revisit any step to add information or to revise the initial problem definition. The key is to have sufficient knowledge and skills to generate the self-confidence and professional mandate to begin the policy analysis (Burch, 1999).

> As an elected member of Watertown's Town Council, my expertise in evaluating social situations is called upon surprisingly often. For example, the town is engaged in litigation against a resident whose home has become uninhabitable because of severe hoarding. I have been able to give the councilors information about the dynamics of hoarding that have helped them to address the situation

firmly but compassionately. In another situation, the town was involved in seizing a property because of failure to pay taxes. Some councilors questioned whether the town was being mean-spirited in its handling of the situation. I was able to point out signs suggesting drug use, which helped councilors decide on the best way to address the problem.

The most helpful aspect of my professional experience is my ability to deal with difficult individuals. I am generally able to stay calm and help de-escalate charged situations where councilors disagree with each other or the town manager—which happens often. Here's an example: The town manager has been pursuing a course of action to move the town's recycling center. Because of something he did two years ago, the council president will have nothing to do with the manager's plan. There is no way the president is going to change his mind, but he does not have the ability, as one vote, to block the manager's plan. Usually, the manager keeps his cool, but sometimes he takes the bait and tries to win the argument about what occurred two years ago. One of those times, I passed him a note that said, "Let it go." He did, and he has referenced that note several times since.

One of the lessons I've learned as a social worker is to cherish small gains. People change at their own pace when they are in therapy. Government is the same. I am currently the chair of the Public Works Committee. Grassroots activists in town are frustrated about many issues: that we use too much road salt, which harms the trees along the streets; we don't employ many traffic-easing measures; the town leaders are not fully committed to maximizing energy efficiency; pedestrians aren't given the consideration they deserve; our stormwater management practices need improvement; etc. As a social worker, I know that respectful dialogue with the superintendent of the Department of Public Works and open communication will be more effective than demanding immediate change. We've opened the conversation on all of these topics, and now we are starting to look at whether the organization of the department can support all of its tasks.

My basic approach to therapy is to "start where the client is," and the same approach is working well with changing the culture of the Department of Public Works.

Susan Falkoff, MSW
Watertown Town Council
Watertown, Massachusetts

Social work knowledge and skills have been lacking in the policy arena during the past several decades as evidenced by the fact that policy agendas have been set by groups whose values are significantly at odds with professional social work values. Consequently, major federal and state legislation has been enacted that is in the best interest of neither social work clients nor social work professionals, widening the gap between the haves and the have-nots. In other areas of policy debate, it has been suggested that domestic social policy development has been in a state of paralysis, using repackaging and window dressing rather than proposing solutions to these social problems (Blau, 1992).

Furthermore, since the 1970s, and with increasing rapidity, social programs have been held to an accountability model. Although it would obviously be politically incorrect to argue that social services should not be accountable or that their success and effectiveness should not be measured, the primary models that have been promulgated often bear little resemblance or meaning to the social services delivered and the problems being addressed.

Even today we have not satisfactorily differentiated outputs and throughput from outcomes. We assimilated the language and accepted the funders' demands for empirically validated measures, but we did less to argue these as reasonable and seldom provided meaningful substitute measures. In addition to the fact that substantial amounts of time may be required to generate less-than-useful measures (e.g., numbers of telephone calls made), what may be worse is that the data give an "illusion of productivity" (Gruber, 1991, p. 181). That is, we begin to believe that making x telephone calls or holding y interviews really measures the effectiveness of our social service programs.

So, as we have argued previously, social workers must be involved at all levels of policymaking, including problem formulation, policy model definition, programmatic solutions, and evaluative designs. And, as with all forms of intervention, the earlier social workers are involved, the better. Policy analysis is embedded with values at each step of the process, as is the clinical model just discussed. If social work values are absent in the problem definition, for example, it will be difficult to design a model that reflects social work values of dignity, self-determination, or confidentiality.

> My husband, the attorney general of Oklahoma, has often said that the practice of law calls for a measure of social work if the practitioner has a heart. He has told me that through my eyes he has been forced to look at causation along with probable cause, at the elements of family stability along with the elements of the offense, at the full paragraph and not just the sentence.
>
> He notes that the law is society's attempt to channel behavior. Social work recognizes that behavior is affected by crosscurrents and eddies of alcohol, unemployment, child abuse, gambling, incest, and cultural patterns that are far stronger than the walls and bars of a dike. If the law is to function, it must forge partnerships with the professionals who are geared by study and heart to focus on the viral agents of crime and not solely on the fever.
>
> *Linda Edmondson, MSW*
> *Oklahoma City, Oklahoma*

To argue that policies are inappropriate and evaluative strategies are meaningless is passive and ineffective; to participate in the development of policies and evaluative strategies is ultimately to better serve our clients. Both CSWE and NASW now emphasize social justice goals and the obligation of social workers to be informed and involved with social and political advocacy. It should be evident from our presentation, analysis, and illustrations that the choice of an appropriate political strategy should be preceded by an analysis and definition of the problem, a selection of the appropriate policy model, and a design for policy evaluation. The prescriptions for advocacy presented in this chapter support the purpose of this book—to teach political intervention skills.

When I decided to pursue a bachelor's degree in social work, I never thought I would be interested in social welfare policy or the policy process. I had every intention of being a medical social worker. I did not see the connection. Social welfare policy as a required course seemed to me a necessary evil on my road to graduation. As it turned out, the course taught me to think a lot about the bigger picture and how social workers can and should be a part of the policymaking process. The course helped me to understand the deep connection between social welfare policy and practice.

Upon graduation, I took a job working for the Girls Clubs of America (now known as Girls, Inc.) as a research assistant. I did investigative work on the social conditions facing girls, particularly girls at risk. What I experienced firsthand is how the numerous local, state, and federal social welfare policies affected the lives of our constituents. During the years I worked for Girls, Inc., federal and state monies for social programs were drying up. This was during the Reagan presidency, an era when we experienced a 30 percent drop in federal funding for social programs over eight years. I saw the devastating impact those cuts had on the girls we served. I knew I wanted to do more, and I believed that with my social work background I could do more. My undergraduate social welfare policy course kept coming to mind when I faced what felt like insurmountable barriers. I decided I wanted to pursue a career change which would bring me into the policy arena so that I could take part in those crucial decisions that affected the social welfare programs so important to the well-being of our nation. Thus, I began my pursuit of an MSW knowing that I wanted to do an internship that would bring me into the policy arena.

While completing my MSW, I served as a public administration intern for the state of Illinois. I was the only social worker in my cohort of interns. Our role was to learn all we could about the operation of state government while participating in the policymaking process. While I focused heavily on policymaking, I also learned the inner workings of every state agency. Social workers were rare in the numerous internships that existed in the governor's office and in the offices of the state General Assembly. Most of the interns had backgrounds in political science or public administration.

One of my most prominent memories of the experience was the value given to my expertise in understanding the social welfare needs of the state. I found my social work training was invaluable to me and the people I worked with throughout the year. The holistic social work perspective of viewing people in their environments provided the tools I needed to be creative in addressing social problems. I had been nervous that my credentials would not be valued, but I found that I was sought out on many occasions to give my opinions and recommendations in matters related to social welfare policy.

It became clear to me that, although social workers are rare, we are sorely needed in the policymaking arena. What we do not realize is that the vast majority of the work done by state legislatures involves social welfare policy. Therefore, we need to be working in staff positions for governors, legislators, and major social welfare committees as well as participating in legislative internships. I found that elected officials and their staffs wanted to do what was best for the people of the state, but they often did not have the expertise that we do to make the best decisions. We can have a serious impact on the legislative outcomes of our states, but we must be willing and not afraid to pursue jobs in the policymaking arena.

Stephanie Brzuzy, MSW, Ph.D.
Chair, Social Work Department
Xavier University, Cincinnati, Ohio

Models Defined

Just as the caseworker chooses a model because of its appropriateness to the client's problem, taking into consideration pragmatic constraints of time, money, or situation, so too the political advocate chooses a model that focuses on what appears to be the most critical area for intervention, taking into consideration whatever practical realities the environment, budgets, or political climate might dictate.

A model is a representation of some aspect of the real world designed to yield insight into or to focus attention on a specific segment of it. Models deliberately oversimplify reality in order to permit understanding and to direct intervention. Therefore, models quite necessarily treat some variables as crucial and ignore others in order to appropriately focus attention on a limited and specific array of determinants (Dye, 1998). For example, the psychoanalytic model deliberately excludes such explanatory variables as environmental and interactional data, but it is nonetheless useful in clinical treatment.

Similarly, policy models should simplify and clarify thinking about social policy and political intervention by identifying the important aspects of a policy and the targets of political intervention and by predicting policy consequences. A useful model should clearly identify the important aspects of a policy using concepts that are testable and have commonly shared meanings. It should be able to explain phenomena, not simply describe them (Stuart, 1999).

Institutional Model

Clearly, much political activity occurs within governmental institutions, such as Congress, state legislatures, courts, and political parties. Technically speaking, a policy does not become a "public" policy until it has been enacted, implemented, and enforced by some governmental institution. The institutional model focuses on policy as the output of these institutions.

This approach may focus on a structural examination of governmental institutions, but to be most useful it must go beyond that to include examination of the linkage between structural arrangements and policy content. This model focuses on questions such as these: Are the policies of federal social agencies more respon-sive to social problems than the policies of state or local social agencies? How does the division of responsibilities among mental health services affect the content of social welfare policy? Both of these questions require not only a description of structural institutional relationships but also a projection of the outcome of the policy as the result of those relationships. When using this model, one effectively focuses on structural arrangements that seem to affect policy outcomes.

For example, most states deliver general assistance to the poor through state or county agencies. However, Indiana still maintains a township trustee system as the vehicle to deliver this service. Consequently, 1,008 separately administered and autonomously directed poor-relief services exist within the state, without any state-mandated standardized procedures for determining eligibility or benefit lev-els. Not surprisingly, this results in extensive variation across townships and unequal and inequitable service to clients. For several years now, political advo-cates have sought legislation that would assign responsibility for general assis-tance to a county-level agency—a structural solution to the problem.

In general, interventive strategies based on the institutional model focus either on altering organizational structures or on choosing an organizational level or division within which to introduce structural change.

Process Model

The process model views policy as a political activity. In contrast to the institu-tional model, the process model focuses on *how* decisions are made. According to this view, it is neither the structure of the organization nor the content of the pol-icy that is of primary interest but rather the activities entailed in the policymaking process. This approach may appear to be of limited use in the analysis of policy, but it is extremely useful to the strategist trying to influence policy.

If, for example, you studied the way in which bills are processed by legisla-tive committees, you probably would obtain information that would prove useful in future efforts on behalf of measures you support. To do so, you need to determine the types of data and evidence the committee is willing to consider. Do committee members assign greater weight to written testimony, expert opinion, or empirical data? Do they regard verbal testimony, client or consumer opinion, and experience as valid evidence? Knowledge of the specific types of data con-sidered and the weight given to each might prove to be crucial information to an intervenor.

For instance, as multiple agencies vie for a limited number of dollars, they often have to make presentations to the funding source to support their budget requests. Understanding the decision-making process is essential for successful competition. One Area Agency on Aging, for instance, obtained only partial fund-ing when it presented its budget and position statement at legislative budget hear-ings. This testimony was fully supported by empirical evidence on the number of elderly in the area, average income, age distribution, and marital and health status. This information documented the need for funding of homemaker, congregate meals, and medical prescreening services. In contrast, the local rehabilitation center had not only prepared verbal testimony accompanied by empirically supported evidence of need and documentation of the number of clients served but the staff also brought to the hearing several paraplegic clients to give personal testimony on the need for extended services. The dramatic emotional appeal of this latter strategy led to full funding of the request from the budget committee.

Additional information useful in this analysis might be data about committee composition, such as the background of committee members and their current positions within the legislature, and knowledge of specific pressures on the committee or on individual committee members, such as the total committee agenda and popular constituent opinions. The strategies likely to be suggested via this model include interventions in the committee process and attempts to influence their outcome, most probably through lobbying.

Group Theory Model

Individuals with shared interests commonly group together to strengthen support for their demands. When these demands are made on a governmental institution, they become part of policy analysis. Sometimes direct-service agencies with similar goals band together (or cooperate) to strengthen their political clout. The group theory model is characterized by its central focus on interaction between political groups.

Often the group is viewed as a vehicle for transmitting ideas and demands from individuals to the government. In this model, politics is seen as a struggle among groups to influence policymaking. Changes in the relative power of one group vis-à-vis another are expected to determine changes in public policy. The relative influence of a group is related to its size, the resources at its command, its leadership, and its access to decision makers.

> Working as a sexual assault advocate in a small community in rural north Georgia, I was part of a system that was not very "child friendly" in terms of child victims. We were a one- to two-hour drive, over mountainous roads, away from the closest children's advocacy center (CAC); in severe cases of abuse, children need to be seen at a CAC. While I was accompanying a 4-year-old to a CAC outside Atlanta, he was crying because he was afraid of "going over the mountain." It was then I realized there was a real need in our community for a CAC. After meeting with my director, I was given the go-ahead to start drafting a proposal to develop a CAC to serve our community. Part of the core components of a CAC is a multi-disciplinary team (MDT), which includes representation from the district attorney's office, law enforcement, and child protective services. Unfortunately, the history of our relationship with these agencies was not so great. For two years, I facilitated the development of a working relationship with these agencies through meetings, training, and team-building activities, always with food. I was trained in the area of forensic interviewing, and we had the CAC facility ready to be renovated; however, we were still lacking the confidence of the district attorney's office, who ultimately would decide whether the protocols were signed and the CAC services would be

utilized. Again, through a series of meetings with the district attorney, I was able to gain his trust in my ability to develop and provide the services through the CAC. Ultimately, the district attorney signed the protocols, as did the other partner agencies. The next election year, the district attorney used the CAC as one of his platforms, and his wife choose the CAC to be the recipient of a fund raiser being held by one of the organizations she was involved with. If there's anything I learned by this experience, it's that persistence and hard work pay off and that relationship building is vital in a small community!

Tina Chiarelli-Helminiak, LSW, MSW
Shippensburg University

In the group model, policy formulation and implementation are the result of negotiations between competing groups. If we were to apply this model in a study of policymaking processes concerning reproductive rights, for example, we would focus attention on the positions taken and tactics used by significant interest groups. Thus, we might examine right-to-life groups and Planned Parenthood coalitions by studying their memberships, tactics, and strategies. We would also be interested in collecting data on the resources available to these groups (such as time, money, or membership) in order to determine why one group may be more successful than another within a given legislative session or have more appeal to a certain constituency.

In the group theory model, the management of intergroup conflict via the establishment of rules (such as a ceiling on campaign contributions) that facilitate intergroup compromise, and the enforcement of such compromises, is seen as the primary function of the political system. Compromise, conflict resolution, and the gaining of victory by one interest group usually are seen as processes that foster the national interest, and the results are said to constitute public opinion. This last assumption, however, is valid only if all groups have or are ensured equal access to power and resources.

Using this model, a policy advocate might try to influence decision making through access to the decision makers or through the control of scarce resources. Intervention strategies could include building coalitions with the controllers of resources or the formation of political action committees. Thus, if a reproductive rights advocacy group was having limited success in legislative lobbying because of its small numbers, active opposition, or public denial of the issue, a possible strategy would be to form a coalition of agencies representing multiple issues. This would provide the advantage of collective persuasive power and might mask the more sensitive or controversial issue.

Elite Theory Model

Elite theory views public policy as largely determined by the preferences and values of a governing elite. Elitists hold that the general population is, typically, apathetic and seldom attempts to make policy or express values. Further, public policy is seen as reflecting the views of the elite, who generally belong to the higher socioeconomic strata and are not representative of the general public.

Consequently, change is slow and the status quo is preserved unless and until societal shifts alter the elite's self-interest. This is not to imply that elites will always work against the general public's best interest but rather that it is this group who defines the public interest.

Because this model assumes that the general population is either ignorant or apathetic and views institutions such as political parties as being primarily symbolic in nature, its focus is on elite behavior and preferences. It also tends to assume a consensus among the elite regarding fundamental norms and values.

Using this model, it is possible to argue that even major pieces of social legislation have been introduced or supported by the elite, not by the masses. This model is helpful in examining, for instance, the relative ease with which Medicare and Medicaid legislation was enacted in the mid-1960s compared to the uphill, and as yet unsuccessful, battle over nationalized health insurance. According to this model, the difference is explained by the fact that Medicare and Medicaid affect the upper-income elite only minimally, whereas nationalized health insurance could jeopardize consumer choice and increase health care costs for all, including the elite.

Using this approach, an appropriate strategy would be to convince the elite group of the value of the desired policy change and to work with them to achieve it, possibly by getting elected to public office and becoming "one of them." One would need to advocate not only why the policy is good, fair, or just, but also, and more importantly, that it is in the elite's self-interest.

Rational Model

The rational model can also be defined as an efficiency model. That is, a policy is most rational when it is most efficient in achieving maximum benefits. Consequently, what characterizes a rational policy is that the ratio of benefits to costs is more positive and higher than for alternative policies.

The model assumes that costs and benefits of a particular policy can be known, that all policy alternatives are available, that all policy consequences are measurable, and that cost–benefit ratios can be calculated. Further, this model assumes that social values can be defined and weighed.

One of the barriers to an informed, rational choice among policy alternatives is that to eliminate a policy already in place may be extremely costly. Another is that long-term benefits, however predictable, must be weighed against current budget considerations. If, for example, we examine the Women, Infants, and Children (WIC) program, we see that despite clear evidence showing that every short-term dollar invested in the program saves three dollars in health care costs in the long run, funding for WIC continues to be stable, whereas food costs have risen, and so fewer people are served. Thus, because funding is limited, fewer than half of those eligible are served. The only rational explanation for this is that current economic decisions outweigh decisions favoring more efficient long-range policy outcomes.

The rational model allows us to calculate and evaluate costs and benefits not only on the basis of the group of clients, consumers, or populace directly affected but also on a larger societal level. Obviously, the definition of beneficiaries will determine the cost–benefit ratio of a particular policy.

Using this model, one would compile information and data to be used for purposes of persuasion. Arguments showing that the advocated policy change is more efficient, that it enlarges the potential beneficiary group and the long-term positive outcomes of a policy, is a strategy for winning policy changes that will increase benefits.

Incremental Model

The incremental model views current public policy as largely a continuation of past policies marked by only incremental changes. One of the best-known proponents of this model, Charles Lindblom, suggests that decision makers normally do not review the entire range of existing and proposed policies, rank-order their preferences among all alternatives, and then make informed choices. Constraints of time, money, intelligence, and politics prevent such a comprehensive, rational approach (Lindblom, 1959).

This model is conservative in that it uses existing policies as a baseline for determining the range of possible policy change. One of the advantages of this approach is that it is less expensive in terms of both the time spent reviewing and projecting alternatives and the costs already invested in existing policies. Consequently, it is a more expedient political model.

This model focuses on new or potential policies only in terms of their relationship to existing ones. An example is the addition of an unemployed parent (UP) clause to Aid to Families with Dependent Children (AFDC) legislation. This clause would enable two unemployed parents to receive AFDC benefits without having to separate. Rather than totally reconceptualizing and dissolving the present AFDC policy in order to enact a guaranteed annual income, some states simply added this UP provision to their AFDC program. Following the incremental approach, one would look for policies not dramatically different from existing ones.

A Proactive Approach to Policy Development

The problem-solving strategies used in any field are only as good as the theories or models available. Social work does not, however, have one model that is adequate to encompass processes and outcomes as well as the etiology of the social problems to be addressed. Most of the previously mentioned policy models can be characterized as follows:

1. Reactive to crisis and remedial in orientation
2. Residual in response, reflecting a reluctance to intervene

3. Based on existing capabilities of special interest groups to influence decisions amenable to them
4. Supportive of stability and, therefore, of existing patterns in distribution of resources
5. Only marginally responsive to inequities in society (Humberger, 1977)

These criticisms imply a need for a systemic or holistic approach to the examination of public policy. Humberger suggests a political–economic approach to examining the dynamics and interrelationships among political, economic, and administrative variables that affect the human service field. He suggests that such an approach is useful for both macro- and micro-level analysis.

Humberger's approach is not significantly different from a systems approach, which, when applied to politics, includes examination of the political system, the external environment bringing pressure on that system, and the output of the political system, that is, public policy. This approach allows, even demands, that variables be examined in a holistic fashion. It suggests the examination of variables not only as they interact within a particular sector, be it administrative, legislative, or executive, but also as they interact across sectors. For example, a state's decision to mainstream children in special education programs would be viewed as a policy decision affecting the special education sector as well as the social welfare and education sectors, involving not only special education students but also mainstream students and, consequently, a broader target system.

A proactive approach not only requires the examination of possible alternatives but also requires the ability to predict future problems, needs, or issues. Forecasting requires assessing or predicting future conditions and anticipating the behavior of individuals and institutions under those conditions. Demographic projections, simulations, or econometric projections are used, along with the more conceptual approach of developing alternative scenarios.

An excellent example of this model is the efforts of social workers to achieve legal regulation of social work practice. Rather than reacting to public pressure regarding services for the poor from untrained workers, or to action by legislators that might encompass a multitude of disciplines under one regulatory structure, practitioners developed a proactive strategy. In the early 1970s, for example, the NASW developed a model licensure bill and promulgated it nationally. Although the process took some time, and states modified this bill to fit their local realities and political climates, eventually all states achieved some form of legal regulation of social work practice. This effort and others like it have not only protected the quality of services to the public but also have regulated service providers.

All of these approaches are used to try to project future needs, problems, or both. Developing policy requires a thoughtful examination of future conditions and needs, a realistic projection of future financial and technological resources, and an approach that accommodates these factors. Knowledge of how social institutions and organizations behave and change is needed to anticipate organizational responses to particular policies.

What should be evident about a proactive orientation is its active approach to policy development, its eclectic sampling of a variety of policy models, and its reliance on a systems perspective. Although use of this approach requires finding reliable, current data to use in projecting future problems and needs, it encourages a posture of initiation rather than one of reaction.

By comparison, without proactive work in the entire policy arena, clients will be poorly served. Both welfare reform and health care reform provide specific illustrations of the worst of partisan politics: victim-blaming ideologies combined with cost reduction as the primary goal. (See Chapter 3 for a discussion of welfare reform.) The problem definition frames the rest of the process. In the case of health care reform, social workers knew that, despite the best efforts of the most dedicated social workers, many people lacked health insurance and that there were two tiers of health care services. Meanwhile, the legislators struggling again with national health care focused on the increasing costs. The resulting primary strategy was not to hold or lower salaries in the health care arena, not to reduce market competition between hospitals, not to regulate the pharmaceutical industry, but to limit consumer choice and restrict available treatments. Social workers and social work organizations were involved in the debate, but once again, without sufficient and sustained effort, they could not succeed.

Policy Analysis

Although policy analysis skills may be covered in the more traditional policy texts, they should be viewed as an essential component of political skills as well. Policy analysis should include analysis of the specific issue or issues as well as analysis of the general political climate (Flynn, 1992).

Traditional policy analysis focuses on the substantive analysis of the issues and on the fiscal analysis of the impact, or lack of impact, of the legislation. However, in including this topic in a political skills text, it is equally important to focus on the analysis of the political processes and likely outcomes of those processes (Kleinkauf, 1989).

According to Kleinkauf, these substantive issues must be examined: What are current statutes and regulations—federal, state, or local? What will this new piece add? What does the bill propose to do? Once the nature and context of the bill is understood, the analysis should proceed to find out who will be affected, positively or negatively: What are the implications of taking no action? Are there any foreseeable unintended consequences of this legislation? Certainly of importance is a consideration of the congruence with social work's mission and value perspective.

Through this initial analysis, the need for additional data regarding the prevalence or incidence of the problem, the current or projected future demand for the service, and the likely supporters or opponents of the bill should be evident. Furthermore, underlying and subtle influences of institutional racism, sexism, homophobia, and ageism, as well as destructive elements of social control, punitive measures, or regressive redistribution of resources should be examined.

The fiscal analysis should include an examination and documentation of any fiscal analysis completed already. This analysis should include start-up and first-year costs as well as ongoing costs. The policy analysis should include the cost of new staff, staff training, public information dissemination, and retraining and educating of existing staff where necessary. Hidden costs should be anticipated and "free" services (such as volunteers) or in-kind contributions should not be underestimated relative to other "real costs."

It is important that the social work policy analyst consider the human cost when conducting the fiscal analysis; that is, what would be the cost to current or prospective clients if this legislation were *not* introduced? Or, put another way, what is the cost of unmet social needs, which may show up in other programs that are not prepared or funded to handle these new needs?

Additionally, the examination of the processes and the likelihood of the bill's passage should comprise the final elements of the policy analysis. An understanding of the assignment to committees may indicate a prediction of the eventual outcome of the legislation. For example, it is commonly understood that the assignment of a piece of legislation to numerous committees increases the likelihood that the bill will die. Conversely, introducing the bill into only one committee, and one whose membership is favorable, is a good sign of quick passage of the bill.

Another indicator of successful passage is the sponsorship of the bill by powerful legislators. Bipartisan sponsorship is an even better predictor. Beyond legislators' support, a thorough analysis should also include an analysis of the bill's support and opposition by community groups and by political parties. The stance of community leaders is critical.

Policy Evaluation

Introducing, negotiating, and implementing policies are important aspects of the policy process, but they do not complete it. If we are to make informed choices among policy alternatives, an ongoing evaluation of established policies is necessary.

Policy evaluation usually requires a review of programs that flow from the policy being reviewed. Consequently, we must be cautious about judging the merit of any policy on the basis of an examination of only one program. Although evaluation has inherent limitations that arise from procedures such as generalizing findings, it is the authors' belief that policy evaluation is nonetheless superior to judgments made simply on the basis of political expediency, intuition, or organizational pragmatics. The merit of a particular program might be measured through examination of that one program, but the success of a particular policy is best determined by multiple program analyses.

Exclusive use of a single evaluation technique reduces, or narrows, the information that can be gathered about the topic under investigation. This practice may be necessary because of limitations on data, time, or money, but it will skew in one direction the data collected and the resulting decisions. Consequently, an evaluation that incorporates multiple types of evaluation techniques is more useful and is preferred, all other things being equal.

Effort

To focus on effort as the primary criteria by which to judge the success of a policy means to collect information about what it takes to deliver the policy in terms of staff, equipment, buildings, and so forth. The basic question, therefore, is "How much?"

Data related to effort include costs of salaries, equipment, fringe benefits, travel, rent, utilities, and supplies. Even such tangible costs sometimes are difficult to ascertain or estimate in multiprogram agencies, in which proportions of all of the preceding expenses may be attributable to different programs in varying degrees.

Sometimes evaluations of effort may focus on the output of a program. In such instances, collecting data on units of service becomes important. Although data collection certainly provides information about the numbers of individuals served or the units of service produced, it alone does not measure the effects of a service. This caution is necessary because it is sometimes inferred that units of service produced equals success or problems solved. That is, projected versus actual output of numbers of clients served often is presented to funders as a measure of success even though such statistics do not indicate whether the clients' goals have been met or their problems solved.

Quality

As policies are translated into administrative regulations and procedures, quality control measures often are included. This may be done through separate legislation on accreditation or licensure. In either case, the basic thrust is similar: to evaluate the policy or program on the basis of the quality of services rendered.

Measures of quality focus not on "How much?" but rather on "What kind?" Indicators of a good program might include level of staff training, education, and experience; worker-to-client ratios; or measures of worker performance compliance with other accreditation measures specific to the program, such as the number of square feet per child in day-care settings or a requirement that workers pass a statewide licensure examination. These are meaningful measures of the quality of any policy, but they may lead to inferences that the higher the quality of the program, the more successful the program or policy is. Often this is a questionable and untested assumption. These indicators are central to the analytic focus only if the policy was introduced primarily to enhance quality in specific programs. For example, if staff educational requirements are raised to enhance the quality of professional service, a measure of proportion of staff with higher degrees would be a reasonable indicator of increased quality.

Effectiveness

A third approach to evaluation is to measure a policy's effectiveness. Using this approach, one would ask the central question, "To what extent are the policy/program goals being met?" Although this approach comes nearest to measuring the "success" of a policy, the ability to collect information on program outcomes certainly depends on the ability to translate program/policy goals and objectives into measurable indicators of success. Ideally, evaluation also requires the collection of preprogram as well as postprogram data.

This may be the most useful type of information about a policy's impact, but it also can be the most difficult to gather. Programs often operationalize shorter-term goals, leaving the achievement of the long-term policy goal to be inferred. For example, although the goal of detoxification might be to reduce alcohol consumption permanently, the measurable indicator might be taken at the point of termination from the program rather than several years later.

When it is impossible or too costly to collect measurable data on program participants before and after their participation, aggregate statistics sometimes are employed. The reduction in teenage pregnancies as measured by health statistics may be used to evaluate the success of a high school course on birth control or the establishment of a local family planning clinic. In both cases, the inference of causality is untested, and the conclusions are, therefore, based on circumstantial rather than direct evidence.

Efficiency

When the primary focus of an evaluation is on cost relative to effectiveness, efficiency is the criterion being used. This type of analysis requires calculating per unit or per client costs for similar programs, consequently facilitating cross-program comparisons. For example, if effectiveness of goal attainment is held constant, it will be possible to compare a unit of adult day care, home-delivered meals, or adult residential nursing home care delivered by different programs.

The analysis might also include the use of cost–benefit techniques in which benefits are calculated in dollar terms. Thus, the evaluator cannot simply say that 60 percent of the elderly population served by a given nutrition program were properly nourished and maintained or that their health status improved. Rather, the evaluator must be able to indicate the worth of this improved health status in dollars. Determining that state and federal governments spent less on Medicaid and Medicare reimbursements as a result of this program would involve translating governmental benefits into dollar terms.

It is even more complicated, but of equal importance, to be able to calculate what these benefits mean in dollar terms to the individual client and to the local community as well as to the government. In the previous example, one might calculate the money saved by an individual client of a nutrition program in terms of reduced medical bills, or the money saved by the community in terms of unneeded ambulance or public health services.

Quite clearly, some benefits are more easily translated into dollars than others. Perhaps one can estimate with some validity the amount of medical expenses saved. Other benefits, such as the saving of a life or prevention of a marital separation, are much more difficult to convert into financial equivalents.

> If you want to be a catalyst for change, the means are at your disposal.... The policy process is complex and people need to be politically involved to begin to understand how the rules of this world affect them and how they are set in motion.
>
> *Adam Alter*
> *Senior BSW Student*
> *Ramapo College (Influencing State Policy, 1999)*

Conclusion

An examination of a variety of policy models and evaluative strategies can help social workers make choices in a more informed manner. Furthermore, by moving beyond theoretical models to prescriptions for professional practice, practitioners can become aware of the linkage between and importance of both theory and practice. Theory and analysis, without subsequent prescriptions for practice, are of limited professional use; wisdom gained through practice, without conceptual underpinnings, may be divorced from both long-term knowledge building and generalizations.

Each of the models discussed in this chapter provides specific prescriptive tactics for political intervention. All require skills and interventive strategies related to monitoring, lobbying, coalition building, and the entering of the legislative arena more directly through support of candidates and the holding of political office. These strategies are described in Chapter 6.

> While working as a children's public policy analyst at a local nonprofit advocacy organization, I had an opportunity to engage in an advocacy campaign that required all of my social work skills and abilities—micro, mezzo, and macro—to succeed. As would happen each year, a review of the proposed city budget revealed not only that dramatic cuts to the health department, specifically the community and personal health services budget, had been implemented during the last budget cycle (post-budget adoption), but also that the cuts were being proposed again that year, making them essentially permanent. As a small nonprofit, we immediately began collecting information and data and talking with our partners. We developed a fact sheet of what we knew from the city budget documents and planned a meeting with our public policy committee. During the committee meeting, we brainstormed our plans for engaging in advocacy and formally adopted fighting the cuts to the city budget as one of several advocacy priorities for the year. We also sought the support from our board of directors, and with its overwhelming agreement that this issue was critical for the health and well-being of our community, the project was initiated.
>
> Our city council budgeting process begins in January and comes to a close in June. In January, departments are given budgeting instructions and guidance by the finance and administration department of the city. City departments then develop budgets for the programs and services within their purview. This is followed with public meetings, departmental budget meetings between each city department, and meetings with the finance and administration department and

the city council. The mayor then proposes a budget; council meetings are held to discuss the budget; the comptroller participates, provides projections, and responds to questions; and finally a budget is adopted. I began my work with the executive director and public policy committee members; we researched and collected the city budget numbers, crafting a method for displaying them that clearly and quickly presented the decline in funding for anyone that reviewed the materials. One thing we were clear of: Even some office staff of the city council members weren't able to take the time to read each and every line in a several-thousand-page city budget proposal. We also developed a concise definition of the community and personal health services programs within the health department budget so that those we spoke with would understand we were talking about dental health services for children, immunizations, well-child checkups, maternity/maternal health visits for pregnant women, and more. Next, the public policy committee members, our MSW Interns, the executive director, and I began a process of collecting data and information. We

- interviewed the director and assistant director of the health department;
- visited health department clinics;
- interviewed the directors of dental and well-child services;
- participated in a "secret shopper" process of collecting data on appointment wait times;
- talked with school social workers and nurses to get anecdotal information on the capacity at the health department;
- met with the director of the finance and administration department to ensure we had all necessary budget information;
- and more.

At each turn, we found different reactions to our questions and inquiries. The director of the health department was skeptical and didn't trust our organization. She was less than willing to share information and materials despite our consistent assertion that we weren't critiquing her services or the way she ran the health department and that instead we were simply advocating for her to have more funding to allow for more services to be rendered. The directors of nursing at the clinics and the director of the dental program were more than willing to talk with us because they were struggling with the consistent cuts to budgets that meant declining services and turning away children in need. We found during our month of research that in the last seven years there had been a 40 percent decrease in encounters in child health services, a 57 percent decrease in encounters in maternal health services, and a 56 percent decrease in encounters in dental health services (an encounter = a visit to the clinic for the indicated service). At the time, the wait for a maternity visit to the clinic was fourteen weeks, or the equivalent of a full trimester. Through our research we also discovered the reduction in provided services was primarily due to personnel cuts. When a position was vacated, the department rather than filling the position, would freeze it—effectively and slowly reducing the capacity to provide needed services. The results were long wait-times and inability of the programs to meet the needs of the community.

Armed with the data and information needed, we began a multi-level education and advocacy approach. We scheduled visits with each of our city council members twice; once early on in the process and once closer to the time of the actual vote on the final budget. The first visit was with the chief of staff of the council members and included me, the executive director, and a member of our public policy team. In this meeting we presented the results of our research, explained our concerns, and asked what their priorities were for their budget review. Next, the executive director and I attended the public hearings for review of each departmental budget, showing interest and engagement in the process. We then called on our network of over 200 identified child advocates, whom we signed up as organizational supporters by emailing fact sheets and mobilizing them to write letters to the city council members expressing their concerns. The second meeting with the city council members happened after all departmental budget hearings had taken place. These meetings were facilitated by me, the executive director, and a member of our board of directors. Rather than meeting with a staff member, we met directly with the council member. In these meetings we outlined our research findings briefly, responded to their questions, and asked them to consider reversing the cuts to the community and personal health services budget in the health department. Next, we scheduled meetings with the mayor pro-tem and the mayor to share our findings, our actions thus far, and our recommendations. These meeting included the chair of our board of directors, along with me and the executive director of the agency. Lastly, the executive director and I testified separately before the city council during their public meetings twice, once each week for the two weeks prior to the adoption of the budget.

In the end, on the day that the city council voted to adopt the budget, it included 1.5 million in restored funds to the community and personal health services budget within the health department budget. It was a wonderful day and an exhilarating experience. Four months of research, visits, education, and advocacy had resulted in a successful campaign. Not all advocacy efforts have a happy ending, but it sure was nice to have accomplished our goal.

As we reflected on the success of the experience, it was clear that several variables contributed to our success:

- We utilized our micro-level skills of engagement to connect with departmental and city council staff, nurses, parents, and others to gather necessary information and to share the findings of our research.
- We included our community partners in the process, collaborating with our public policy committee (professionals from local human service agencies), our network of supportive child advocates, and other providers within the community to help shape and share our message.
- We worked diligently to be clear that we supported the city health department staff and that we were in no way attempting to critique their service delivery system, emphasizing that we in fact wanted to partner with them to help them.
- We included the local business leaders on our board of directors when visiting with the decision makers, such as the mayor and the council members. It was essential that those in power understand that this issue was not just of concern to child advocates and social workers, but rather was a community issue.
- We were present at meetings throughout the process and consistent in our commitment to answer questions and to find the information requested if we didn't already have it.
- We were careful to present our research findings via simple and straightforward messages, but we always had the detailed and in-depth information available in the event it was requested.

- Perhaps most important, we continuously framed this as an issue of quality of life for all children in our community. We would not let those we talked to dichotomize the issue into one of "us versos them" or "those children."

   This experience was one I will never forget. There were hours of research, weeks and months of preparation, meeting after meeting, and visit after visit—all over in one "aye" vote by the city council. It reinforced the notion that in advocacy you cannot be concerned with instant gratification. It was a great four months of work that in the end would benefit thousands of low-income women, children, and families in our community.

Heather Kanenberg, Ph.D., LMSW
Director of Field Education and Assistant Professor
University of Houston–Clear Lake BSW Program
Former Children's Public Policy Analyst at Children At Risk

The only way that social workers can be effective advocates for their clients, can move private troubles into the public arena, and can "affect change" is to understand the frames or lenses through which to view social policy. With that understanding, and with the skills of social work that place person in environment and fosters a systems perspective, policy creation, analysis, and/or evaluation can be done within the framework of social work values.

All Social Work Is Political, So . . .

1. Attend a city council meeting, a county government meeting, or a state legislature subcommittee hearing. What kinds of information were used to make a decision: demographic data, research findings, personal stories, testimonies? Which, in your opinion, seemed to influence the participants most?

2. Choose a newly enacted state policy.
    a. Use two of the models to analyze it.
    b. Identify a strategy for changing or modifying this policy as suggested by the model.

3. Identify a potential future social problem.
    a. Predict the future extent of the problem.
    b. Describe the type of policy necessary to resolve the problem.

4. Choose a current state policy and use efficiency criteria to analyze it.
    a. Suggest ways of costing out benefits to clients as well as to society.
    b. Describe elements you would include as costs in delivering policy.

Suggested Readings

Figueira-McDonough, Josefina. 1993. "Policy Practice: The Neglected Side of Social Work Intervention." *Social Work* 38 (2): 179–188.
Gil, David. 1970. "A Systematic Approach to Social Policy Analysis." *Social Service Review* 44 (4): 411–426.
Sosin, Michael, and Sharon Caulum. 1983. "Advocacy: A Conceptualization for Social Work Practice." *Social Work* 28 (1): 12–18.

References

Blau, Joel. 1992. "A Paralysis of Social Policy?" *Social Work* 37 (6): 558–562.

Burch, Hobart A. 1999. *Social Welfare Policy Analysis and Choices*. Binghamton, NY: Haworth Press.

Dye, Thomas. 1998. *Understanding Public Policy*. Englewood Cliffs, NJ: Prentice Hall.

Flynn, John P. 1992. *Social Agency Policy*. Chicago: Nelson Hall.

Gruber, Murray. 1991. "In and Out of the Rabbit Hole with Alice: Assessing the Consequences of Efficiency Prescriptions." In *Efficiency and the Social Services*, Robert Pruger (ed.), pp. 175–192. New York: Haworth Press.

Humberger, Edward. 1977. "A Political–Economic Approach to Human Services." Paper presented at the American Society of Pubic Administration National Conference. Washington, DC: Human Resources Administration.

Influencing State Policy. Fall 1999. "Student Projects." *Influence* 3.2: 10.

Kleinkauf, Cecilia. 1989. "Analyzing Social Welfare Legislation." *Social Work* (March): 179–181.

Lindblom, Charles E. 1959. "The Science of Muddling Through." *Public Administration Review* 19 (Spring): 79–88.

Stuart, Paul H. 1999. "Linking Clients and Policy: Social Work's Distinctive Contribution." *Social Work* 44 (4): 335–347.

6

The Practitioner's Influence on Policy

Social workers cannot afford to stand by and allow others to make policies that we are expected to implement. Social workers, those who have studied and implemented the policies, have seen the effect of the programs and the defects in the programs and know the unfulfilled needs of the people and thus ought to be able to initiate legislative efforts to form new programs or revamp old programs.

—Edolphus "Ed" Towns*

The general social work practitioner presumably is equipped with a framework and an array of roles that allow for intervention at the macro as well as at the micro level. Policy analysis, policymaking, and political intervention must be a central part of this framework (Pierce, 1984).

As subsequent chapters point out, data on social problems or needs is absolutely crucial to effectiveness in political intervention. A lobbyist cannot sway a legislator on a piece of legislation on day care, for example, without statistics, scenarios, or both to back up his or her position, and the practitioner is the best source of such data because the practitioner is on the front line. In contact with clients on a daily basis, the practitioner often develops particular insight into social problems as well as firsthand knowledge of the target population.

The purpose of this chapter is to emphasize the importance of the practitioner, both directly and indirectly, to an array of political activities. Practitioners can have tremendous impact on legislative, administrative, and fiscal decision making simply by using their practice knowledge and clinical data.

It is unfortunate that not all social work practitioners have within their repertoire of knowledge and skills an array of solutions to social problems, from case- or micro-level to political interventions. This would not necessarily add additional tasks to the practitioner's role or require the learning of new skills; the

*Ed Towns is a U.S. representative (New York).

actions involved consist primarily of information dissemination and client empowerment strategies. As noted in Chapter 2, the profession is beginning to emphasize the importance of such skills, given the CSWE Curriculum Policy Statement (2001) and the revised NASW Code of Ethics (1999). Additionally, if a study of political participation of social workers in the health care field is generalizable, there is hope that social work practitioners now engage in more and more diverse political activities than they did in the past, with voting, lobbying, campaigning, and collaborating among the most frequently noted activities (Domanski, 1998; Homan, 1999b).

Information Dissemination

Documentation

Regardless of work setting, the practitioner continually encounters unmet needs, social problems, and gaps in or barriers to service. However, recognition of such needs and problems seldom results in collective, public activity by practitioners. More commonly, practitioners treating problems such as marital conflict, poor family communication, or parenting difficulties may look to a new treatment approach, read or write an article, or develop or attend a workshop. Macro-level solutions, such as changing a policy or program, or establishing a new program or agency, seem to come less readily to the practitioner's mind.

No matter what form of intervention a social worker may undertake—community organization, casework, administration, or political activity—the resource most needed and used is information. Before any diagnosis can be reached or community organization strategy developed, information about the client's background and presenting problem or the community's problem and demographics must first be obtained. Intervention in the political arena has the same basic requirement because the same processes are used by the social worker in the political arena as in case or community work.

Also important is the social worker's daily interaction with clients, not only for the purpose of data collection but also to facilitate the organization or mobilization of clients on their own behalf. The practitioner's relationship with clients or client groups provides clients with additional insight and motivation, both of which help to enable clients to advocate for themselves.

Social workers, practicing in a variety of settings (hospitals, juvenile homes, the courts, public schools, mental health clinics, and so forth), are in a position to respond quickly and authoritatively when asked about the major difficulties they face in serving clients: lack of time to adequately help people, too large a caseload, insufficient resources. Each practitioner is an expert on problems, needs, and resources. Clearly, therefore, the practitioner can become an ideal conduit between those who have problems and needs and those who are politically active. Social workers are also good resources for what works. Unfortunately, this doesn't often occur because the practitioner's knowledge and expertise usually remain at the case level. The missing link to bridge the gap is to aggregate individual practitioner's diagnoses and data into the kind of information that is necessary in order to function in the political sphere. Part of the solution was the creation of NASW's National Center for Social Policy and Practice.

Increasingly, agencies have some form of system by which to gather data that justifies expenditures to funding sources and describes activities to boards and to the community. Most of these information systems, whether simple and idiosyncratic to the program or highly complex or standardized, are constructed to depict or describe the existing activities of the staff (management information systems) or the characteristics and problems of the clients (client information systems). Consequently, even the most comprehensive and technical of these do not always identify unmet needs or adequately illuminate the overlapping dimensions of a problem.

The practitioner can pull together case statistics and scenarios that clarify, expand, or redefine a problem area in ways that an information system cannot. For example, as the number of teen mothers who choose to keep their babies increases, public school policies need to be changed so that these young women can continue their education. Working with individuals, practitioners might find solutions for each young mother. Because the problem is both a social and an individual one, social and political solutions, such as public school policy changes, are needed. Thus, a major requirement of advocacy for policy change is documentation by practitioners of needed services (Briar and Briar, 1982).

Because information systems are initiated to serve either agency documentation or clinical diagnostic needs, it is not surprising that the use of these in political testimony, legislative support, or administrative rule writing and program implementation may appear to be an afterthought. However, documentation is a primary step in any problem-solving process in social work, and systems should be designed for multiple purposes, including clinical, administrative, and political activities. Social work staff at all levels should be able not only to input data but also to manipulate it to create categories and groupings that answer many questions, problems, and needs in various dimensions.

If practitioners become imbued with the idea that they have a unique and essential role in the documentation of needs, problems, and resources, they may find the task of "paper pushing" less cumbersome, boring, or unessential. Although their documentation skills and their information are essential to the political process, practitioners themselves do not need to be directly involved as political activists or advocates in order to contribute to political solutions.

> In 2006, 45 percent of Latino children were eligible for Medicaid, but only 10 percent were enrolled. Latino children typically comprise fewer than half of the children served in the various Regional Behavioral Health Authorities (RBHA), but in Maricopa County, Arizona, the disparity is greater.
>
> Arizona has been a pioneer in implementing managed care in its Medicaid program. It was the last state to adopt Medicaid, and it utilizes a capitated managed care model. Furthermore, behavioral health is a carve-out, meaning that it is

administered by the state health department instead of by the managed care single state agency (called the Arizona Health Care Cost Containment System). Even more complicating, today this delivery system is administered through two private for-profit corporations and two nonprofit corporations.

The above mentioned health disparity for Latino children in Maricopa County has existed for at least fifteen years. I have been advocating in Arizona to get the Latino Caucus of the state legislature to address this health disparity. The Latino Legislative Caucus has met on at least five occasions over the last two years with representatives of the Arizona Department of Health Services and the local RBHA. I have been retained as an informal consultant to them on this issue due to my know of, and interest in, this health disparity issue.

Recently, the immediate past minority leader in the state senate has been having meetings with the governor's policy advisory on health to discuss this issue. Meeting with the new RBHA in Maricopa County have been discouraging because the RBHA has their hands full in implementing their new contract. The Latino Legislative Caucus leadership has given Senator Garcia, who is an MSW, the lead on this policy issue. He has taken it on himself to host meetings with the governor's policy advisor and the division director responsible for behavior health.

Although no legislative remedy has been proposed, Senator Garcia has been assured that the new RBHA's contract has provisions addressing this policy issue. The issue appears ready to move to the next level, which would require a legislative resolution. Given the economy and the Republican control of both houses, we are skeptical that any legislative remedy will be given priority. But I and others remain vigilant and continue looking for opportunities to make a difference for our Latino children.

Manuel Medina, Ph.D.
Multicultural Associates, Eloy, Arizona

Testimony

Given that legislators possess limited knowledge of the wide variety of subjects about which they must make decisions, testimony from the field is an essential part of political deliberations. Here is another opportunity for practitioners to effectively use their experience, expertise, skill, and knowledge to influence decisions made in the political arena.

Presentation at a legislative hearing of testimony using scenarios can have a major impact. Because the practitioner has access to clients who may be affected by a current or future policy, testimony can be enhanced by the inclusion of documented statistics, scenarios, and case illustrations, as well as by the presence of the clients themselves. The practitioner may speak on a client's behalf or have the clients speak for themselves. Either of these tactics can be used in a highly persuasive manner.

Of concern to the practitioner is the client's potential loss of confidentiality and anonymity through the use of client information, client profiles, case illustrations, and the client's presence. The social worker must be cautious about jeopardizing any individual client's privacy.

It is essential to keep in mind the basic principle of client self-determination when decisions are made about a client advocating on behalf of his or her own best interests or on behalf of other clients. In fact, having clients take matters into their own hands to affect a solution is a recommended part of the helping process. Consequently, the role of enabler is an essential role for the social worker practitioner. If they are not already aware of the possibilities, clients should be shown that it is possible to implement situational, environmental, political, and organizational solutions to problems, as well as personal solutions. The introduction of macro-level solutions in turn helps to reinforce in clients the idea that their problems may not be caused by their own inadequacies.

Testimony by both the practitioner and the client is an extremely dynamic lobbying tool and is most dramatically done by the practitioners and clients directly affected. It may be more persuasive than the most expensive lobbyist, who, after all, must rely on secondary sources, such as aggregate data or "secondhand" stories. Thus, the client or social worker who can present facts, personal vignettes, and scenarios, and who also is a constituent, can play a significant role for clients and in major policy settings—a role that no other individual or group can fill.

> I have been employed as a transplant social worker since 1985 and a dialysis and transplant consultant since 1998. While my primary job is to provide direct services to kidney, pancreas, and liver transplant patients, as well as living kidney and liver donors, I increasingly was asked to provide consultation and expert advice in this field. As a result, I have moved from clinical social worker to social work advocate and back again many times.
>
> Although my clinical work is very important and was the specialization I chose, advocating for the expansion of the state Medicaid program to cover heart, heart-lung, lung, liver, and bone marrow transplants for the working poor has been, undoubtedly, my most significant accomplishment to date. This advocacy also resulted in a provision allowing patients waiting for transplants to remain on the waiting list even if they lose their Medicaid eligibility. My advocacy has also recently resulted in a coalition of transplant hospitals and related nonprofit health associations, which has promoted living donor leave for Arizona State employees and has been successful in having two bills introduced in the 2008 Arizona State Legislature.
>
> *Charles Thomas, LCSW, ACSW*
> *Banner Good Samaritan Medical Center*
> *Phoenix, Arizona*

Expert Witness

Legislative committees may request testimony or allow designated time slots for organizations and individuals to give testimony about an issue currently before that committee. Expert witnesses usually are called by invitation, and the expert must hold certain credentials—educational or experiential—to be deemed "expert." Sometimes legislators will undertake trips to seek information, witness events, or experience a particular social problem, so that they can themselves provide this firsthand type of information.

Information is crucial to policymaking. It is the practitioner who is the expert on many client needs and problems, far more so than the social work administrator or the paid professional lobbyist. The role of expert usually excludes clients because the term often implies possession of specific educational credentials and a breadth of professional experience. Part of the verification of one's qualifications as an expert might include the ability to project the course of future events if a problem or need were to go unattended and to show that these predictions have empirically demonstrable bases.

Although, as mentioned, the role of expert witness usually is undertaken at the invitation of a legislative or administrative group, social work practitioners should make themselves more ready to undertake this role and better prepare themselves to serve as expert witnesses if asked.

Written Communication

Writing letters to legislators is another important professional role that practitioners can fill. Many practitioners do not realize the potential impact of one letter from a professional. Nor does letter writing take much work: Legislators want to know as concisely as possible which bill one is writing about and the position taken; they want brief documentation for that position and enough identification so that the writer can be contacted for additional information. This type of letter is not difficult to write. Letter writing is discussed more fully in Chapter 7 on lobbying.

Many human service organizations have newsletters or house organs that can and should routinely be disseminated to state and federal legislators and relevant decision makers. The potential payoff in visibility for the organization, its clientele, and the services it provides is well worth the modest investment required. Increasing a public official's awareness of the services an organization provides is as important as documentation of existing unmet needs. Both pieces of information are essential to informed decision making.

Client Empowerment

Enabler/Advocate Role

Inherent in the general social work practitioner's functions is the role of enabler or advocate. One of the basic social work principles is to help clients move toward independence from the social worker, to enable clients to define and resolve their own problems, and to help them become self-advocates (Mickelson, 1997).

These roles require more than the collection of data and the subsequent assessment of the situation or problem. They require the practitioner to imbue clients with the ability to "own" their problems and to identify client strengths for overcoming them. In the role of advocate, the practitioner moves from analysis to action, requiring clients to identify resources and assert their rights.

Although the advocate role is most commonly used with individual clients to move from case (individual) to class (group), advocacy requires no additional skills other than the ability to aggregate data or mobilize clients. Community organizers build on these basic principles as a practice specialization, but specialization is not required.

Practitioners must not be so constrained by their therapeutic specialization or by an agency's policies on eligibility or service modalities that they become unable to see that macro-level problems require macro-level solutions. For example, an elderly single person who is depressed because of isolation from the community and loss of independence is treated for depression. This may well represent an example of the inability to recognize macro-level solutions. The astute practitioner might also examine community resources to ascertain whether adult day-care centers and accessible transportation are available. If not, practitioners in similar agencies could be queried to see whether a sufficiently large client group exists to warrant further strategies, and, if so, the social worker could advocate with them or on their behalf for the development of these services.

An additional benefit of enabling clients to advocate on their own behalf is that it not only gives clients a sense of ability to control their lives but also gives them skills that are useful and transferable to various other situations.

> The work done by nonprofit and community organizations is vital to a healthy community. When public policies adversely affect the work done by human service organizations, the impact is felt not only by the organization's constituents, but also by the larger population. There is no profession better equipped or more qualified to impact policy makers than social workers.
>
> *Mary Nienow, MSW*
> *Chair of Grasstops*
> *Minnesota*

Evaluator/Consultant Role

Practitioners also are in a central position to identify and evaluate the effects of legislative policies on their organizations and to determine whether the rule-writing and implementation phases have been logically interpreted and consistently followed. Chapter 9 on monitoring describes these processes in greater detail.

Once policies have been passed or services have been introduced or redesigned, the practitioner delivering those services is presumed to be the person best placed and qualified to act as an evaluator and consultant to determine whether new policies or services follow the intent of the legislation. Do the rules prescribe services that will overcome the barriers and issues articulated? Is access assured to the targeted client group? Are clients better off now that the service is available (Homan, 1999a)? This is not to suggest that agencies necessarily will invite or encourage this type of critique. However, evaluation is a vital function in policymaking and a logical role for the practitioner.

Voter Registration

The central premise of the democratic process is that of freedom of individuals to choose among candidates who represent an array of political ideologies. Voting is the mechanism by which citizens have the opportunity to voice their opinions, make decisions, and elect those who shall represent them. Our system requires voters to be registered before they can vote in an election.

Promoting and enhancing client self-determination is a basic value of social work. Voting is one of the mechanisms that permits the citizens in a democratic nation to have a voice in determining the nation's domestic and foreign policies (Jansson, 1999). Nonetheless, a large proportion of citizens are not registered to vote, and not surprisingly, a disproportionate number of these unregistered voters are social work clients: the poor, the young, the elderly, the unskilled.

It is consistent with social work principles to assist clients to exercise their democratic right to self-determination. One way to do so is to help them register to vote. In the past, voter registration activities undertaken by some social workers and schools of social work have been opposed by members of the profession. They argue that registration is a partisan act and, therefore, is unlike other enabling activities, such as assisting clients to obtain a food stamp identification card, secure necessary documentation to rent an apartment, or file a death certificate so that insurance claims can be processed. Also, arguments have been made, often based on misconceptions about state Hatch Acts, that public employees are prohibited from undertaking voter registration activity.

In reality voter registration is quite legal as long as it is nonpartisan. The National Voter Registration Act of 1993 (also known as "Motor Voter") was enacted to address the problem of declining voter registration and to ensure the participation of all citizens in this country's political process. The act (which took effect in 1995) requires states to register clients at state-funded offices that provide service to people with disabilities and services related to Temporary Assistance to Needy Families (TANF), food stamps, Medicaid, and WIC. In addition, states must permit people to register to vote when they obtain or renew their drivers' licenses (hence the nickname Motor Voter). Clearly, social workers and human service agencies that have a tax-exempt 501(c) (3) status can participate in voter registration as long as the drive remains nonpartisan. Neither the Hatch Act nor the IRS can prohibit such efforts.

Hatch Act

In 1939, Congress approved legislation known as the Hatch Act, which limits the political activities of federal employees, employees of the District of Columbia government, and certain employees of state and local governments. The Hatch Act was enacted out of concern that governmental employees were participating in political activities and might cause problems in public institutions. Therefore, the act limits governmental employees' partisan political activities. In 1993 President Clinton signed into law a revision and simplification of the 1939 act. The Hatch Act falls under the authority of the Office of Special Counsel, which should be consulted for specific questions and concerns. With very few exceptions, all employees in the federal executive branch or in state and local executive agencies are subject to the act. A key point to remember is that the act is mostly concerned with partisan political activities, which means the election or political action connected to a political party whose presidential candidate received electoral votes in the most recent presidential election. The Hatch Act is confusing both in terms of who is covered and because of its restrictions (Thompson, 1994). The following lists of dos and don'ts should help to clarify permissible and prohibited activities covered by the act.

May register and vote as they choose

May assist in voter registration drives

May express opinions about candidates and issues

May participate in campaigns in which none of the candidates represents a political party

May contribute money to political organizations or attend political fund-raising functions

May wear or display political badges, buttons, or stickers

May join political clubs or parties

May sign nomination petitions

May campaign for or against referendum questions, constitutional amendments, or municipal ordinances

May not be candidates for public office in partisan elections

May not campaign for or against a candidate or slate of candidates in partisan elections

May not collect contributions or sell tickets to political fund-raising functions

May not make campaign speeches or engage in other campaign activities to elect partisan candidates

May not distribute campaign material in partisan elections

May not organize or manage political rallies or meetings

May not circulate nomination petitions

May not work to register voters for one party only

This summarizes the law governing political activities of governmental employees. Clearly, the act does not keep employees from any kind of activity. Social workers who are employed by the government should seek additional information to advocate for social change within the law.

The Executive's Role in Influencing Policy

Unfortunately, in the past, social work administrators have been stereotyped as conservative and part of the status quo. Probably a central explanation for this description is that these executives are seen as representatives of recalcitrant and unchanging organizations—the very same ones that are often targets for social work activists (Richan, 1980).

Although there has been some empirical evidence to support this stereotype (Epstein, 1981; Heffernan, 1964), research indicates that this perception has changed. In one study of advocacy organizations, for example, it was found that the effective organizations were more likely to have social work administrators than were the less effective ones (Reisch, 1986). In another survey (Ezell, 1989), it was found that administrators devote significantly more time to advocacy on their jobs than do micro practitioners and that these macro practitioners use more of their time for class advocacy. One survey (Pawlak and Flynn, 1990) showed that 77 percent of the sample wrote letters and 43 percent talked with officials. About a third used intermediaries in their political activities.

According to Ezell's work, "it appears to remain true that no social workers are very active in political campaigning, litigating, representing clients in hearings, conducting issue research, influencing media coverage of an issue, or attempting to influence administrative rule making. Administrators were significantly more likely to engage in the last three" (Ezell, 1989, p. 13). When asked why they engage in these efforts, the macro practitioners more routinely saw advocacy as part of their jobs and were more likely to belong to other organizations that take stands on public issues.

One potentially simplistic explanation for the administrators' increase in political activity is the growing decentralization of decision making and funding to states and localities and the pressures of an organization to survive. Consequently, social work administrators have had to learn to compete effectively in this arena. The "ability to assess the structure and operation of power in an organization and skill in coalition formation are two central attributes of the organizational politician" (Gummer and Edwards, 1985, p. 18). This leadership is most likely to take the forms of working with the state system, redesigning the voluntary sector, mobilizing external constituencies, and pursuing legal options; this type of advocacy is externally directed and takes political sophistication (Perlmutter, 1985, p. 4).

I was the executive director of the Community Service Council (CSC) of Central Indiana and vice president for planning at the United Way of Central Indiana. I had observed human service programs developing incrementally in Indiana. Programs were scattered over at least six state departments, with many operating outside the bounds of any of these bureaucracies. Neither planning, cooperation, nor consolidation were even issues. I decided that the CSC should conduct a needs assessment of the eight-county central Indiana region, funded by the various stakeholders who agreed to do so. I wanted to ensure that indirect services such as planning and information and referral were addressed.

An implementation phase followed the completion of the needs assessment, and promoting action on state planning was a priority issue. A prominent businessperson, chair of the implementation phase, arranged a meeting with the governor and his executive staff to talk about interdepartmental planning. While these state officials were not terribly receptive to this concept, they were concerned that some clients were abusing the system and that others were not really being helped because of the lack of coordination among state services. I suggested that CSC should research what other states were doing and provide the governor with a report. Funds for the implementation phase were shifted slightly to provide for this research. After I completed two papers on this topic, I met with the staff director of the statewide human services coalition and the heads of two key human service departments. Although state officials were not extremely supportive, they did agree to fund one position for a planner to work with the Interdepartmental Board for the Coordination of Human Services. Although this position became institutionalized, there still was no attention to statewide structure and policies in the state's human services system.

Thus, United Way of Indiana approached the governor to initiate a statewide public–private strategic planning process for human services. I was a member of "Hoosier Initiative," and we made sure that both candidates in the gubernatorial election were included in the process. Legislation that would lay the groundwork for implementation was championed by CSC and the United Way and was made into law.

The new governor recognized the partnership achieved through Hoosier Initiative and named me and the three other leaders to four of the seven citizen seats on the interdepartmental board. The state is now engaged in serious study around reorganization and I, as vice chair of the board, will chair the subcommittee responsible for this plan.

Although incremental, the achievements are significant: from a dilemma identified locally, to a position held by a coalition made up of diverse constituencies, to a state priority. Additionally, my role as an agency executive working from the outside and trying to persuade state bureaucrats what to do has shifted to that of an inside leader, helping the state decide which path to take.

Irv Katz, MSW
Chief Executive Officer, National Human Services Assembly

Influencing Policy: An Illustration

Sara L. Barwinski, MSW, was the advocacy facilitator at Lutheran Family and Children's Services in St. Louis, Missouri. She provides an illustration of the process of influencing policy.

I work with the unit that addresses low-income clients, crisis intervention, homelessness, case management, and resettlement. When the federal cuts came, we started seeing more and more homeless families. It was very frustrating to discover that the people who needed resources after losing their shelter were not receiving food stamps. The fact that I was fairly green in the field was helpful in a lot of ways. I decided to take advantage of the caseworker training provided by the Department of Social Services. I thought that if I was going to work directly with clients in these situations, it would be helpful if I really understood the rules and regulations.

I was confused. I knew that, technically, homeless people were supposed to be able to get food stamps, yet my clients kept coming back stating that they had been denied food stamps. State officials assured me that the homeless people in Missouri were not being denied food stamps because of homelessness.

Through networking with other organizations addressing hunger, I found that, indeed, the federal food stamp program was there for the homeless, but in the streets of St. Louis the homeless were not getting food stamps. I then interviewed clients about the process and their experiences, and I discovered the problem. The clients were not allowed to apply in the first place! This explained why the state officials at the capitol were saying that there was no problem. They never received any applications; therefore, no problem existed.

When clients came into the welfare office, the first order of business was to put their names and addresses on a waiting list from which they could be called to fill out applications. Of course, those with no addresses to put down would never get to the application phase. They were told that they could not be seen until they came back with addresses. That was the loophole—there was no paper trail, there was nothing that could be legally appealed, and consequently the state was ignorant of their problem.

If you don't have an address, you have to establish residency. This is a matter of concern to the counties, especially in cities like St. Louis, which borders on Illinois. How do the intake workers know whether a person is really a resident of the county? The state manual provided no clarification. On the one hand, clients could not be denied because they were homeless. On the other hand, clients needed an address to prove residency in the county in order to apply in that county. The issue was not something that the state had been challenged to clarify.

It was time to take on this issue. I needed a client to use as a test case. I didn't think it was wise to use a homeless family because of the possibility of having the children removed from their parents. I needed an unmarried person who was willing to fight the bureaucracy.

I asked one particular client, a young person who had been through the foster care system—I'll call him Jeff. At 18, all of a sudden he found himself on his own, unprepared to do anything. By the time I worked with Jeff, he was 20; he had drifted for a few years and was living on the streets. He agreed to be the test case.

I went with Jeff to apply, and we used the agency's address to get through that first loophole. When we actually saw a caseworker, we were received with anger as it was realized that Jeff was using the agency's address. But I had done my homework, and it was going to come in handy. I explained to the caseworker what my real concern was: I wanted the caseworker to clarify the policy and make a decision to either accept or reject the application for food stamps. I had already talked to people at legal services. They were prepared to take legal action, but we needed a formal refusal first. If the caseworker accepted the application, then we had a precedent that we could use to change the overall policy.

The caseworker did not want to take the application. I knew that the law was absolutely clear: Everyone had the right to apply, and each applicant had the right to a written rejection. When the caseworker asked us to leave, I held my ground and gently demanded his decision in writing. I had with me the names and telephone numbers of the people I had contacted at the state capitol who had assured me that this was not happening. I suggested that before he refused to take this application, he might want to call some of them just to check because they had assured me that I would not have a problem. He made the calls. He wasn't really happy, but he came back a few minutes later and took the application.

Legally the state had to respond within the next five days. However, it took seven days before the city office got the approval to issue food stamps. The state decided to get around the issue of Jeff's not having an address by using the Department of Social Services county office address and having Jeff pick up the stamps there. This then established a precedent, allowing homeless people the option of either using the county social service office address or other addresses that they could arrange with their caseworkers.

Although the system was now in place, we had only one caseworker who knew of the new system. I am not so naïve as to think that this action would make a difference for all homeless people in Missouri. It was only the first step.

Next I convened a group of service providers who worked with the homeless to walk them through the process that I had developed with Jeff. I explained what the state policy was now and trained them to do the exact same thing with their clients. From that meeting a dozen people or so took homeless clients to the welfare office. This procedure was not without problems; it took several months to obtain our goal of having the process well ingrained in the county welfare department so that eventually we would not need to accompany the clients. We met with county officials to discuss the system and to show them that we wanted to help make the new system work. However, I let them know that we were very serious by bringing an attorney from legal services with me. It was all very pleasant, but the officials knew all along that there was the real potential of a lawsuit. The attorney's presence was like having an iron fist in a soft glove—we came as friends, but we let them know we meant business.

At that meeting we identified the main concern, and we worked out different ways for clients to verify county residency. One progressive approach we came up with was to allow social workers to serve as collateral contacts. We produced a form on which a social worker could state that to the best of his or her knowledge, this homeless person, whom our agency had been serving for a certain amount of time, was a resident of this county.

I had been in communication with people in other cities around Missouri, who assured me that this was not just a St. Louis problem. It was necessary to formalize the policy change and make it permanent by incorporating it into the manual, which would go out to workers and be included in their training.

To start this next step, we successfully got a policy clarification memo and a manual change that accompanied the memo. The memo clearly stated that homeless people were not to be denied food stamps and that they were entitled to receive the stamps at the county offices. To put the final touch on this policy change, I invited state officials to take part in a news conference with us. It was not the intent to embarrass them or to take legal action, although we had been prepared throughout this fight to go to court. We felt now was the time to lay the foundation for further efforts on behalf of our mutual clients, and the purpose of the news conference was to announce this new policy. This was a far more effective strategy than blasting the officials for not rectifying the problem in the first place.

There was another positive outcome from this experience. Including the client Jeff in the news conference, and crediting his collaboration in our efforts, provided an incredible boost for his self-esteem. It is a social work value to empower clients, and I see advocacy efforts to be no exception.

From a practitioner's standpoint, I could have stayed in St. Louis giving out bags of food and not touched anywhere near the number of people I did by getting this policy changed. This experience taught me how important it is for practitioners to keep tabs on their clients as well as on the bureaucracy.

Sara L. Barwinski, MSW, a NASW social work pioneer, was the advocacy facilitator with Lutheran Family and Children's Services, St. Louis, Missouri.

Ms. Barwinski kept up her advocacy efforts on behalf of clients in need of food stamps. Twice she testified before the U.S. Congress on legislation that resulted in the Stewart B. McKinney Act and the Hunger Prevention Act of 1988.

Conclusion

It should be evident that the practices and processes advocated throughout this chapter are already in place and part of the intrinsic fabric of social work. Like so many of the skills and techniques discussed in this book, they require only the ability of the social work professional to translate them from the micro- to the macro-level arena of practice.

Furthermore, we have seen that intervention in the policy or political arena need not be direct. Repackaging existing information in a slightly different manner and enlisting other individuals in coalition building or problem identification may be all that is necessary.

The empowerment of clients may be strategically used or may occur as an outgrowth of other activities. In either case, it is a core social work principle, not an ancillary function.

All Social Work Is Political, So . . .

1. Think of a high-ranking elected official you would like to influence. Then determine who you know who knows someone who knows that elected official. See if you can make it a very short list. Then try making such a list for the president of the United States.

2. Examine the client data collected by an agency where you are interning or to which you have access. Does the agency collect sufficient information to document a need for new services, policies, or both? If so, explain how. If not, what kinds of information does the agency need to collect?

3. Identify an unmet need among your client population and present a political strategy for filling this need. Describe the steps that are necessary in the process.

Suggested Readings

O'Connell, Brian. 1978. "From Service to Advocacy to Empowerment." *Social Casework* 59 (April): 195–202.

Sunley, Robert. 1970. "Family Advocacy: From Case to Course." *Social Casework* 51 (June): 347–357.

References

Briar, Katherine Hooper, and Scott Briar. 1982. "Clinical Social Work and Public Policies." In *Practical Politics: Social Work and Political Responsibility,* Maryann Mahaffey and John Hanks (eds.), pp. 45–54. Washington, DC: National Association of Social Workers.

Council on Social Work Education. 2001. *Educational Policy and Accreditation Standards.* Alexandria, VA: CSWE.

Domanski, Margaret D. 1998. "Prototypes of Social Work Political Participation: An Empirical Model." *Social Work* 43 (2): 156–167.

Epstein, I. 1981. "Advocates on Advocacy: An Exploratory Study." *Social Work Research and Abstracts* 17 (2): 5–12.

Ezell, M. 1989. "Administrators as Activists." Paper presented at the National Association of Social Workers Annual Conference, San Francisco, California.

Gummer, B., and R. L. Edwards. 1985. "A Social Worker's Guide to Organizational Politics." *Administration in Social Work* 9 (1): 13–21.

Heffernan, W. J. 1964. "Policy Activity and Social Work Executives." *Social Work* 9 (2): 18–23.

Homan, Mark S. 1999a. *Promoting Community Change,* 2nd ed. Pacific Grove, CA: Brooks/Cole.

Homan, Mark S. 1999b. *Rules of the Game: Lessons from the Field of Community Change.* Pacific Grove, CA: Brooks/Cole.

Influencing State Policy. Fall 1999. "Student Projects." *Influence* 3.2: 10.

Jansson, Bruce S. 1999. *Becoming an Effective Policy Advocate.* Pacific Grove, CA: Brooks/Cole.

Mickelson, James S. 1997. "Advocacy." *Encyclopedia of Social Work,* 19th ed., pp. 95–100. Washington, DC: National Association of Social Workers.

National Association of Social Workers. 1999. Code of Ethics. Washington, DC: NASW Press.

Pawlak, Edward J., and John P. Flynn. 1990. "Executive Directors' Political Activities." *Social Work* 35 (4): 307–312.

Perlmutter, F. D. 1985. "The Politics of Social Administration." *Administration in Social Work* 9 (4): 1–11.

Pierce, Dean. 1984. *Policy for the Social Work Practitioner.* White Plains, NY: Longman.

Reisch, M. 1986. "From Cause to Case and Back Again: The Reemergence of Advocacy in Social Work." *Urban and Social Change Review* 19 (Winter/Summer): 20–24.

Richan, W. C. 1980. "The Administrator as Advocate." In *Leadership in Social Administration: Perspectives for the 1980's,* F. D. Perlmutter and S. Slavin (eds.), pp. 72–85. Philadelphia: Temple University Press.

Thompson, Joanne J. 1994. "Social Workers and Politics: Beyond the Hatch Act." *Social Work* 39 (4): 457–465.

Influence through Lobbying

Legislative advocacy can be at its best when it advances the goals of the advocate, the social work profession, and when it connects to the legislator's concerns.

—Patricia Ewalt*

In a noisy back room of a restaurant directly across the street from the capitol, a group of legislators continues a debate started earlier in committee hearings. The unresolved issue they are discussing is whether to appropriate additional revenues for services to children who are learning disabled or for highway repair and reconstruction.

Several legislators believe children who are learning disabled do not deserve special services. In their opinion, the problems of these children are laziness and inattentiveness and, therefore, the educational system should deal with them as disciplinary problems. Others believe the money would be better spent on highway and road repair—a significantly more visible project that would affect all constituents.

A lone voice among the group speaks in support of appropriating the funds to children who are learning disabled, citing physical disabilities as well as difficult home environments. When asked why he takes this position, the legislator describes a child who lives next door to him who has a learning disability and tells how the parents are struggling to pay for private tutors and services.

The others conclude that this is only one example and may be the exception, not the rule. None of the legislators seems to know exactly how many other children who are learning disabled are in the state or what problems they and their families face.

Earlier a lobbyist for the highway repair appropriations bill had persuasively demonstrated the degree of popular concern for this legislation and the number of complaints received about present conditions and had argued the cost

*Patricia Ewalt is the former dean of the School of Social Work at the University of Hawaii.

effectiveness of undertaking these projects now rather than waiting until the next legislative session. The lone legislator sympathetic to the children with learning disabilities cause, however, reluctantly admits that he does not know the extent of need and does not have significant constituent support for the proposal. In the absence of additional information or persuasive advocacy, and in light of the legislators' indifference to and ignorance of learning disabilities, the group supports the highway repair bill. In the real world of political processes, decisions are influenced and made by those who work the system in their favor. This chapter discusses what is commonly known as "politicking" or, as it is more professionally termed, *lobbying*.

The term *politicking* is used frequently and indiscriminately. It is sometimes used as a personal adjective: "He (she) is really political." Unfortunately, this usually suggests that the individual is attempting to make contacts and influence individuals in order to enhance a personal position. This may give negative connotations to politicking, suggesting that it is selfish and possibly underhanded.

Indeed, lobbying presumes the persuasive presentation of one side of an issue, primarily to influence decision makers. Because of this, many people, especially social workers, may refuse to participate in what may be viewed as selfish, untruthful, or conflicting practices. However, the American system of government was constructed on the notion of pluralism. In other words, it was designed to encourage and accommodate the expression of conflicting views, group conflict, negotiation, bargaining, and compromise. Lobbying is not a straightforward presentation of all positions on an issue, nor does it have as a goal the enhancement of influence or position. It is our contention that lobbying is a legitimate, fundamental, and powerful practice in a pluralistic society and that social workers and their clients will continue to lose politically if they do not enter this arena.

Social workers often perceive lobbyists as representatives of special interest groups, failing to realize that they themselves are a special interest group also, with beliefs and values that prescribe goals and positions. Unlike other groups, however, the special interest of social workers always has been society's disadvantaged and disenfranchised members. Thus, the social work profession's special interest is not self-interest but rather a concern for individuals, groups, and communities who cannot lobby for themselves.

There are myths about the political process that often discourage social workers from participating in it. One myth is that social workers need specialized training in the political process before they can intervene. They fail to recognize the value of their knowledge and understanding of a community, of individuals, of an individual's functioning within the community, and of group interactions, but this knowledge is the most valuable tool that a social worker can bring to the lobbying process.

Another myth is that a large group of individuals with a lot of money is needed to influence legislators. In fact, there are numerous ways in which a single individual or a few individuals, with the right timing and the right information, can affect social policy. Although it may dishearten many social workers to oppose groups that have more resources and money, it should not be cause for retreat.

Social Work Skills in the Political Process

Because our political structure is both representative and pluralistic, it requires, and even demands, that some individuals speak on behalf of others and that opposing groups resolve conflicts. The very nature of the political process is one of individual interaction, and this clearly implies the importance of social work skills.

Social workers are trained to understand how individuals relate and interact, how groups form and change, how miscommunication can alienate people from each other and from society, and how motivation affects behavior. These are the resources unique to social work advocacy. Social workers can use this knowledge and their corresponding skills to understand and to intervene in the political process.

In the committee process, for example, a social worker who has background information on the committee members (such as district composition, the members' previous voting records, education, training, and previous professional experience) can observe and understand committee member interactions. In many cases, the social worker will be able to predict what approach and what factors may persuade a given legislator to support the social worker's position.

> To be an advocate for the poor requires a kind of lobbying that's different from that which comes to mind when one talks of peddling influence at the state capitol. Social service lobbyists cannot compete with the wining, dining, and campaign contributions of the numerous and powerful lobbyists that have achieved the status of the "third house of Congress." Social workers fail when they play in that league. Our strength and success is in facts and figures, not dinner and drinks.
>
> *Sandy Ingraham, MSW*
> *Social Services Consultant*
> *Harrah, Oklahoma*

Social workers also receive in-depth training on one-on-one interaction. These skills are certainly transferable to interactions with legislators. Equally important are the other basics of social work, such as knowledge of social problems, social interaction, and the social environment. This knowledge can be very beneficial to the legislator in the difficult task of legislative decision making.

> While reading a report of the U.S. Public Health Service Act, I noticed that, even though provisions were made for training funds for eleven other health professions, social work was not mentioned at all. I was concerned that social work students would not have access to resources available to other health professions students, for example, scholarships and loans for disadvantaged students and training for health care in rural areas and for working with people with AIDS.

I had previously made a point of maintaining contact with my senator's office by telephone and mail, as well as by in-person visits whenever in Washington, D.C. Now I wrote to the senator inquiring why social work was not included among the professions funded for training.

As it happened, Senator Inouye has a strong interest in increasing the availability of nonphysician providers, such as social workers and nurses. He is very interested in opening doors for disadvantaged students. And he is very interested in services to disadvantaged populations, including people of color, people in rural areas, and people with AIDS.

Senator Inouye responded that the underlying legislation, the wording that defines health professions, would have to be changed. Social work had not been defined as a health profession. Without this basic change, federal officials would not be required to give consideration to social work training. The senator asked for increased help from the social work profession to bring about the needed change.

The social work profession, represented by the Government Relations Department of NASW at the national office, had already been advocating in Congress for the needed change. The new ingredient at this point was the constituent's request for the senator's advice and help to change the definition, a goal of interest to the constituent, the senator, and NASW.

Consequently, the senator asked for the constituent's as well as NASW's increased assistance to gain allies for the desired change. He gave continuing advice about actions that needed to be taken with members of the Senate and House. NASW implemented the senator's requests and I was able to enlist the assistance of members of an additional organization, the National Association of Deans and Directors of Schools of Social Work.

After two years, the Health Professions Education Amendments were passed, including the definition of social work as a health profession.

Patricia Ewalt, Ph.D.
Former Dean, School of Social Work
University of Hawaii

It should be noted that at certain times and in some situations, the fact that a social worker is not primarily working as a lobbyist can work in favor of influencing a legislator. This is so because the legislator will know that the social worker is lobbying because he or she is truly concerned, has a special interest, and is knowledgeable, not because he or she is being paid to lobby or acting out of self-interest. This should not suggest, however, that it is not important for social workers to build and maintain continuing relationships with legislators.

Throughout this book, we indicate the distinct importance of social work values. It bears repeating that the fact that social workers as lobbyists are less self-interested than are many other special interest groups may be an extremely influential factor. Some have charged that lobbying by social workers to continue or to implement a program is self-serving because such a program creates or maintains jobs for social workers. This argument should not be allowed to cloud the issue. The main reason for lobbying for programs is to provide needed services to people.

The Political Process

A formal process exists by which all legislation must proceed. Legislators must follow rules, regulations, and procedures before a bill can be voted on and passed to the executive branch. This procedure includes checks and balances to ensure input from multiple sources and conflict resolution between groups. The essence of the legislative process is making choices between conflicting objectives. Coming to a compromise on a specific piece of legislation can be an extremely time-consuming process. It is true that sometimes a bill can pass through Congress or a state legislature with lightning speed, but usually these are bills that either respond to very critical situations or have great public support.

To influence legislation effectively, social workers must understand precisely how the legislative process works. Each state has its own rules or procedures; the state printing office or state chamber of commerce will have this information or know where it can be obtained.

In general, legislative bodies are composed of committees, each with a separate jurisdiction and substantive area. It is in the committee that a bill is given its most thorough review or reading. A primary method by which committees obtain information is from public testimony; thus, the committee is a key public access point. One individual who acts at the right time with precise and persuasive information can have a tremendous effect on the committee process.

However, there are inherent problems with this process. First, committee agendas can change without notice. Second, committee meetings can be canceled without notice. Third, bills sometimes are not placed on the committee agenda at all. One must keep informed about committee activities and be ready to counteract these problems.

The key person in the committee quite obviously is the chairperson. The chair has sole discretion over the committee and can choose to present a bill in such a way as to have a tremendous impact on the action taken by the committee and may not even place it on the committee's agenda. The array of options that a legislative committee can undertake are as follows: (1) report on the bill favorably as is; (2) report favorably, with amendments; (3) report favorably on a substitute bill; (4) report on the bill unfavorably; (5) send the bill to another committee for review; or (6) table the bill.

Depending on the committee's recommendation, the next step is for the bill to go before the first house for full review. At that time, the general legislative climate should be assessed to determine whether a great amount of public support is needed.

From the first house, the bill must proceed to the second house for approval, and finally to the president or governor for signature. This process provides several key points at which intervention can take place.

The Politician

The key component within the legislative process is the politician. As legislators, they represent large constituent groups having a diversity of positions, values, and ideas. Politicians vary in age, experience, training, political ideology, and party affiliation. In order to understand the political process, one needs to know not only the rules and regulations but also the players.

External to but influential in the political process are such other factors as public opinion, media involvement, the activities of special interest groups, and informal coalitions among legislators (such as the African American caucus, the liberal caucus, the senior legislators' caucus, and so forth). Knowledge of these factors assists lobbyists in influencing legislators.

Politicians have diverse constituencies to whom they feel accountable. First, politicians are responsible to those who voted for them. Second, they have a responsibility to the population within their geographic district. Third, they feel a responsibility to those individuals who campaigned for them. And we must not forget that there is an accountability to the party the politician represents as well, and the planks, or core policy values, represented by that party and, therefore, that politician. If politicians are listening to opposing opinions from these diverse constituent groups, decision making becomes difficult.

Another set of concerns involves limitations on the politician's time. Politicians have very little time to go out and seek problem areas and concerns that need correcting. They must rely on individuals, constituents, lobbyists, and others to bring problems to them and to supply them with detailed information about the problems or concerns on which they are working. To further complicate matters, many state representatives have either no aides or only one aide to do research, to investigate, and to advise them. Some have access to staff members hired by the legislative body, but the scope of this assistance is rather limited. Clearly, given the variety of issues that face any one legislator, often there is not enough time or staff to go around, especially when one realizes that politicians frequently are unfamiliar with many issues about which they must make decisions.

Legislators also must deal with constant public exposure. Many hours of work are allocated to understanding and dealing with conflicting views and interests. They must meet with their constituents and with special interest groups, all of whom want to advise them. As a result they may find themselves immersed in such complex social issues as abortion, euthanasia, the death penalty, and terrorism. The advice and pressure from the groups supporting and opposing these issues often is contradictory.

Furthermore, because any individual who becomes a legislator goes through a very lengthy and costly process to get elected, a frequent concern for politicians is to maintain their positions by being reelected. A candidate for the U.S. Congress may spend almost half of a term campaigning and may either avoid difficult and controversial issues during campaign years or assume a popular, noncontroversial position.

Anyone who wants to become an effective lobbyist must have a general knowledge of the factors that influence politicians' behaviors. Some individuals become politicians because they want to be in the limelight and to have constant public exposure, some are deeply concerned about issues and want to make changes, and some find themselves in politics because of their family's name and prominent status. Such issues may influence how a legislator perceives legislation or acts on issues; thus, lobbyists must understand these factors in order to have a total grasp of the politician and the political milieu.

The Informal Political Process

Lobbyists must be aware of formal legislative procedures and processes, but they also should be familiar with the informal processes. Usually viewed as "politics," the informal processes actually are individual-to-individual or group-to-group influences, motives, or relationships that affect the outcome of legislation. When attempting to influence legislation, one needs to consider both the formal and informal processes.

For example, one group of legislators trying to push through a bill to create public jobs in order to decrease the unemployment rate may be opposed by another group of legislators who wish to increase a certain defense budget item. These two groups may come together and compromise by creating defense-related jobs, thus enabling both groups to obtain their desired outcomes. It is also possible, of course, for this scenario to result in the defeat of both pieces of legislation.

In addition to caucuses or groupings of legislators by state, by party affiliation, or by issue, other influences exist that can have an informal affect on legislation. First, the piece of legislation in which you are interested may not have as high a priority in the eye of the public as does other legislation. Second, because legislators may have so many other items to deal with, your piece of legislation may be dealt with only superficially in order to appease you. Finally, legislation will be dealt with by politicians in respect to its possible impact on their careers and reelection.

Lobbying Groundwork

Goal Setting

Once a social worker/lobbyist understands the formal and informal processes a bill must go through and has a grasp of the players (politicians, aides, other lobbyists), the next step is to formulate a clearly defined goal. One must decide whether to influence already-proposed pieces of legislation, modify present legislation, or develop a new piece of legislation. To enlist others in a lobbying effort, one must have an explicit goal. Whatever the goal, it should be stated clearly and, ideally, in measurable terms so that it is possible to know whether the goal has been achieved.

Strategy Setting

Setting strategy is a critical and often neglected part of lobbying. Without it lobbying may be ineffectual. *Strategy* is a plan of action for the achievement of a goal. As soon as the goal has been identified and operationalized, the strategy should be determined.

A parallel can be drawn between strategy setting and management by objectives, where the goal is defined and the various steps to reach that goal are stated. It is clear to all participants what steps are needed in order to proceed to the goal. In the delineation of strategy, any complicating factors or unforeseen obstacles that may delay or block action should be spelled out, and alternative strategies should be developed in case complicating factors or obstacles arise.

For example, legislation is introduced at the state level to restore allocation levels for primary and secondary public education. Passage appears likely, despite the state's fiscally constrained condition, because it is difficult to oppose education for young children. However, the state is plagued by high rates of unemployment, and several mayors have requested the governor proclaim a state of emergency because of the decreasing nutritional level of a large segment of the state's population who are unable to afford adequate amounts of food. This crisis could overshadow concern for public education.

It is impossible to describe all alternative strategies that could be adopted. A strategy must be developed after a review of the policy and the politicians involved, an assessment of the bill's likely trail, an understanding of potential legislative and community climates, and an assessment of what possibilities are realistic for the social worker/lobbyists.

One strategy may be to work with and educate key legislators as the legislation is developed, amended, and passed through committees—that is, a strategy of working within the legislative system to overcome resistance and to educate. An alternative and potentially conflict-producing strategy at the opposite end of the continuum is to amass public support and encourage numerous contacts with legislators (Ornstein and Elder, 1978).

This strategy has become popular and may indeed be the strategy of choice, under the name of grassroots advocacy. Usually, however, it is desirable to first attempt to work within the system, and then, when and if opposition develops, to move to an external strategy. A middle approach might be used in a situation in which a piece of legislation appears to have majority support but faces a potential floor debate. In such a case, a letter campaign to the general assembly or the presence of concerned citizens during a legislative session may prove effective.

A social worker/lobbyist should keep in mind several essential concepts. First, it is important to be honest and factual whenever a legislator or legislative aide is contacted. Second, and perhaps more important, it is well to remember that straightforward presentations with data generally provide the most persuasive approach and maintain the credibility of both the social worker/lobbyist and the social work profession. Finally, any presentation should include answers to two questions of critical concern to legislators: (1) What will this proposed legislation cost? (2) What is the social impact of this bill? It is particularly important not only to anticipate the answers to these questions, but, if the costs appear high, also to provide information about the costs of allowing the social problem or need to go unresolved.

At the beginning of any lobbying effort, the social worker/lobbyist must keep in mind that many checks and balances are built into the legislative process and that legislators can be influenced in numerous ways. The process is complex, with formal as well as informal variables; hundreds of concerns and points of view are concurrently presented before any legislative body. Thus, a social worker/lobbyist must have two important qualities, patience and persistence, and should bear in mind the following guidelines:

1. Know your issue thoroughly. Anticipate the opposition's claims and formulate persuasive counterarguments. Be prepared to provide technical information that will be useful to the politician(s) involved.
2. Identify a core group of committed and effective workers who will lead a coalition of interested groups and individuals who can be called on to write letters, lobby, or publicize the issue.
3. Locate a lawmaker who is sympathetic to your issue and is likely to be effective in advancing the cause, and continue to work with him or her for the duration of the process.
4. Be familiar with the formal legislative structure and the procedural steps a bill must take to become a law.
5. Spend as much time as possible at the capitol, both to answer legislators' questions and to be in a position to intervene effectively at the critical moment by offering advice or information before decisions have been made. (Michigan Sea Grant Advisory Service, 1981)

In addition to patience and persistence, another extremely important attribute of a social worker/lobbyist is the ability to acknowledge the merits of competing proposals. Although a lobbyist's role is to mobilize the strongest and most persuasive arguments for a particular position, when a lobbyist becomes unable or unwilling to acknowledge the merits of an alternative proposal, he or she is seen as a propagandist, and any credibility and eventual utility may be reduced (Patti and Dear, 1981).

The Internet is an important tool for understanding your issue thoroughly and to become familiar with the formal legislative structure, procedural steps, and alternate positions and competing points of views (and players). Drawing on the educational resources of various libraries, think tanks, businesses, government offices, advocacy organizations, and legislative resources themselves, every aspect of lobbying, organizing, and electoral politics can use web resources, including recruiting volunteers and securing contributions for particular causes (Schneider and Lester, 2001).

Lobbying Methods

There are a number of ways to communicate your viewpoint directly to elected officials. To understand which kind of communication method has the most impact, imagine being asked to volunteer for a committee. Which of the following approaches would be most likely to get you to agree to the request?

1. A typed letter from someone you have never heard of or met
2. A handwritten letter from someone you met briefly last week
3. A visit from a longtime acquaintance
4. A visit from someone you have never met before
5. A telephone call from someone you have never met

Clearly, the more personal the relationship and the means of communication, the greater the impact. The same holds true for elected officials. This does not mean you have to be personally acquainted with legislators in order to lobby effectively. At the very least, you may be a constituent or a professional with valuable information, which is an important relationship for the legislator. By building a relationship with a legislator, perhaps through meeting at a community forum or by working on the legislator's campaign, you will enhance your influence. An email message from a campaign worker is far more effective than a visit from a constituent the legislator has never met before. The following methods provide different approaches to communicating with a legislator.

Letter Writing

It is commonly believed that letters to legislators are never read. This is a myth. The fact is that they are read most carefully, particularly if they come from constituents. Letters indicate that constituents are sufficiently concerned about an issue to take the time to write (McInnis-Dittrich, 1994).

Letters to legislators should be short, to the point, and credible. Write one or two pages at most. Confine yourself to one subject area or bill. Write different letters for different bills or issues. Legislators are quite busy, and long letters are time consuming. However, do not sacrifice clarity and completeness for brevity. Describe your position exactly and, if necessary, provide documentation. State your purpose in the first paragraph and then elaborate in the text. The use of facts combined with personal experiences, whether yours or your client's, is most effective. State the action you want the legislator to take: whether you want him or her to vote yes or no on a bill or to cosponsor legislation, be specific. (See Figure 7.1.)

Although form letters, postcards, and telegrams are usually read and sometimes answered, they do not carry the weight and persuasiveness of a personal letter and should be avoided. These are viewed as efforts by groups and not as opinions of individuals. The more personal the letter, the greater the impact. Legible handwritten letters on your own stationery are the most effective.

Attitude is important; positive communication works best. Never threaten a legislator: This will be counterproductive and will cause you to lose your credibility and to be discarded as an "angry individual." If you have assisted in a campaign or on passage of another bill, remind the legislator of your support in the past and how you are counting on him or her. Thank the legislator for

Honorable Elected O. Ficial
Texas House of Representatives
P.O. Box 2910
Austin, Texas 78768-2910

Dear Representative Official:

As a parent of your district, I have a deep, personal interest in H.B. 1001 which will do away with the use of corporal punishment in the public schools. I strongly advocate its passage.

I recently had my son come home from school after receiving three "hits" with a wood paddle from the principal for talking during class. I agree that my child, who is ten, should not be misbehaving. However, children need to learn to follow rules, not learn that you solve a problem by using force. Under current Texas law I have no power to stop the use of corporal punishment on my child.

Please vote for H.B. 1001 when it comes up for a vote next week.

Thank you in advance for your consideration.

Sincerely,

I. Am Right
2424 Most Streets
Anywhere, Texas 77001
713–555–5555

TYPING IS NOT ESSENTIAL, LEGIBILITY IS.

LIMIT LETTER TO ONE PAGE

PARAGRAPH ONE: *Identify yourself, state the subject, state your connection to it.*

REFER TO A SPECIFIC BILL NUMBER. *One issue per letter.*

CLEARLY STATE YOUR OPINION.

PARAGRAPH TWO: *Explain your position, why you feel as you do, present your reasons, use personal examples.*

PARAGRAPH THREE: *Ask for specific action from your elected official.*

WRITE YOUR NAME, ADDRESS, AND TELEPHONE NUMBER CLEARLY. YOUR LEGISLATOR MAY WANT MORE INFORMATION.

FIGURE 7.1   *Sample Letter to Communicate with an Elected Official*

Source: Reprinted from James S. Mickelson, *Speaking Out for Houston's Children*, Houston: CHILDREN AT RISK, 1995. Used by permission.

considering your views and, if you are comfortable with such a statement, for the hard work he or she has undertaken on other issues of concern. A short thank-you after any vote on a piece of legislation with which you agree will testify to the depth of your interest and may enhance your credibility when other issues arise.

When writing to elected or appointed officials, the following forms of address and salutation are recommended:

To: The President
The President
The White House
1600 Pennsylvania Ave., NW
Washington, DC 20500
Dear Mr./Ms. President:

To: U.S. Senators
The Honorable (insert full name)
United States Senate
Washington, DC 20510
Dear Senator (insert last name):

To: U.S. Representatives
The Honorable (insert full name)
U.S. House of Representatives
Washington, DC 20515
Dear Representative (insert last name):

To: Cabinet Members
The Honorable (insert full name)
Secretary of (insert department)
Washington, DC (insert zip)
Dear Secretary (insert last name):

Email advocacy is increasingly more common. Particularly at the congressional level, its use became more necessary when mail to legislators began to be routinely screened after the anthrax scare of 2002. Email allows communication in a quick and easy manner, but the volume of email that legislators at the state and federal level receive (thousands a day in many cases) means that its impact is far less than in email's earlier days. This does not mean that email is useless as a lobbying tactic—it takes large amounts of email dedicated to a single issue to catch a legislator's attention. The result is that personalized letters from constituents now receive more attention than massive quantities of electronic mail. Elected officials are likely to see a number of short comments on an issue as not much more substantive than a printed postcard or form letter. To have the strongest impact when emailing, keep the following recommendations in mind:

- Consider email the same as sending a written letter by fax or the U.S. Postal Service.
- Always include your street address as well as daytime and evening telephone numbers. This information confirms that you are a constituent; in addition, some elected officials like to follow up on electronic correspondence through regular mail.

- Email only your own representative, and personalize your messages. Never "broadcast" form letters to the entire legislative body; such messages are not effective.
- Include a clear and concise statement in the subject line of the email message, for example, "Vote Yes on HB18" or "Concerning Medically Uninsured Children."
- If you are emailing a chair of a committee or its members about a subject that will be considered by the committee, send a copy of the message to your representative even if he or she is not on that committee. Most likely you will not get a reply, but the numbers of pro and con comments from constituents will be tallied and considered.
- Avoid sending attachments of supporting documentation. Instead, provide a summary of supporting documents in the email message and offer to supply them. Attached documents can overload an email system, and some recipients are concerned that an attachment could contain a virus and will not open it.

Telephoning

A telephone call does not have the same effect as a paper letter. However, phone calls, timed correctly, can be most effective. Usually 48 hours before a vote is taken is the best timing. The constant ringing of the telephone with people asking for a "yea" or "nay" vote can move an undecided legislator to making a decision.

When calling, you will undoubtedly get a staff member or a receptionist. Simply state who you are and the message you wish to convey: "I would like the representative to vote yes on bill XX. This is important to the many. . . ." Be sure to leave your name, address, and phone number, which will confirm that you are a constituent.

Face-to-Face Lobbying

Social workers who are naïve about politicians and the political process may believe that politicians are so powerful that they are unapproachable. It seems easier to these social workers to write letters, sign petitions, or join coalitions than to interact directly with legislators. Nevertheless, legislators need direct interaction and may, in fact, even seek it out from various individuals and groups. Legislators realize that they are very much isolated and protected from what is really occurring in society and, therefore, must rely on input from credible sources.

In face-to-face lobbying with a legislator whom the lobbyist has never met, one must establish credibility by identifying who is being represented as well as one's personal expertise and experience. Particularly if the lobbyist is a constituent of that legislator, a basis for rapport may already exist. Having been visibly active in a legislator's campaign is certainly beneficial in establishing a relationship; campaigns are expensive, and politicians generally dislike fund-raising, so they are likely to remember those who assisted and supported them in that process (Mahaffey, 1972).

It is unnecessary to buy a legislator lunch. It is also unnecessary to bring gifts to a legislator—who will also have to report such gifts (in most cases, gifts worth more than $50) and would rather hear what you have to say than to see what you brought. Straightforward, factual, and well-presented information is most effective. Although legislative offices and surroundings might be intimidating to the beginning social worker/lobbyist, remember that the representative needs your information and assistance. Legislators are extremely busy and often must deal with a multitude of subject areas. Thus, they might switch subjects during an interview. Also, they sometimes deliberately take a contrary stance, but this may be because they want to learn how to argue effectively on behalf of your position.

Developing a good working relationship with a legislator's scheduler and/or staff should not be overlooked. These individuals are gatekeepers. As such, they represent a potential access point to the legislator and a channel through which information can be transmitted that may influence the legislator.

Many social worker/lobbyists focus their efforts on legislators who share values and goals similar to their own. Although such legislators are valuable, they may not be the most important target of influence (Patti and Dear, 1981). When deciding who to contact, you should compile several lists: one consisting of legislators overtly supportive of your position, another of those who are explicitly opposed, and a third list of those who are undecided. The third list is the one that should be targeted for intensive effort. At the same time, keep in contact with supporters through informative letters, phone calls, and the like.

Before a face-to-face interview with a representative, preparation is in order. Determine what particular issues are of interest, how the legislator approaches certain subjects, and what position he or she has taken on similar legislation in the past. This will allow you to present material in a way that encourages the legislator to listen to your position. Present the information to the legislator, keeping in mind the particular importance of the cost of the proposal and its social implications.

Almost all legislators will grant an appointment to constituents on request. However, in dealing with members of Congress, particularly if you are attempting to see them in Washington, time constraints may require that the appointment be with a legislative aide. Do not be dismayed. In most cases, the aides are the ones who formulate policy and persuade the legislator to take a position. It may also be useful to ask for an appointment in the legislator's home district, where committee pressures and other responsibilities are somewhat reduced. Remember that the legislator is in the home district to get constituents' opinions on issues.

Because the length of appointments is likely to be limited, it is an excellent idea to provide written material and supportive documentation. Be sure that this material is as succinct as possible. A copy of all written material should also be provided for the legislative aide. Remember that it is important to use case examples from the legislator's district whenever possible.

Obtaining an appointment with state and local officials is usually easier, and these meetings often occur in less formal settings, such as political gatherings, receptions, or in the corridors of the statehouse or county building. However, do not invade the politician's personal life with a confrontation at the grocery store or

theater. In all settings, common courtesy should be used, and, regardless of the outcome of the discussion, you should thank the legislator for the appointment and for
his or her open-mindedness. Follow up the meeting with a thank-you letter that
includes a synopsis of the position taken by the legislator during that meeting as
well as a reminder of your position. Finally, follow through with anything that you
agreed to do. If you fail to do so, your credibility will quickly deteriorate.

> I was inspired by my experience at Lobby Days while completing my MSW
> program—I got a thrill from speaking to a legislative assistant about the four bills
> NASW-CA had designated for us to advocate for. I felt that it really gave me an
> opportunity to have my voice heard and to fight for causes that I believed in and
> held so close to my heart, such as foster care and transitional housing. So as a stu-
> dent completing my final year, I decided to take on the role of student liaison for
> NASW-CA at San Jose State University. Alongside a few other inspired classmates
> of mine, I helped to organize 130 students from our school and prepared them
> for their own experiences at Lobby Days. I wanted to get even more out of this
> experience, so I chose to be a team leader this time. I was very nervous, thinking
> that I would have to lead a team of students into the legislative offices and help
> them to learn the basics of advocacy and lobbying.
>
> Little did I know that I would end up taking a team of migrant women from
> a small community in the Central Valley of California into the legislative offices.
> I had to face the challenge of language barriers, but because I had met these
> women before, I knew they had powerful stories to share that address the bills we
> were to lobbying on. I witnessed first-hand what an impact these women had as
> we translated their experiences and feelings on what the bills would address. I felt
> so proud afterward, I knew that they had the experience of having their voices
> heard, and knowing I was a part of empowering them made Lobby Days more
> rewarding and powerful experience for me as a social worker.
>
> *Jennifer Tan, MSW*
> *Milpitas, California*

Testifying

A legislative committee struggling to understand the intricacies of a complicated
piece of legislation will solicit testimony as a way of gathering as much information as possible on various aspects of the legislation in the shortest amount of
time. Indeed, if the legislators had endless hours to sit and talk with a variety of
individuals, testimony would be much less useful, but because time is limited, testimony provides an excellent opportunity for the general public to have input into
a committee's decision. Hearings often are conducted in various parts of the state
or nation to ensure access to more people and to a diversity of points of view
(Homan, 1999; Sharwell, 1982).

In the testimonial process, the committee listens to statements about the
legislation and on information helpful to their decision making. The legislators
can ask questions of the person testifying, and any legislator can request that
particular individuals appear before the committee or subcommittee to testify.

Hearings are an ideal way for the media to gather public opinion and for individuals to have a tremendous amount of input into legislative decisions (Richan, 1996). The following are some reasons why written testimony should be provided:

- It demonstrates professionalism.
- It shows a more than casual interest in the legislative matter.
- It ensures that the committee record of the testimony will be accurate.
- It can make the oral presentation to the committee more effective because some of the committee members and the committee staff will read the written statements in addition to listening to the testimony.
- It permits the advocate to say all he or she wants to say in the written statement while still being able to meet the time constraints often imposed on oral testimony.
- It provides flexibility in that the advocate can cover all the issues in the written statement but can highlight points in the oral portion that are particularly responsive to points by opponents.
- It provides greater assurance that media coverage of the testimony will be complete and more accurate because media representatives can work from the written statement rather than from hastily penciled notes.
- It enables the advocate to inform members of the organization represented and other persons and organizations about the content of the testimony.
- It provides a better record for the advocate's own organization than do notes from memory. (Sharwell, 1982)

If you are asked or plan to testify before a federal, state, or local committee, remember this: The key to effective legislative lobbying is preparation. Although preparation takes a considerable amount of time, it is necessary in order to increase the chances of success.

Once you have written the testimony you will give the committee, it is time to outline what you are going to say. During the testimony itself, you will only be given a very short time to talk—from two to fifteen minutes, depending on the situation and how many people will testify.

Begin by introducing yourself: *"My name is I. Am Right."* Tell who you are and what program you represent: *"I am with the B.A.B.S. That stands for the Bay Area Bee Sting support group."* Acknowledge your appreciation to the panel for taking time to hear about the issue and allowing you to testify. Let them know briefly that you are knowledgeable on the subject and how many people you represent: *"I am a social worker with B.A.B.S. and have been working with bee sting victims for three years. We have served more than 2,300 people who have been stung by killer bees."* This should not take more than a few sentences.

State your goal and outline your major points. In a sentence or two, tell the committee what your major concern is: *"I come before you today to alert you to the growing problem of killer bees. They are a real threat, and the problem is growing."*

Tell them how many bees have entered the country; give them some personal examples of people who have been stung; describe the limited success of the current program; offer specific recommendations as to what legislators can do to solve the bee menace:

> In the past five years the killer bees have been migrating north and will soon be reaching the larger cities in our state. Many do not know that more than 400 people have had to go to emergency rooms because when the bees attack people can receive up to 100 stings. Imagine the fear of a fifteen-year-old girl, when she was babysitting a two-year-old and the bees started to sting the child; the sitter started hitting the bees to get them away from the toddler. All the sitter could do was to cover the child with her body and let the bees sting her. She was taken to the hospital and spent two days nursing 230 bee stings. This is only one of the many who have come to B.A.B.S. for help because they fear the outdoors.

Outlining your major points assures the legislators that you are organized and that your testimony is relevant. Talk about the problem. Discuss the national (or local) significance of the issue and try to relate it to your state and community. Try to relate the problem to the states or districts of the legislators before whom you are testifying:

> It is time for a Ban the Bees bill. We are ready to support such a bill that will give the local authorities the resources to trap and kill these killer bees. The time to act is now before bees reach the cities. Once that happens, many more citizens will be demanding something be done. Your district, Senator Official, is just on the route the killer bees have migrated.

Mention current efforts to resolve the problem. Describe experimental or demonstrational solutions. Explain why the efforts are insufficient or how they can be improved. This should not take very long. Keep it simple and to the point. Before you are through, summarize your major points and let them know that you would be happy to answer any questions. Then, thank the committee for their time.

> In closing, if we can stop the killer bees now, we will not only save people from pain and suffering but we will also save money in the long run because the killer bees are multiplying rapidly. Please consider our proposal for a Ban the Bees bill. Thank-you for your time. I would be happy to address any question you may have.

Do not be afraid no matter how large or imposing the hearing room is. Remember that your elected representatives are people too, and they are there because they want to do what is best for the community.

Do not read your testimony because your legislators prefer to be talked to rather than read to. Your hope should be that they will be interested enough in you and your subject to ask you questions after you finish. If you bore them, they will be become disinterested in your testimony. Keep your oral presentation brief and conversational.

Do not spend more time describing your own qualifications or your agency's than you do describing the problem. Focus on the specific issue of the hearing.

Do not assume that the panel or committee members are experts. All legislators vote on a wide variety of issues, from water projects to interplanetary space programs. Although you certainly do not want to talk down to them, you should also not assume that they know all that you do about the issue. Be careful not to use acronyms. Do not try to tell them everything you know—simplify, simplify, simplify.

Do not only use statistics. They are helpful but it is best to personalize your testimony. One way to assist elected officials (and get their attention) is to let them know how the issue at hand affects their constituents. A personalized example of someone affected by a problem or someone helped by a proposed solution often carries more weight than the results of ten national studies.

Do not guess at an answer to a question. If you do not know the answer, say so, and indicate that you will find out the answer and get back to them. Then get back to them. It is your credibility at issue. Anticipate questions your testimony may prompt and have good answers in mind.

Do not leave after you have finished your testimony. Sit down for at least fifteen minutes. It will show that you are interested enough to stay through other testimony, and sometimes a committee member may want to talk to you about the issue after the hearing.

Lobbying and Nonprofits

When it comes to lobbying by nonprofit organizations, there exists a myth that this is prohibited and will jeopardize funding. It is true that there are some laws and procedures that an organization classified by the Internal Revenue Service (IRS) as a 501(c)(3) must follow, but lobbying is by no means illegal or totally prohibited (Hopkins, 1992). Foundations, which are subject to several restrictions that do not apply to nonprofits, can make grants to charities for lobbying and advocacy efforts (Asher, 1995). Although there are social and political concerns a nonprofit may face in undertaking a lobbying effort, legal restrictions are usually used as an excuse rather than being a reality. It is recommended that before a lobbying effort is undertaken that might use more than 5 percent of the total agency budget, the law should be reviewed. What follows is a simple summary of laws affecting lobbying efforts by a nonprofit.

The IRS defines lobbying as the attempt to influence legislation on the local, state, or federal level. This means trying to influence policymakers to vote for or against a certain item that comes before them, for example, approval of a budget. If the nonprofit can "educate" the elected official on the needs for expenditures for a program to remedy a social problem and the specific program budget is not before the legislature to be voted on, then this activity is public education and not lobbying. The rule of thumb is the action of a vote.

The law is clear on how much a nonprofit can spend on lobbying. The law divides lobbying into two categories: grassroots and direct. Grassroots refers to influencing legislation through communications with the general public. Direct is lobbying directly with legislators and their staff (Amidei, 1992). There are two ways that the IRS determines how much lobbying is permissible. First, if the organization includes lobbying as part of its efforts to meet its mission, then the nonprofit may "elect" by filing a simple form that tells the IRS that you are lobbying and wish to be reviewed under the "expenditure test." Electing with the IRS gives the nonprofit permission to spend more of their total budget on lobbying. The expenditure test is very precise in determining the amounts allowed. Second, if the nonprofit does not "elect," then the nonprofit is more limited on expenditures and the interpretation of lobbying is done by the IRS. Electing does require more documentation and reporting to the IRS (Alliance for Justice, 2001).

Nonprofit organizations must operate within the regulations set by the IRS or they may be categorized as action organizations, losing their tax-exempt status. This, however, should not be construed as prohibiting lobbying efforts. Although the regulation may seem confusing at first, once a clear understanding of the organization's direction and how it fits within the law is determined, the nonprofit can and should enter the political arena to affect change. A good resource to help nonprofits with the regulations is the Alliance for Justice (www.afj.org), which produces a number of publications on the subject.

Conclusion

Lobbying efforts can be seen as manipulative and self-serving. However, the reality of the American political system is that these efforts are part of the legislative process.

The social work profession needs to become more astute in the practices and skills involved in lobbying. The various facets of the political process, legislative and committee rules and regulations, and formal and informal decision-making processes have created a milieu that social work professionals have avoided. Lobbying for human service legislation is not self-serving but rather is consistent with client advocacy.

If more social workers were to acquire the techniques outlined in this chapter, the authors are confident that more humane social policies would be developed and enacted. Lobbying is, indeed, an essential interventive strategy in social work.

> As a longtime member of the Kentucky House of Representatives, I have come to rely on individuals, especially constituents, who come to me with concerns and issues, as I have to vote on a lot of different items from bridges to health care. Social workers are experts and need to realize that elected officials need their counsel on many human service and social justice items.
>
> When someone comes to "lobby" me, I am most appreciative if they talk to one issue in a concise and straightforward manner. I have come to trust those that will provide me with more information on both sides of an issue if I call on them.
>
> *Jim Wayne, MSW*
> *Kentucky House of Representatives*

This chapter has only touched on the various aspects of lobbying techniques. It is a primer for social workers who wish to advocate for human service goals. The skill with which social workers participate in the political system is an important factor in determining their influence on the formation of social policy.

Immense resources neither are required nor will guarantee social workers significant influence in the political arena. Rather, the success of the profession's endeavors will be determined by social workers' abilities to use both effective lobbying skills and their unique mix of professional skills.

All Social Work Is Political, So . . .

1. Learn how a bill becomes a law in your state.

2. Call the election commission or go online to learn who all your elected officials are, from local to federal.

3. Determine when a hearing for a bill you are interested in will occur. Develop a position statement, and then testify at that hearing.

4. Develop a position on a current legislative issue and make an appointment with your own state legislator to influence his or her vote.

Suggested Readings

Jackson-Elmoore, Cynthia. 2005. "Informing State Policymakers: Opportunities for Social Workers." *Social Work* 50 (June): 251–261.

Patti, Rino, and Ronald Dear. 1981. "Legislative Advocacy: Seven Effective Tactics." *Social Work* 26 (July): 289–296.

References

Alliance for Justice. 2001. *Worry-Free Lobbying for Nonprofits: How to Use the 501(h) Election to Maximize Effectiveness.* Washington, DC: Alliance for Justice.

Amidei, Nancy. 1992. *So You Want to Make a Difference: Advocacy Is the Key,* 3rd ed. Washington, DC: OMB Watch.

Asher, Thomas R. 1995. *Myth versus Fact: Foundation Support of Advocacy.* Washington, DC: Alliance for Justice.

Homan, Mark S. 1999. *Rules of the Game: Lessons from the Field of Community Change.* Pacific Grove, CA: Brooks/Cole.

Hopkins, Bruce R. 1992. *Charity, Advocacy and the Law.* New York: Wiley.

Mahaffey, Maryann. 1972. "Lobbying and Social Work." *Social Work* 17 (January): 3–11.

McInnis-Dittrich, Kathleen. 1994. *Integrating Social Welfare Policy and Social Work Practice.* Pacific Grove, CA: Brooks/Cole.

Michigan Sea Grant Advisory Service. 1981. *How Citizens Can Influence Legislation in Michigan.* Lansing: Michigan State University Cooperative Extension Service.

Ornstein, Norman, and Shirley Elder. 1978. *Interest Groups, Lobbying and Policy-Making.* Washington, DC: Congressional Quarterly Press.

Patti, Rino, and Ronald Dear. 1981. "Legislative Advocacy: Seven Effective Tactics." *Social Work* 26 (July): 289–296.

Richan, Willard C. 1996. *Lobbying for Social Change.* New York: The Haworth Press.

Schneider, Robert L., and Lori Lester. 2001. *Social Work Advocacy: A New Framework for Action.* Pacific Grove, CA: Brooks/Cole.

Sharwell, George. 1982. "How to Testify before a Legislative Committee." In *Practical Politics: Social Work and Political Responsibility,* Maryann Mahaffey and John Hanks (eds.), pp. 85–99. Washington, DC: National Association of Social Workers.

8

Tools to Influence and Organize Others

Politics is the public side of social work. It is nothing more than the bringing together of people in a public setting to try and solve problems and/or to develop social policy. I think that social workers have excellent skills to build consensus and to solve problems.

—Debbie Stabenow*

As mentioned in Chapter 7, there is a great deal that one person can do to make programmatic changes and policy changes using the skills of lobbying. However, there are beliefs and systems that are so ingrained in the American culture that the only way to bring about social change regarding such policies and national attitudes is to educate and organize constituencies. One person can start a movement, but it takes others to fully implement the changes. The power of organizing others was clearly demonstrated by President Obama in his presidential election campaign. There is a difference between organizing and mobilizing the community. *Organizing* is the process of empowering individuals in the community to address their needs. *Mobilizing* is activating the community around a predetermined cause or issue. This chapter reviews some of the tools and methods that can be used to influence others.

Whereas Chapter 7 discussed specific techniques and skills for individuals to use to have an affect on programs and policies, this chapter deals with the tools of influencing groups. With their training and experience in community organizing, advocacy, budgeting, planning, and evaluating, social workers already have the basis on which to build the skills necessary to affect change at this larger scale. The old saying that "there is power in numbers" is exactly the message of this chapter. The greater the number and diversity of individuals who are united in support of a policy, the greater the likelihood of making the change.

*Debbie Stabenow is a U.S. senator (Michigan).

Organizing others is important because "social developments are part of a total economic and political system—a political economy—in which all strands of life, from the national to local level, intertwine with each other. Most problems that contemporary communities face manifest themselves at the neighborhood level but result from city, state, national, and even international factors. What is most striking, however, is how immune we think we are from the penetrations of the national political economy into daily lives" (Fisher, 1997, pp. xvii–xviii).

All social changes or movements go through a series of phases. Some movements take longer at certain phases or may even become stuck in one phase and die. All depends on the economic factors related to the need, societal concerns toward the need, and the effectiveness of the organizing efforts to address the need. All must be present, but one or two factors can dominate to ultimately address the need.

Ten Phases of a Social Movement

The following phases of a social movement are overly simplified but are offered for consideration when the need arises to organize others. They are adopted and modified from many sources as early as the works of Lindeman (1921).

Phase 1: A consciousness of a need or problem is developed. This may begin with only one person expressing a need. In many cases it comes from a practitioner or client identifying a need or problem that then is expressed to others for validation and clarification of the need. In short, the "idea is born."

Phase 2: Consciousness of the need is conveyed to a larger group that incorporates the idea and takes ownership of the issue. This could be a formal organization or institution or an advocacy group that is already addressing a related issue. In some situations, a new group or organization is developed or founded to address this concern.

Phase 3: The group that has now adopted the consciousness of need begins to define the need to selected leadership. At this point, the issue becomes more general or the original concerns now include more issues relative to the need, depending on the amount of fact-finding the group undertakes.

Phase 4: The issue now experiences an influx of emotion and the effort to enlist a quick answer to the need. This emotional energy stimulates the next phase and could cause a faction of the group to separate and become the emotional extreme group or spokesperson on the issue.

Phase 5: As the issue is presented to more groups, institutions, and individual leaders, an increased presentation of solutions emerge. Hence, there are now several approaches to address this new consciousness of need. Additional groups may form supporting their solution.

Phase 6: Conflicts between the various solutions emerge, and more solutions may be presented that will further the debate. This phase can last for some time given the three factors of economics, societal concern, and the effectiveness of the organizing efforts.

Phase 7: In an effort to sort out the conflicts to the solutions, a phase of investigation may occur. This can be most helpful to the process or it can stall the movement indefinitely. In some situations, this phase may be skipped, depending on the fact-finding efforts of organizers.

Phase 8: The public has open discussion of the issue. This can range from public meetings or hearings, to editorials, to national debates that last for years. Groups with the most influence attempt to secure the support of the public to adopt their plan or solution.

Phase 9: Once there is some testing of solutions and their integration, a practical resolution to the issue can emerge. Efforts to retain something from each practical plan are necessary before the next phase can occur.

Phase 10: Certain groups will relinquish their positions in order to save themselves from complete defeat, and a compromise on a plan occurs that most players will support.

Organizing is not always as systematic as these phases would make it appear, but the course of change from the perceived need to the implementation of a solution requires that all phases be included. If the strategy is well planned and if the social factors are favorable, then change can occur quite quickly. However, all too often, for issues such as civil rights, corporal punishment of children, or abortion, a great deal of effort and time is required before achieving a consensus relative to a solution.

Strategy

As discussed in the previous chapter, a strategic analysis is a straightforward, useful way of examining the helping and hindering forces that will impact on any change effort (Staples, 1984). Somewhere between phases 2 and 3, it is important that the group think through how the organizing efforts will be orchestrated. The centrality of a strategy for the organizer is important. Without it, convictions and commitment are nothing but empty hopes. Actions without a strategy are merely ad hoc "targets of opportunity" without any sense of how they fit into some larger scheme.

One question that will arise in developing a strategy is whether to use consensus or conflict methods. A total reliance on a strategy of either consensus or conflict will, in most circumstances, be unsuccessful. In organizing others it is clear that consensus building among groups and individuals is necessary. However, there will come a time in the process when some conflict methods may need to be employed.

> Plan everything. Planning skills are very important to impact social policy. Most people think that the legislative process is coming up with a great idea, throwing it into this system, and then sort of nursing it along. What you have to really do is determine what's likely to happen, what kind of problems you're going to face, and plan alternative solutions, alternative approaches. It is extremely important to create an entire strategy before you ever start.
>
> *Sandy Ingraham, MSW*
> *Social Services Consultant*
> *Harrah, Oklahoma*

Any development of strategy must begin by clarifying the problem or issue. A common statement as to what the need or situation is that should be rectified must be agreed on. Data must be gathered and presented succinctly for others to digest. The proposed plan or solution must be conclusively stated. Although many organizational efforts are in the best interest of others, it is necessary to clarify or articulately state a contract with those from whom you want support. How will their efforts toward this movement benefit them? All of this should be taken into consideration during the strategy development.

There are many ways to influence others to take action on social change. Not all methods are covered here, but these samples will help the reader understand the need to seek out different approaches to garner support. Of course, part of the strategy of a movement is to understand who you are trying to organize into action and what is the benefit for their actions. Once this is clear, one can determine which tool or method will yield the most return for the effort.

Coalition Building

A *coalition* is a loosely woven, ad hoc association of constituent groups, each of whose primary identification is outside of the coalition (Humphreys, 1979). Social workers, when coalition building, usually seek linkages with those who are most sympathetic to their ideas, values, and philosophies, such as mental health associations and the Children's Defense Fund. But all too often, social workers overlook potential alliances with groups that may, on the surface, appear unlikely to be supportive of social work policies. Thus, all aspects of a given issue should be carefully examined to identify points of potential commonality. For example, when Congress was considering an increase in the gasoline tax to generate revenues for the improvement of roads and bridges, this effort was supported by human service professionals because it would create jobs for the unemployed. Although this was the central issue that garnered the support of human service professionals, road builders and construction workers also supported the legislation, forming an otherwise unlikely coalition.

A true coalition is time-limited, with a specific issue or social change in mind. Too often, formal organizations are formed under the identity of a coalition. Such groups are really more of a formal association that works on areas of mutual concerns. These groups meet to share ideas, information, or approaches to a problem. Such organizing efforts may be helpful but are not a true coalition. A key point to remember when building a coalition—the more diversified the groups in a coalition, the more powerful the coalition becomes. Conversely, the greater the diversity, the more vulnerable it is to being splintered by outside and opposing groups. If an organization or coalition is splintered at a critical moment, it can undercut support for the legislation; without unanimity of support, legislators may not even bother to discuss the legislation (Mahaffey, 1972).

Gimmicks

With the multitude of issues facing legislative bodies, it is a challenge to make your issue stand out not only with the legislature but also with individuals. Gimmicks are just a ploy to direct attention to an issue. They will not affect others unless information and organizing action follow. Gimmicks can range from catchy phrases, to using an object as a symbol, to activities.

In one state campaign to pass the Children's Health Insurance Program, commonly referred to as CHIP, a group used the phrase "Don't gamble with our children's health" printed on a card with a poker chip glued to it. Large numbers of these CHIP cards were mailed to state legislators.

Various objects have been used to symbolize an issue. One group used a tongue depressor with the phrase "Put a plank in your platform for kids." Another mailed old shoes to a Washington, DC, organization, which placed the shoes on the steps of the Capitol to illustrate the number of homeless people. Demonstrations or activities, although not used much today, range from the Million Man March to the Stand for Children. More destructive actions have been taken by protesters throwing red paint on fur coats in demonstrations against the killing of animals for furs. Gimmicks like these attract media attention and bring an issue to the public's attention.

Other gimmicks are used only to get the attention of policymakers. One group working on infant and maternal health issues delivered apple pies (a symbol of motherhood) with a copy of the group's position on legislation taped to the box containing the apple pie. The social worker who delivered the pie would only give it directly to the elected official to make sure that he or she saw the position paper. This tactic worked because staff members, who wanted to eat the pies, would get a legislator to leave a meeting to receive a pie. Although gimmicks can be effective attention-getters, they must be evaluated in terms of their positive or negative impact on the public and on policymakers and in terms of the desired outcome.

Technology

Social workers are so people-focused that historically they often overlook techno-logical developments that can enhance their efforts greatly. This is also due in part to the fact that social workers lack budgetary resources for state-of-the-art technology. This is unfortunate given the advancements in computers, Internet, and communication technology. Clearly the 2008 presidential election is an exam-ple of just how much can be accomplished in organizing efforts if the current technological advances are used. The Obama campaign exploited the biggest technological shift in national politics since the rise of television. Obama amassed an army of 750,000 supporters who signed on to his website and participated in 30,000 off-line events. His YouTube videos reached 37 million viewers alone (Scherer and Newton-Small, 2008).

Technology has played an important role in the political process.

> Franklin Delano Roosevelt used radio to get his message across effectively to vot-ers. Lyndon Johnson rode a helicopter to get him around Texas in his famous race for the Senate. John F. Kennedy understood the power of television better than Richard Nixon during the race for the Presidency in 1960. And Republican opera-tives in the 1970s built direct mail into a fund-raising behemoth that powered party gains for 20 years. (Hoffman, 2008)

In a review of previous editions of this text, we have moved from saying little about technology to extolling the virtues of new advancements such as the fax machine, the Internet and email, all of which is now commonplace or even outdated. Given the rapid advancement of technology, we can no longer write about specific technologies as the "tool" to influence others, but we can simply state that technology must be used to enhance and expedite the real process of influencing others—connecting people to rally behind a cause. People influence people. No amount of new technology would have caused the historic event of November 4, 2008 (election night), if President Obama had not had the ability and the message to influence others.

As social workers, we need to look at the new technology and ask the question: "Will this technology connect our message with individuals?" Face-to-face inter-action is the most effective form to influence others; however, it is not the most cost-effective of today's technology. As one uses different technology, the effec-tiveness of message communication can diminish. Consider the impact of a phone call compared to an email. But if the email contains a customized text or video, the influence of the communication increases. Here, then, is the advantage social workers have in understanding people and identifying which technology will bring the most "human" touch to influence their action. Obama used social-networking features on his website; John McCain did not.

As Internet bandwidth expands and more people have high-speed access, the amount of data that can be communicated increases, which will allow for videoconferencing not only one-on-one but also with a larger number of individuals. It will be possible to make collaborative decisions quickly, thus meeting the goal of social work to be inclusive.

Keeping abreast of innovations is time consuming, but it should be considered a requirement for the professional and supported by social work organizations. Integrating technology knowledge in the continuing education of the social worker is the most effective way to address the issue of keeping abreast of technological advances. As with all technology, it is important to ensure that the individuals with whom you are organizing have the same technology as you have or similar technology that is compatible. In some cases, there may be a large digital divide.

> While the future of social work is not totally dependent on changes in computers and technology and their impact on society, it is one opportunity to begin to move the profession into the next century with new vigor and energy. If we can take full advantage of this new product of technology, the personal computer, and put it to use helping us operationalize our vision and implement our mission, perhaps it can be the key to opportunity for the next century. (Raffoul, 1996)

Using the Media

An important factor in organizing and making issues known is the use of the media. In some cases, without the assistance or attention of the media, a movement may become stagnant. We may view the mass media warily, yet we also know that the media is a powerful force in our society—a force for change (Pertskhuk and Wilbur, 1991).

Social workers need to understand how the media function, and they need to "work" them just as they would a legislative body. In media advocacy one must identify the objectives, target an audience, and tailor the message to that audience. As social workers we must learn from other professionals whose expertise is mass communications, public relations, or media consultation. However, a social worker's skills in working with people will pay big dividends if used with those who control the media.

Newspapers

Although newspaper circulation has decreased over the years—indeed, several disappeared in 2009—they should not be neglected in an effort to affect change. Newspaper readership is still high among older and more powerful citizens. Other than the Internet, newspapers are perhaps the easiest and most thorough medium through which to tell your story or to raise the public's consciousness. Letters to the editor are also effective, and policymakers read them! Another way to tell your story is in "op-ed" articles. Op-eds—articles that appear opposite the editorial page—can be a powerful and remarkably cost-effective way of getting

Don't Shortchange Texas Children

The Ways and Means Committee, chaired by Houston's Representative Bill Archer, has approved a bill (House Resolution 4) that reforms the welfare system and restructures child welfare programs as part of the GOP "Contract with America." This stampede for reform shortchanges Texas taxpayers and children.

This sweeping reform, titled the Personal Responsibility Act, proposes to give program control to the states. Title I (Temporary Family Assistance Block Grant) and Title II (Child Protection Block Grant) of the bill would cap entitlements and establish a block grant to be distributed to the states.

Under the proposed legislation, Texas would get $558 million annually for its children. The distribution for these block grants is based on the amount of federal dollars each state had used in previous years. The Title I distribution is calculated by averaging the states' expenditures for fiscal years 1991–1993, for aid to families with dependent children, and Title II by using the amount the states received in 1993. Traditionally, Texas has not concentrated on pulling down the federal dollars because of the federal rules and regulations involved. For years we have been sending money to Washington and getting less in return. Now that the federal rules are to be changed, we still get the short end of the stick. Under this bill, Texas will be able to build programs based on our needs, but we will have to do so without an equitable share of the pie. Texas tax dollars will be used to take care of New York and California children.

Not long ago Texas became the second most populous state. Additionally, we have a greater ratio of children than most states—to be exact, 5.2 million according to the 1990 census. This means that Texas has 7.3 percent of the U.S. child population. New York has 4.4 million children or 6.8 percent of the U.S. child population. California has long been the most populous state and accounts for 12.9 percent of U.S. children. But New York and California have been spending more than Texas on federally funded welfare programs and, under the new plan, would get a much larger share of the funding pie than Texas. Thus, some of the welfare funds that should go to Texas—under equitable funding—will be going to those states.

This is the intent of the "Contract with America." In Congress's exuberance, an equitable approach to block grants seems to be overlooked. For fairness' sake, Congress should use the formula of child population parity, shifting completely to this priority by the year 2000. By using child population as the formula for distribution of federal resources, Texas tax dollars would be used for Texas children. This would mean an additional $864 million for the state.

Let me be clear about the issue of using our tax dollars for our kids. I am not addressing the size of the pie, but the allocation of the pie. CHILDREN AT RISK is not alone on this issue; United Way of the Texas Gulf Coast and the Joint City/County Commission on Children support this position. Because of our outcry, a provision of $100 million for fast-growing states has been included, which still would be only 12 percent of what Texas alone would receive under child population parity.

It's time that Texans make it known that we want our tax dollars used fairly for our children.

Jim Mickelson

FIGURE 8.1   *Example of an Op-Ed Piece*

Source: Reprinted from the *Houston Post*.

your message out to a variety of audiences, providing information, and shaping opinions (Zeck and Rennolds, 1991). Figure 8.1 gives an example of an op-ed piece. The op-ed section is used for columns that address concerns of the community in an editorial or opinionated format. Major newspapers have an op-ed editor to whom you can send your article. Of course, newspapers also cover special events. You can take time to explain the issue to a reporter and give any necessary background information. Editorials, like coverage of media events, are more likely to be included or covered if they are timely and take a position ("attitude") on an issue that is current and of public interest. Figure 8.2 provides an example of an editorial.

Inhumane How Texas Treating Its Downtrodden

Amid the barbs of partisan politics over the proposed size and solution to the Texas Department of Human Services' [TDHS] budget deficit is this reality: No cutbacks can be withstood by our state's at-risk populations: our children, elderly, and medically indigent.

While turning away federal dollars is unwise, cutting funds from state-supported programs such as Children's Protective Services and foster care can in no way be considered a solution, since that strategy will only further reduce our ability to help and will ensure a future of even greater problems.

In recent years, Texas has faced this dilemma: Increased stress on families from the economic downturn, which subsequently creates increases in many social problems, while critical public agencies charged with the responsibility of preventing and/or alleviating those problems have had drastic budget reductions.

Private-sector initiatives should be applauded. But these cannot—indeed should not—take the place of responsible government to care for all its citizens. The importance of prevention and early intervention is well understood; so are the realities of systemic and interlocking problems. To allow these conditions to exist for any Texan is not only a terrible statement about Texas, but puts us all in jeopardy.

Unfortunately, our nation trails behind many others in the care of children and atrisk families. Unfortunately too, the data are clear: Even with our "kinder and gentler" focus, poverty is on the rise nationally, disproportionately affecting some (minorities, children, and the elderly). More than half live in a household where at least one member works.

What is worse, in a nation that trails other developed nations, Texas ranks at the bottom compared to other states on all the major indicators of caring for its population: infant mortality, teen pregnancy, high school dropouts, welfare payments, expenditures on child protection, substance abuse.

I am not proud that Texas ranks forty-sixth in what it pays "needy" families on welfare, forty-fifth in what it does to help people with medical needs, forty-seventh in meeting mental health needs, and forty-ninth in terms of services to the elderly. I am not proud that Texas ranks in the "terrible ten" or the "filthy fifteen" because proportionately our poorest citizens are being taxed much higher than our wealthiest.

The relationship of multiple problems forms an insidious web. Low-income families are likely to be unemployed or marginally employed, have no health insurance, have low rates of completed education, and live in substandard housing. As a consequence (and, I would contend, through no fault of their own), they become imperiled for problems such as substance abuse, teen pregnancy, domestic violence, illiteracy, and chronic unemployment or underemployment.

Any cuts in any programs have an effect on all other services. Reducing or discontinuing services to one population will, without any doubt, increase the demands elsewhere. We in Texas have watched, but not learned from, other states who had the shortsighted belief that social problems were not socially caused, were mutually exclusive, and could be remedied with Band-Aids.

Texas has always been perceived as a strong state. But we are unlikely to maintain that image with a future labor force that is unskilled and untrained, in the face of enormous and untreated inner-city problems, and in the face of other more accurately descriptive adjectives such as "cruel and uncaring." What is real is our inhumanity to our fellow Texans.

The current projected budgetary deficit for TDHS is in large part the result of effective and much more comprehensive strategic intervention. For that improved intervention I applaud the TDHS chairman, Rob Mosbacher, Jr., its board, commissioner Ron Lindsay, and other executive staff.

The solutions I offer are not "quick fixes." They are not an abrogation of public and social responsibility. They are not the total reliance on privatization and philanthropic "do-gooders." The shortsightedness of current and past legislators and our citizenry is incomprehensible to someone whose life training and experience bring me face to face with the extent and depth of human suffering amid Texas' relative affluence.

The concern of the governor and much of the legislature about the unpopularity of taxes is a narrowly focused definition of taxation and an ill-conceived notion of future economic growth and improved quality of life. For example, if we propose the course of budget reductions in the area of services to the elderly, we will force many of these people back on to families probably already stressed, creating personal economic hardship, a likely increase in family stress, and therefore, increases in elderly or child abuse. Likewise, if we remove funding from quality day care, we will either remove women from the labor force and force them into other public support—Aid to Families with Dependent Children—or create situations in which there are more unsupervised children in our communities who, in turn, may find themselves victims.

There are no easy, quick fixes to human suffering. To disenfranchise a large segment of our population from rights to health care, safe environments, and a minimum standard of living isn't just inhumane, it is shortsighted and ignorant.

I was not born a Texan, but I have twice chosen Texas as my home, based upon a belief that it is a great state. I want to be able to say that Texas is a powerful and strong state because it cares for its own.

Karen S. Haynes

FIGURE 8.2   *Example of an Editorial*

Source: Reprinted from the *Houston Chronicle.*

Radio

Talk radio can be a powerful force for political action, but more often it works as a forum in which issues can be legitimized as part of the public policy agenda (Aufderheide and Chester, 1990). In this format you can personalize the message and address the issues in more depth than on television. The best example of how effective talk radio can be is illustrated by how right-wing conservatives have used radio to get their message to millions. Today the left-wing progressive talk shows are using this medium as well, giving social workers more opportunities to speak out on issues. This is not to say that social workers should avoid either "side," but rather that they should take every avenue to deliver their messages. Social workers have not used this medium to its fullest, and they should consider it. Talk radio is great for public service announcements (PSAs), which can be helpful in educating the community about concerns or actions that need to be taken.

Television

The most powerful of all the media is television. In order to stimulate the public or to pressure policymakers, the evening news is what you want to use. However, social workers are not knowledgeable or skilled in the use of television. A social worker's best skill is to use words and take time to help a client or community. In television, time is absolute. After you subtract commercials, weather, sports, and the goodnight comments, a thirty-minute newscast contains only about seventeen minutes of news (Jones, 2005). Every issue within the profession should have hours of television time devoted to it, but that's not how it works. It is in television that social workers need to learn the "ten-second bite." In other words, each message must be effectively delivered in ten seconds or less. If a story is really big, it might get fifteen seconds. Most stories will run for thirty seconds; only a major story gets ninety seconds. When the question is asked and the camera is running, ten seconds is all you get to put your message across. Additionally, it must be delivered with as much flair and emotion as possible. Otherwise you'll end up on the editing room floor (Jones, 2001; Shook, 2000).

Examples of Organizing Others

A Competency Issue Becomes Reframed as a Staffing Crisis

During my tenure as assistant secretary of Children, Youth and Families for the state of Washington, I was asked to represent NASW and its Commission on Families at a national conference of the American Humane Association on the competence needed for child welfare practice. This panel on competencies involved representatives from the American Public Welfare Association and its affiliate, the National Association of Public Child Welfare Administrators, as well as the Child Welfare League of America. This panel shifted from skills to the crisis and the gap between available positions and workers to fill them.

Across the country the vacancy rate was estimated to be as high as one-third. It was here that we pledged to take the crisis to the Children's Bureau. With leadership from the NASW commission, we presented to the Children's Bureau both the crisis and the solution involving the use of Title 4-E funds for training and recruitment of social workers from schools of social work. The response from the child representative at the time (also a social worker) was one of puzzlement and surprise that these funds might be used to prepare social workers for child welfare practice.

*Vacancy Rates Symptomatic of the Rising Challenges Children
and Families Are Enduring, Rising Child Deaths,
and Fear of the Practice Arena*

My own appointment as assistant secretary was the result of a tragic child death in the state of Washington. The Commission on Families heard about the growing crisis in communities across the nation. Commission members carved out an agenda involving the building of a cross-organizational campaign among national agencies, the Children's Bureau, state and local NASW chapters, and units to address reprofessionalization and staffing. The NASW commission held several historic meetings to ground the agenda both in NASW and among the other national associations.

Once the Children's Bureau saw the social work profession's readiness to act, a grant was awarded to host a small national conference. Expecting twenty-five attendees, the conference attracted over 200 from forty states representing commissioners of child welfare, deans, directors, and faculty. Eight states were featured for their model partnerships. Within a year, through a Ford Foundation grant to CSWE, seventy to eighty exemplars had been documented.

Many of the strategies drawn upon were good "family-centered practices." Another grant made it possible to host fourteen conferences, and by 1993, nationally we were collectively drawing down over $100 million in 4-E funding across child welfare agencies and social work education. Additionally, the Children's Bureau had funded fifty schools to promote training and curriculum-building initiatives.

The thrust moved to expanding partnerships with other professions involved with vulnerable children and families. A national conference, cohosted by fourteen national associations representing social work, education, and health, attracted more than 300 participants. Voices of consumers of services were heard as presenters and as participants. Attorney General Janet Reno also made a historic presentation on the responsibility that we all share for these most vulnerable children, youth, and families.

Family-Centered Practice Strategies Used to Build a Movement

Again, like good family-centered practice, unless there is cohesion on how we treat children and families, there will be poor results and we may inadvertently undercut each other. Now that the collaboration movement is building, we are undergoing even greater challenges in the simultaneous renewal and change of health, social service, and education, and the counterpart disciplines in universities and colleges. What began as a journey to deal with the crisis of recruiting qualified staff in child welfare instead was symptomatic of the need for a much deeper movement and ground swelling in rebuilding our professions and our service delivery systems. My personal role has been to serve as one of the many facilitators of this movement and to nurture and cajole, when I can, as well as to celebrate the many successes and achievements led by colleagues in the country.

Katharine Hooper-Briar, Ph.D.
Chair, Family Studies and Social Work
Miami University, Oxford, Ohio

The Children's Presidential Campaign

It was seventeen months before the presidential election day when a group of people came together at the Child Welfare League of America (CWLA). We knew that in order to continue to improve the lives of children in this country, the next president had to be sensitized to children's issues. The question we asked ourselves was: "How does one assure that the next president will make children a national priority?" The answer was: "If the public is informed and concerned about the plight of children, then the presidential candidates would more likely respond."

After much thought and discussion I decided that the CWLA would run a campaign of children's issues in conjunction with the presidential campaign. In other words, the issue would be handled similarly to that of the candidates' campaign. Thus, the Children's Presidential Campaign was born.

I had experience with campaigns, having been a state legislator in Massachusetts and having worked for a governor. However, this was the first time that I was running an "issues" and not a "person" campaign. But, like all campaigns, it had to educate and convince the voters to support the issue. Once the presidential candidates embraced the issue, the CWLA would be in a better position to influence whomever the next president was on policies regarding children.

We needed people, time, and money. We had people, mostly league member agencies, but a broader base was needed. We had the time, and we needed to raise money, which we did. The strategy was to create media attention so that the general public would ask questions about children's issues and ask the candidates questions about children's issues, forcing the candidates to make statements on how to address these issues. The campaign targeted not only the media, but the candidates and the general public as well.

The first step was to develop a list of critical issues affecting children which we felt needed to be highlighted in the campaign. We built the campaign around a twelve-point program. The list included such issues as income security, housing, nutrition, child care, and adequate health care for all children, with special emphasis on abused and neglected children, adopted children, and those who are physically and mentally challenged.

To assist in organizing and recruiting, we developed a brochure that outlined the campaign, a newsletter to communicate with our supporters, a fact sheet to educate the candidates, a list of items that member agencies could use to help the effort, and a solicitation approach for money.

We now had all the ingredients of a campaign: time, money, and people. Not only did we use the hundreds of member agencies across the nation, but we sought out others who were interested in joining the movement.

We started with a press conference announcing the Children's Presidential Campaign (CPC). Staff sent out fact sheets, brochures, and information on the CPC to the media and to all candidates who had announced. The campaign was then off and running.

Since the CPC was aimed at the presidential candidates, it should not be surprising that our efforts were targeted at key caucus states and primary states like Iowa, New Hampshire, Florida, Texas, New York, Pennsylvania, and Ohio. There were a number of special events that occurred in these states, starting with Iowa where the media was focusing on the presidential race.

In Iowa, 150 child advocates, adults, and children showed up for a rally at a day-care center to kick off the CPC. The event did attract a fair amount of media interest, and by doing so, we knew that we were on the right track. This initial success was not without an inordinate amount of organizing effort by a local executive director of a children and family agency to assure that there would be a turnout of both the public and the media. In addition to television and radio spots, the Des Moines *Register* ran a strong editorial on the need for a children's agenda by all the presidential candidates.

From Iowa our efforts spread to every targeted state. As the nation focused on each state's race, so went the CPC. One by one each of the targeted states had a special event, each one with its own unique approach. In fact, Oklahoma, not one of the targeted states, had a big event because they wanted "to be part of the action."

There was one event in particular in Texas that received more media coverage than any of the other special events. When one of the CWLA member agencies heard about the CPC, the executive director called together the managing staff of the agency, who felt that this was a prime time for the agency to do something in their community. It was the first time that Texans would be voting in the "Super Tuesday" primary election. Texas was being focused on by the nation as a key state that could influence the primaries.

This group decided that they would hold a presidential debate in the high school gym, which would make a great setting for television. During a meeting with the superintendent of schools, they explained how it would be a great educational experience for the students to see history in the making. It became clear, however, that the superintendent would not support such an event. His rationale was that it was "too political." The agency staff went to the school board. They were met with the same response.

Now, more determined than ever, they developed an alternative plan to have children march on the county courthouse lawns advocating for candidates who supported children's issues. It was a Tuesday, which assured as much media coverage as possible, since Tuesday is usually a slow news day. The date was exactly two weeks before the primary election. The rally would be at noon to make it convenient for the reporters to make their deadlines. Through day-care centers, parochial schools, and the children at the agency, 400 children and 100 adults showed up for the rally. The children made posters that read "We count too" and "America's Future." The children demonstrated to music, yelling "We count too" Not only did these children make a statement about the need for candidates who supported children, but they also told themselves that they are important.

They asked me to speak to the group, along with the mayor and several other folks. Seeing all these young children and young people participating with enthusiasm was exciting and moving. From that one event, twenty-two media "hits" occurred, not only in the local area but mostly in the urban community fifty miles away. One media hit was an unusual three-minute segment on a major TV channel about the demonstration and the problems facing children. Although the organizing efforts were complicated, particularly when using children, the event was very successful and effective.

In New York a coalition of nineteen organizations came together to work on the New York CPC. The New York campaign organized several successful events; however, we experienced one setback. The coalition set up a presidential debate on children's issues, which was canceled at the last minute when the organizing committee realized that the candidates were not really committed to showing. This only proved to us that a continued effort was needed to get and keep children's issues in front of the presidential candidates.

As the presidential campaign swung into the total nation, the CWLA realized that more participation from the general public was needed. We knew from a Harris poll that the public was concerned about child welfare, but we also knew that to get people involved, the approach needed to be simplistic yet effective. After considerable thought and discussion, we realized that postcards, letters, and other such traditional approaches were not going to capture the candidates' attention. After all, there were many groups trying to get their concerns heard, about everything from abortion to gun control to space exploration.

During a brainstorming session the words *platforms* and *planks* kept coming up, which is language often used in campaigns. The idea of a piece of wood or something wooden, like a plank or platform, emerged. The idea of using a tongue depressor was conceived. This would not only catch the attention of the candidates, but also the public whom we wanted to mobilize. The phrase "Put a Plank in Your Platform for Children" became the slogan written on the tongue depressor.

The plan was to use those people who had already signed on to the CPC to host a "Plank Stuffing Party." This effort would quadruple the number of people involved in the campaign and thus broaden the base from child welfare professionals to the public at large. Some 200 persons expressed interest and each was contacted by phone to explain the process. The CWLA would supply the planks, the addresses of each candidate's campaign headquarters, and some sample notes that could be written and sent with the planks. This, then, was the first phase of our public campaign to reach the candidates.

The effort caught on because as people came together to stuff planks, they talked about children's issues. Each participant had an opportunity to have other parties or to find individuals who would stuff planks on their own. The effort multiplied and 300 such parties occurred across the nation, which resulted in about 105,000 wooden planks and personal notes being sent to the presidential candidates.

So successful were the planks that phase two of the planks came after the political parties had nominated their candidates. A new slogan was printed on the tongue depressors: "I'm voting for a children's president." The strategy was to show each candidate that there were a great number of voters interested in children as an issue. CWLA wanted the candidates to talk about their agenda for children. On the back of the plank was printed "Please send me a copy of your children's platform" and a space for each person to write their name and address.

Phase two had three effects: (1) The candidates knew voters were concerned about children; (2) this then required the candidate to formulate a platform so that it could be sent to the voters; and (3) the voters could see for themselves how the candidate viewed children.

It must be noted that while the CPC was very political, the campaign remained nonpartisan. Never did the CWLA show any favoritism to any party or candidate. We encouraged all candidates to address children's issues, whether they were Republican or Democrat, liberal or conservative. Every candidate was also provided with needed information and technical assistance. Our goal was to get as many candidates as possible talking about kids.

We discovered one day just how successful the planks had been. With only a few weeks left in the campaign, the staff at the CWLA in charge of the CPC received a call from the correspondence officer for the Bush campaign headquarters who asked, "What are all these tongue depressors doing in my office? I have 10 to 15 thousand of them. Just who are you people? Is this some kind of a gimmick?" It was from that conversation that President Bush put together a platform on children and responded to each person who sent a plank.

Soon after the call from the Bush headquarters, another call came from a Massachusetts post office that serviced the Dukakis national headquarters, stating that the planks were jamming the postal machinery and asking us to stop all these planks being sent.

At the peak of the CPC, both candidates knew that there were voters who cared about children. The campaign picked up where it left off with the next election, to keep the pressure on so that voters would consider candidates who commit themselves to work to improve the quality of life of children and their families.

David S. Liederman
Former Executive Director
Child Welfare League of America, Washington, DC

Conclusion

Truly one person can start a movement. In fact, all change is started by one person seeking to inspire action among others. Certainly advocacy has been a central concept within the base of social work practice. Organizing others is one end of the continuum of the political involvement. The intent of this chapter was not to be a primer on organizing but to point out that such efforts are indeed part of the total political picture. Further, we must not neglect the fact that the use of today's technology can enhance age-old organizing skills. Lastly, it is our hope that we have shown that no issue or social change effort is out of the reach or beyond the skills of social workers to accomplish.

All Social Work Is Political, So . . .

1. Find out how one registers to vote in your state and how you can get others to register. Take the necessary action to register ten new voters.

2. Choose an issue, and determine what groups would make a good coalition to have an impact on the issue. How would you get these groups to work together on the issue?

3. Review the website of a candidate for public office or a group advocating for an issue, and determine whether they are using the latest technology effectively.

4. Write an editorial on a subject, and submit it to your local newspaper.

Suggested Readings

Jones, Clarence. 2005. *Winning with the News Media: A Self-Defense Manual When You're the Story*, 8th ed. Tampa, FL: Video Consultants. (www.winning-newsmedia.com)
Staples, Lee. 1984. *Roots to Power: A Manual for Grassroots Organizing*. New York: Praeger.

References

Aufderheide, Pat, and Jeffrey Chester. 1990. *Strategic Communications for Nonprofits: Talk Radio*. Washington, DC: Benton Foundation.
Fisher, Robert. 1997. *Let the People Decide: Neighborhood Organizing in America*. New York: Twayne.
Hoffman, Auren. August 25, 2008. "It Takes Tech to Elect a President" *Business Week*, www .businessweek.com/technology/content/aug2008/tc20080822_700775.htm
Humphreys, Nancy. 1979. "Competing for Revenue Sharing Funds: A Coalition Approach." *Social Work* 24 (January): 14–18.
Jones, Clarence. 2005. *Winning with the News Media: A Self-Defense Manual When You're the Story*, 8th ed. Tampa, FL: Video Consultants.
Lindeman, Edward C. 1921. *The Community: An Introduction to the Study of Community Leadership and Organization*. New York: Associated Press.
Mahaffey, Maryann. 1972. "Lobbying and Social Work." *Social Work* 17 (January): 3–11.
NpowerNY. 2001. *Mobile Technology in the Non-Profit World*. www.NPowerNY.org.
Pertskhuk, Michael, and Phillip Wilbur. 1991. *Media Advocacy: Strategic Communication for Nonprofits*. Washington, DC: Benton Foundation.
Raffoul, Paul. 1996. "Social Work and the Future: Some Final Thoughts." In *Future Issues for Social Work Practice*, Paul R. Raffoul and Aaron C. McNeece (eds.), pp. 293–299. Boston: Allyn & Bacon.
Scherer, Michael, and Jay Newton-Small. April 23, 2008. "Why Dems Rule the Web." *Time*, www .time.com/time/magazine/article/0,9171,1731879,00.html
Shook, Frederick. 2000. *Television Field Production and Reporting*. New York: Longman.
Staples, Lee. 1984. *Roots to Power: A Manual for Grassroots Organizing*. New York: Praeger.
Zeck, Denice, and Edmund Rennolds. 1991. *Op-Eds: Strategic Communication for Nonprofits*. Washington, DC: Benton Foundation.

9

Monitoring the Bureaucracy

Bills are made into laws with good intentions. Those good intentions can become lost in the complex process of rule writing, administrative orders, and budgetary constraints. All can be lost if not monitored.

—Ciro D. Rodriguez*

After months of hard work, a social worker who had been lobbying for passage of a bill was informed that the state senate had passed the bill and the governor had signed it. Much effort had resulted in legislative victory. Or had it?

On the contrary, social workers all too often win the legislative battle and proceed to lose the war by assuming their work is finished (Curren, 1982). Legislatures must not only pass bills but also fund them, and if they do not fund a bill after passage (as sometimes occurs), that bill effectively is killed. Nor is funding the last of the hurdles. Administrative rules may be written that misinterpret the legislators' intent, or agencies may implement the regulations in a manner that differs from the intent.

The purpose of monitoring the bureaucracy is to ensure that the intent of the legislation is carried out. The social work lobbyist needs to monitor four areas after a bill has been passed: (1) promulgation of rules, (2) implementation and adherence to the rules by agencies, (3) the budget allocation process, and (4) executive orders and administrative changes.

Monitoring should not be confused with lobbying. Monitoring is the process of keeping a watchful eye on the government to see that the legislative intent is carried out, whereas lobbying is the act of influencing legislation. Monitoring and lobbying have some elements in common, yet they are distinctly different activities. For example, a social worker who discovers an inconsistency between the intent of the law and its subsequent implementation might use the

*Ciro D. Rodriguez has an MNS and is a U.S. representative (Texas).

lobbying techniques described in Chapter 7 to rectify the situation. The greatest overlap between the two activities occurs when the administrative rules are being promulgated for a recently passed piece of legislation. During this period, a certain amount of lobbying as well as monitoring may take place. In either case, the social worker must develop an interventive strategy, deciding how most effectively to induce others to modify their policy in the desired direction (Dluhy, 1982).

Throughout this chapter we refer to the *intent* of legislation, by which we mean the ultimate goal the supporters of the original bill had in mind. Throughout the entire legislative process, from the initial drafting of a bill to its funding and implementation, various interpretations, modifications, and deliberate misconstruals can result in a program whose characteristics are inconsistent with the original intent of a bill. Consider tax bills: Congress attempts to stimulate certain business or economic activities through tax breaks but finds that, because of regulatory loopholes or misinterpretations, not only have government revenues been reduced but other unintended tax breaks also have been created.

It is important for the social worker to understand that certain formal and informal steps related to policy adoption and implementation apply to all levels of government: (1) rule writing and promulgation, (2) rule implementation, and (3) budget allocation. In addition, one must be aware of the importance of executive orders and other administrative changes that subsequently may affect program implementation.

Rule writing and promulgation occur shortly after the bill is signed by the president, governor, or mayor. The promulgation processes usually occur only once, although legislation may be amended, repealed, or replaced at any time, after which the promulgation and implementation process will recur. Administrative orders, agency compliance, and the budget allocation process require more continuous or at least repeated scrutiny. In addition, even after a law has been enacted, a continuous surveillance of the program and the budgetary process is necessary to ensure that the services and benefits that were the intended result of the law are being provided.

The intent of this chapter is to inform the reader about the complex processes that occur after a bill is passed and the effect these can have. Monitoring skills are essential in the repertoire of political interventions. We provide strategies for effective monitoring in the three areas listed previously and indicate how social work skills can be used in the monitoring process.

Promulgating the Rules

A law is a mandate from a legislative body that provides guidelines to govern behavior and decision making, whereas administrative regulations provide directives for the law's implementation. A bill is usually vague in its content in order to avoid political debates over smaller issues. Additionally, legislators do not have the knowledge to write a bill that would cover every aspect of implementing a program. Therefore, the purpose of rules is to inform both the general public and those who administer the legislation how the law will be implemented and enforced.

> With respect to monitoring the implementation of policy, I believe that there are three aspects useful for social workers to think about. These are (1) the decentralization of policymaking functions, (2) increased auditing requirements and local public scrutiny, and (3) increases in consumer participation in local decision making. What these three elements mean for professional social workers are opportunities for more direct involvement in policymaking and policy-monitoring activities, having public support for performance as well as fiscal audits, and increased opportunities for coalition building and community organizing.
>
> *Dennis Jones, MSW*
> *Former Commissioner*
> *Texas Department of Mental Health and Mental Retardation*

Regulations may be perceived as additional policies that transform the legislative ideal into practical design and delivery stages. Regulations usually sharpen and clarify staffing requirements, service provider responsibilities, client eligibility, treatment modalities, and accountability and reporting mechanisms. These regulations are not merely simplistic extensions of the legislation. Indeed, this power to guide the behavior of others and the opportunity to make decisions about the basic allocation of services are powerful tools that can considerably alter the original intent of the legislation.

Public input is always sought during the rule-writing stage, through written commentary directed to the administrative staff engaged in rule writing or at public hearings scheduled by the agency. Usually, there is no time limit on how long it can take to write the rules to satisfy all concerned with a particular law. A delay in rule writing may be a means to weaken or skew the law's intent.

The substance and political importance of public input are weighed by the agency prior to issuing the formal regulations (Pierce, 1984). It is possible for the president or a governor to implement emergency rules while awaiting the final draft from the appropriate agency. Such an action can undoubtedly have long-term effects.

The rule-making process varies from state to state and in city and county governments. Procedures articulated in the Administrative Procedure Act (APA), passed by Congress in 1946, are the model most used by other levels of government.

The first decision made in the rule-writing phase is which agency will be assigned the task. On the national level the Office of Management and Budget, under the president, monitors all rule making. Once responsibility has been delegated to a specific division of an agency, agency personnel are assigned to complete the task. Contrary to what is commonly thought, agency personnel do not exist for this function alone. The assignment of rule writing is often added to their other job responsibilities. Regulations reflect the values, knowledge, and expertise of these staff members, as well as any ignorance or unconcern.

Once a draft of the rules has been developed, public input is sought. All rules for the federal government are published in the *Federal Register*. The final draft must be published not less than thirty days before the rules are to be administered. On the local level, one must monitor to determine when and where public hearings will be held and how they will be published.

Now the rules and regulations can be implemented. When implementation begins, and even after services have been started, the legislative body can make changes in the regulations by passage of an amended bill or by budgetary allocation. Any of these processes can alter or qualify the intent of the initial bill (Curren, 1982).

Within the rule-writing process there are multiple points at which a social worker may find it necessary to monitor or intervene. Clearly, one point of intervention is with the staff assigned to write the regulations. A weakness of the system is the lack of personnel who understand how statutory design influences program implementation (Gimpel, 1991). An excellent approach at this stage is to set up an appointment with the staff members to provide brief and factual input. A straightforward strategy of showing an interest in the process and a willingness to assist could have a great influence on staff members because they may have limited knowledge and expertise on the subject of the rules and limited time to complete the task (Curren, 1982). Prior to a meeting, think through and write out a proposal, if possible. These individuals may willingly incorporate your ideas in order to minimize their efforts. Most states require that any input given to those who are writing or promulgating the rules be considered and evaluated.

Providing input at public hearings is another opportunity to influence the direction of administrative regulations. It is essential to keep track of times, dates, and locations of public hearings related to legislation of interest to you to ensure that your representatives are present. Written positions or recommendations are important given the time limitations on verbal presentations.

For the sake of illustration, let's assume that a law was enacted to establish a drug treatment program in an inner city. Regulations should specify the types and qualifications of administrators, therapists, and support staff and should establish the targeted clients, eligibility standards, fee schedules, operational procedures, hours, and service parameters. All of these decisions can dramatically affect the services provided by the program. For example, charging a fee for such treatment would most assuredly be a disincentive to poor inner-city residents and would dramatically reduce the program's effectiveness. Not providing evening or weekend services would have an equally devastating effect. However, evening hours, drop-in policies, and outreach efforts might improve service delivery and increase program effectiveness.

Rule Implementation and Agency Compliance

Once the rules have been written, their implementation must be monitored. This is best done at the beginning, when it is easier to make changes, rather than after programs and procedures have become firmly established.

To be sure, there is an inherent contradiction in rules related to human services. In order to ensure that the intent of the law is carried out, it may be desirable to promulgate detailed and possibly restrictive rules. Some degree of flexibility in the interpretation of those rules, however, may well allow the program to address more adequately and equitably over time a variety of individual client concerns and problems and allow the program to respond to changing client needs as well. Loose regulations may suit the agency's interest in having administrative flexibility while easing the agency's drive for political survival (Bell and Bell, 1982). The pitfall is that this flexibility may allow services to change as popular opinion dictates, regardless of recipients' needs.

The issues involved in specifying staff qualifications for a particular human service program offer a useful illustration of this type of dilemma. For example, a rigid requirement that only MSWs with mental health training will be acceptable as therapists in a drug treatment program, when applied statewide, may represent an unfairly restrictive qualification if such personnel are not available in all areas of the state. However, the often-used alternative of establishing "minimum qualifications" (e.g., a minimum requirement of a high school diploma or 12 credit hours of human service training) may result in untrained staff providing services and even therapy to program clients.

Monitoring rule implementation is necessary not only to protect the general public's rights but also to ensure agency adherence to the regulations. Some of the major reasons implementation may deviate from legislative intent are as follows:

1. Legitimate differences in interpreting legislative intent can occur. For example, the use of flexible terminology in listing requirements, such as "social work degree or the equivalent," could be interpreted to mean "MSW" but also legitimately could be taken to mean "MSW or MA in psychology or sociology" or even "BA with life or professional experience equivalents."

2. All agencies, including human service agencies, have vested interests to protect—not only their budgets, but also their organizational structure and general service delivery design. After an organization is established, any modification, whether it be expansion, contraction, or extinction, will create a great deal of resistance. When states enacted child abuse legislation, strong resistance arose when the responsibility for investigation, and reporting was assigned to state public welfare departments or child welfare agencies that already were overburdened.

3. Social agencies, despite the lofty language in their charters and in social legislation, are not necessarily benign with respect to protecting clients' rights. Once reimbursement for the services has been exhausted, the client all too often is disregarded or referred to another agency. When the Title XX amendments to the Social Security Act mandated that 50 percent of all funded services be delivered to current welfare recipients, several states initiated "head hunts" to increase welfare rolls so that they would have more clients to serve.

4. State and federal budgetary oversight agencies have veto power over state agencies when it comes to administrative decisions made in the course of implementing social legislation, and this power is sometimes exercised to the detriment of groups of clients who were intended to benefit from the legislation. For example, mothers in the program often are directed by agencies to find work, when in fact the intent of the law that established the program

was to encourage mothers to stay home and raise their children. In such cases, budgetary agencies need to be challenged on their interpretation of legislative intent (Bell and Bell, 1982).

5. Public pressure caused by a misunderstanding of a program might cause legislators, administrators, and agency staff to make changes that ultimately alter the intent and effectiveness of the program. For example, encouraging Temporary Assistance to Needy Families (TANF) mothers to find work, without also providing adequate day care, will result in less adequate care for the children involved than was the case before the program was enacted.

6. The covert purpose of the law differs from the public justification for it, thus complicating the measurement of its effectiveness. For instance, many job training programs for the poor were enacted not to assist people to become economically self-sufficient but rather to stimulate the economy or reduce welfare rolls.

In sum, agencies may deliberately or mistakenly misinterpret administrative regulations, which can result in deviation from legislative intent at the point of program initiation. Social workers within and outside the organizations who administer such programs must monitor and intervene at this stage to ensure consistency with legislative intent. A number of monitoring operations may be legislatively mandated, such as administrative auditing, program review and evaluation, or compliance with quality control measures. Also, state "sunset laws" may require external review of the agency. Getting appointed to an advisory committee with oversight functions is one important and powerful method of monitoring these necessary internal or external review processes. Social workers may also use whistle-blowing from within the organizations they serve as a form of advocacy in monitoring the compliance versus the intent of the law (Greene and Latting, 2004).

Budget Allocations

The budget is the clearest and most measurable indicator of governmental priorities. It lies at the heart of the political process and requires a great deal of continuous monitoring (Wildavsky, 1979). Legislators have the opportunity, either annually or biannually, to enhance or undermine the effectiveness of a program or agency via budget allocations. For example, Congress once passed a bill that allocated $1.25 per capita for health services. But it was cut to $0.38 per capita two years later, leaving the agency unable to meet the goals originally established in the legislation.

The size and design of a budget are a matter of serious contention in our political life (Wildavsky, 1979). The budget not only proposes what is to be expended but projects revenues as well. The federal budget, which can have a deficit, follows an atypical budgetary process because most state, local, and private budgets must be balanced or show a reserve. On the state and local levels, overly optimistic revenue projections by a governor or mayor may cause the administrative branch to react by reducing expenditures in order to maintain a balanced budget. Thus, revenue projections are just as important as proposed expenditures.

Just as flexibility in interpretation of legislation can have both positive and negative consequences, flexibility in how budgets are presented also can have contradictory effects. Budgets may be presented and approved as lump sums for entire state administrative units, by line items, or by departmental functions. If budgetary oversight, approval, and allocation is by line item or by departmental function, legislators can provide more direction and input over agency priorities. A lump-sum budget appropriation process, however, may allow for too much latitude and administrative discretion by the agency chief executives.

The budget allocation process can be influenced in two ways. One way is to influence the type of budget that will be presented and approved. If social workers want extreme latitude, they should lobby for lump-sum budgets. Second, because department heads make funding recommendations to the budget director, the strategy used by the department head can be crucial. For example, if a department head requests an extremely large increase after several years of small, incremental budget increases, this will create legislative interest. If the need for the request is well documented and publicly supported, it may be granted. However, it is likely that undocumented requests for large budget increases will be disregarded.

As mentioned earlier, budget allocations have a great impact on policy implementation. For that reason, monitoring of the budgetary process is highly important, even crucial, to program maintenance and service delivery. Social workers have both firsthand experience and aggregate data from previous budget cycles on the impact of differing funding levels on client service. This information should be supplied to the legislative budget office before a new budget is proposed. Presented regularly, such information can be used to sensitize fiscal planners to the impact of funding levels on client services and to projections of future demand. After the budget is proposed, the next logical intervention is lobbying the legislature; after the budget is amended and approved by the legislative branch, it is returned to the administrative branch for signature and implementation, and further intervention becomes difficult.

The most obvious and yet most controversial issue in budget allocations for human services is to define and operationalize "adequate standards and services." *Operationalization* refers to staff size, staff qualifications, caseload ratios, and hours of service delivery. A common value dilemma faced by social work program staff is how to deliver quality services to all needy clients when funds are limited or decreasing, without turning clients away. Although in the short term it is not in the best interest of the client to be denied service, waiting list figures indicating unmet needs can be powerful indicators to legislators of the need for increased funding to expand a particular service.

Administrative Changes or Executive Orders

Once a bill has been enacted, responsibility for the programs it creates rests with the chief executive officer or the department head, who often is empowered to make certain administrative changes. If any changes in the rules are then made, the same process mentioned earlier will be followed. However, there are ways in which administrators can affect a program without changing the rules. One is to recommend a reduced budget.

Another subtle mechanism for circumventing legislative intent is to exercise power over the way responsibilities for the program are assigned. To take an extreme example, assigning program responsibilities to one agency, or to one agency staff member, may signal limited interest in effective program implementation. Likewise, assigning responsibility for the program to an inappropriate agency could predetermine its failure. Therefore, monitoring such administrative actions is a critical interventive task.

Nonenforcement of the rules through administrative oversight is another way to undermine the intent of a piece of legislation. If the law does not include evaluative or accountability requirements or procedures, noncompliance is likely. For example, Congress allocated funding to some hospitals and required them to provide a percentage of their health care services free to the poor in exchange for federal support. Under the act, participating hospitals were required to inform poor patients of the availability of the free services. However, because no agency was designated to oversee the hospitals on this point, many hospitals did not comply with the regulation.

Other unobtrusive methods can be used by an executive to alter the outcome of a program: placing a freeze on staff replacements, overloading a specific agency subdivision, rewarding noncompliance, changing eligibility requirements, and reducing publicity and outreach. All of these methods will alter the amount and pattern of services provided.

Social Work Skills

All of the rule-making and rule-implementing processes mentioned in this chapter require consistent monitoring in order to ensure that the intent of the law is carried out and that the clients targeted by the legislation receive mandated services. Because elected officials, agency staff, public opinion, and society's needs change, social workers must monitor from both outside and inside the bureaucracy. They also need to use social work skills to ensure that program goals and services remain appropriate. Although this type of ongoing monitoring can be difficult and tedious, it is nevertheless essential and is quite compatible with social work skills as well. The same basic problem-solving approach that social workers use with clients can be employed in monitoring a program: Identify the problem, gather information, make an assessment, and develop a plan of action.

Problem identification may seem to be the most straightforward of the stages because usually it is evident that clients have unmet needs or are falling between service areas. What may not be evident is where the problem lies—legislative enactment, program design and delivery, or budget allocation. After this has been determined, appropriate information can be collected and presented.

Information is the key to effective advocacy. Persuasive information comes in many forms. Quantitative data may be collected and presented, such as the percentage of the population in need, the number of clients served, or the number of people at risk. Information may be presented comparatively, in the form of data specifying proportions of the population in need or as ratios of clients served county to county or state to state. The same information can also be collected and presented in qualitative terms, by citing case illustrations or by projecting additional problems or future scenarios if the current need is not met.

Regardless of type, information gathered by social workers can increase their ability to influence public officials. Facts collected about community problems will generate questions, identify hidden problems, and support or challenge government policies and explanations. Information lends credibility to opinions. It also enables one to reveal officials' evasions, question their assumptions, and, if necessary, expose errors or inconsistencies in their figures (Shur and Smith, 1980).

Today, comprehensive data can be located quickly through use of the Internet. However, a word of caution: As with traditional library and reference searches, you must always consider the source of information. Are sources or references provided so that you can tell where or how the data were obtained?

Another way to get information is to join a newsgroup or subscribe to a mailing list. Individuals interested in the same subject subscribe to these services. You can send an email message to the entire list of individuals to request information, or you can post a note for the subscribers to view. Subscribers can respond to your request for information and provide knowledge they have or tell you where to find additional documentation.

Today's technology is a useful tool in monitoring. One can follow budgets, expenditures, and services performed or not performed. A word of caution: Even with the advantages of quickly accessible data, one must still consider the source and how those data are interpreted and stated.

Clearly, much information is readily available. But because fewer reporting requirements are being enacted or mandated, the kinds of data that could be helpful to advocates are no longer available to the public. This may seem in contrast to the increased accountability being placed on social workers. The question is what *kinds* of data are collected. For example, the number of people who leave the TANF caseloads is an accountability issue. Both the reasons for closing cases and what happened to the individuals are important to anyone interested in monitoring the bureaucracy and for revising policies and procedures, but this information is not necessarily being collected. Social workers must support both data collection and evaluation of program outcomes, which are essential for monitoring legislative intent and for advocating the expansion or modification of services.

Whenever secondary sources of data are used, the inherent biases in the collection, collation, and analysis must be taken into account. Particularly when using state agency plans and reports, be aware that the need to justify a program may bias the presentation of information. Using census data, government reports, and state plans, both a projection of needs and an assessment of output and outcome can be obtained for the purpose of defending the existence or expansion of any program or service. After the information is collected and tabulated, the position must be presented in a style and format that is persuasive to those responsible for decision making. For example, stating that 0.003 percent of all children in a particular county were sexually molested last year may be accurate, but this approach is less effective than dramatizing the problem. You can make this point more effectively by stating that for each member of the six-person committee, 100 children were unwillingly forced into sexual acts by an adult. The general problem is to decide when statistics are useful, which statistics will be most persuasive, and when a more dramatic and personal approach will be more effective.

A word of caution is in order here: Rhetorical excess and incorrect or purposeful misuse of factual data can discredit even the best lobbyists. Trite phrases can divert attention from the issues. Although personalizing statistics may be a persuasive tactic, sensationalizing them could be detrimental to your cause.

The final stage in the monitoring process is to develop a plan of action, not only for the presentation of information but also for ongoing monitoring and lobbying to ensure that a particular position is carried through.

An illustration of monitoring agency compliance with administrative regulations can be drawn from the Hill-Burton Act. With the economic downturn of 2009, the need for federally funded health services has greatly increased. One regulation created by the Hill-Burton Act states that hospitals must post a sign in their emergency department and waiting rooms stating that they are Hill-Burton hospitals and that services are available without cost to those without funds. However, many hospitals did not comply with this regulation. It was only through monitoring of hospitals and the threat of a lawsuit by a group of social workers that hospitals were forced to follow through with their obligation to advertise and provide these services to the poor.

> When I started graduate school, there were jobs for every social worker who was graduating. Then in my second year at the University of Oklahoma, all of a sudden programs were being cut. It occurred to me that if the programs were being cut, social work students weren't going to have jobs, and poor people weren't going to get services. I then could see that political influence was needed. I talked the School of Social Work into doing a very creative placement, sort of turning me loose at the statehouse to see if there was a way to make an impact on that system.
>
> They hooked me up with a local social action agency that had never been involved in state capitol issues but was very interested in the possibility. That was the beginning of a twenty-year career as a political social worker.
>
> Today I have, in essence, a business that is a legislative monitoring, consulting, and training enterprise. It keeps me involved with social service agencies and supports me while I am able to do lobbying, sometimes paid, sometimes just as part of the process that I'm involved in.
>
> On a regular basis, I have about twenty contractors, if you want to call them that. I read all of the legislation that affects social services and summarize it based on what effects it has on social services. This review is sent to the different groups based on their needs. I meet with their boards or associations on their time schedule and have a briefing, helping them figure out how to advocate for themselves.
>
> For example, Monday mornings I meet with the Oklahoma Alliance on Aging. Around the table are representatives from every senior citizen group in the state: AARP, retired teachers, the area-wide aging agencies. They look at and discuss all of the bills relevant to gerontology. I help them plan what they're going to do to lobby for themselves.

After many years of working, I enjoy an excellent reputation in the Oklahoma state legislature because I put together information and deal with information in an extremely credible way. So most of the time I get asked for information instead of trying to force it on somebody. After a while if you're very consistent and responsive, people will start coming to you and asking. Legislators today come off of the floor to find me and say, "I'm just about to argue a bill on so-and-so; tell me what the issue is here, give me some information." And, you know, all of a sudden, I end up being used as a staff person for every house member and senator who is interested in promoting a piece of progressive legislation.

Sandy Ingraham, MSW
Social Services Consultant
Harrah, Oklahoma

One social worker monitored a state commission that oversaw the implementation of block grants. She diligently attended every meeting to ensure that the commission was complying with the original intent of the legislators. She became so skilled at monitoring individual commission members that she could predict their decisions and individual preferences by their posture, facial expressions, and gestures, and subsequently could alter her interventive style or content. What is *not* said often can be a clue to a person's attitude, as can body posture, gestures, and word usage. Awareness of the external factors affecting committee members or chairs can be important in determining the most appropriate interventive strategy. The ability to observe and understand group processes, formal and informal leadership, and committee members' personal goals and ambitions are all essential in effective intervention.

It should be obvious at this point that individuals, either alone or as part of a decision-making body, are the primary actors in all of the monitoring processes discussed in this chapter, from legislative enactment to rule writing to agency compliance. Social work skills and social workers' experiences are tremendous assets in the monitoring stages.

There is one additional area of monitoring where social workers must be vigilant. With the increase of anti–social service sentiment, numerous legislative attempts, usually in the form of last-minute amendments to unrelated legislation, have been made to constrain or block social workers and social services organizations from influencing the political arena. Only through continuous and vigilant monitoring of all legislation have such efforts been averted or aborted. Without such monitoring efforts, the ability of social workers to advocate on behalf of their clients would have been greatly constrained.

Conclusion

Monitoring is the process of overseeing that rules and regulations, budget allocations, and agency compliance are consistent with the intent of the law. Social work skills are very effective in all stages of this process.

Monitoring all of these stages takes time and a great deal of patience and is probably the most detail-oriented of the political interventive techniques, yet it is a necessary step to ensure that the original intent of a piece of legislation is indeed implemented. The affect that an individual can have on the outcome may be even greater than during the initial legislative process. This is not to say that lobbying for the passage of a bill is not necessary, but many mistakenly think that once a bill is signed, no further advocacy is necessary.

All Social Work Is Political, So . . .

1. Call your member of Congress, and ask that he or she keep you informed of some legislation that is being discussed. Track to ensure that this is done, and see what kind of information you receive and from whom.

2. Choose a recently enacted piece of state legislation, and follow it to the agency that is assigned to write the rules. Obtain a copy of the administrative regulations, and assess how closely they appear to follow the intent of the legislation.

3. Identify individuals or formal organizations in your state that monitor human service legislation and implementation. Describe the processes they use.

Suggested Readings

Albert, Raymond. 1983. "Social Work Advocacy in the Regulatory Process." *Social Casework* 64 (October): 480–481.
Prigmore, Charles S. 1974. "Use of the Coalition in Legislative Action." *Social Work* 19 (January): 96–102.

References

Bell, William G., and Budd L. Bell. 1982. "Monitoring the Bureaucracy: An Expression of Legislative Lobbying." In *Practical Politics: Social Work and Political Responsibility,* Maryann Mahaffey and John W. Hanks (eds.), pp. 118–135. New York: National Association of Social Workers.
Curren, H. Patricia. 1982. Speech to the Michigan Political Action for Candidate Election Committee.
Dluhy, Milan J. 1982. *Changing the System: Political Advocacy for Disadvantaged Groups.* Beverly Hills, CA: Sage Publications.
Gimpel, James. 1991. "Congressional Oversight of Welfare and Work: Fundamental Flaws Make Legislative Efficiency Nearly Impossible." *Public Welfare* (Summer): 10 (49): 3: 8–11.
Greene, Annette D., and Jean Kantambu Latting. 2004. "Whistle-Blowing as a Form of Advocacy: Guidelines for the Practitioner and Organization." *Social Work* 49 (2): 219–230.
Pierce, Dean. 1984. *Policy for the Social Work Practitioner.* White Plains, NY: Longman.
Shur, Janet, and Paul Smith. 1980. *Information Resources for Child Advocates.* Washington, DC: Children's Defense Fund.
Wildavsky, Aaron. 1979. *The Politics of the Budgetary Process.* Boston: Little, Brown.

10

The Campaign

I have found that social work skills were most useful in campaigning. Each of my six campaigns would legitimately be described as grassroots campaigns. In the last one, we ran a campaign that was a full citizen empowerment effort and a good example of organizing techniques.

—Ruth Messinger*

Whenever you think about a political campaign, you most likely conjure up a picture of bumper stickers, balloons, hats, rallies with impassioned speeches, and cheering crowds. But this is only a small component of what a campaign entails. This chapter provides an overview of campaigning designed to encourage social workers to participate in this aspect of the political process. The purpose is not to educate you on how to run a campaign or to discuss the intricacies of campaign strategy at different governmental levels, but rather to reduce the fears and disillusionments that volunteers, especially social work volunteers, are likely to feel when working on a campaign.

You might ask, "Why is it necessary to become involved in a campaign?" The answer is that it is essential to elect individuals to office who will listen to the concerns of both clients and the social work profession. To have such persons in office makes the social worker's task easier when monitoring and lobbying. For a social worker to have the politician's ear, the politician needs to know that person put forth a certain amount of effort and time to help the candidate obtain the office. The earlier the volunteer's support, effort, and time are put forth, the greater the return and the greater the influence on the politician. This is not to suggest that you are buying legislative votes. Presumably, the reason you work on a campaign is to get into office the kind of person you want as your representative. By being involved at the beginning of the campaign, which is the most difficult stage, as

---

*Ruth Messinger is former Manhattan borough president.

well as in the later phases, you reap the rewards that come to those who jumped on the bandwagon early. Also, such people are much more likely to have the candidate's ear, to be granted access when key issues are discussed, or perhaps to be offered a position than those whose support was given later or perhaps not at all.

It must be remembered that campaigns differ depending on the level of office being sought, the intensity of the issues, and the constituencies that the candidate will represent if elected. Generally speaking, the higher the office, the more complex the campaign becomes.

The object of any political campaign is, quite simply, to win. One must be elected in order to introduce, modify, or vote on legislation. No candidate expects or needs 100 percent of the votes; to win, one must receive only a majority of all votes cast. The remainder of this chapter explains the strategies by which this goal is met, and Chapter 11 shares some insights on being a candidate.

Components of the Campaign

The campaign is the vehicle that initiates and communicates a consistent message to enough voters to convince a majority to vote for the candidate. As in all endeavors, information, planning, organization, and management are required.

Every campaign has a particular message, or theme, that communicates everything about the candidate: not only occupation, activities, and positions on the issues but also the nature and substance of the candidate's relationships with volunteers, organizations, and constituents. Consequently, the campaign theme is much more than a slogan, although it can sometimes be captured in a slogan.

Because a candidate's theme transcends all other aspects of the campaign, it should never focus on detailed positions on any one or two specific issues or pending laws, but rather should describe the style of leadership the candidate will provide on issues in general. For example, during a deep recession one gubernatorial candidate's campaign slogan was "Jobs, Jobs, Jobs." Though it may appear that this slogan was rooted in one issue, actually it indicated that the candidate understood unemployment, the problems of the poor, economic conditions, business, the state's budget deficit—in short, everything related to earning a living, including the need for human services. The message this slogan conveyed was one of hope: that the candidate was the one who could restore the state to economic health. Consider President Obama's 2008 campaign theme—"Change"—and the message it sent. Note that the theme did not itemize the many areas that needed change. To do so might have caused the campaign to lose some supporters, either because they did not agree with all of the points, or because the list omitted an area that a supporter felt most important. Change, short and simple, spoke to many and could incorporate the overall sentiment that change in leadership style, administrative priorities, and governmental oversight was necessary. Also, this message incorporated the more subtle message of "hope."

A campaign must be more than a series of contacts and a hodgepodge of bumper stickers, press releases, posters, telephone calls, and mailings—no matter how frequent, consistent, or effective. Above all, a campaign must establish an emotional connection between the candidate and the electorate, a connection that actually allows people to comprehend the differences among candidates and to choose from among them by voting for one (Libby, 1999). To establish this connection, the candidate cannot rely on the communication of facts alone. Instead, there must be contact with individual voters where they are, in terms of both geography and interest. It must be as persuasive a contact as possible to gain their support on election day (Kleinkauf, 1982). As social workers, we understand the power of emotions, and campaigns rely on this fact. The challenge for the campaign is to determine what will generate enough emotion for a citizen to vote for the candidate (Reisch, 1993). One emotional issue used by many candidates is crime. Even though the national crime rate has decreased over time, the emotional fear of becoming a victim of crime is a powerful motivator. The more information you have, the better able you are to tug at the strings that lead a voter to behave as you wish (Selnow, 1994). This may seem unethical to the social worker, yet a basic premise of practice is to start where the client is. In a campaign, a candidate must know where the voters are.

In addition to an emotional connection with voters, a campaign must have a strategic management of resources. Irrespective of its level, intensity, or field, the major resources of a campaign are time, money, and people. Because these resources are limited, they must be mobilized, developed, and stretched as far as possible to enable the campaign to contact and persuade enough voters to provide the winning margin.

The amount and use of each of these resources depends on each of the other resources, as well as on external factors influencing the campaign. For example, when time is short, more people are needed to work on the campaign, whereas when time is plentiful, tasks can be spread among fewer people. Alternatively, when money is plentiful, time and people are less crucial.

No matter how abundant these resources are, all campaigns strive to increase the supply. And finally, no campaign can survive without access to all three types of resources.

Time

After the campaign has begun, time becomes limited. The election date represents a deadline that cannot be changed. Therefore, the amount of time available will greatly influence how money and people are used. Most election races are about five or six months long. However, the higher the office being sought, the more time the campaign will need to plan strategy, raise funds, and recruit volunteers. Presidential campaigns, for example, now tend to begin as much as four years before election day.

Some campaigns are relatively brief—for instance, when a legislator resigns, dies, or is impeached and a special election is held, or when a primary election occurs in a district where one party predominates. When time is available, money can be raised and volunteer activity can be extended over the full length of the campaign. The longer the time frame, the easier it is to raise funds, plan strategy, or even do with less money and fewer people.

All too often, as election day approaches, the working days of the campaign staff and volunteers become longer, with everyone involved working sixteen- to eighteen-hour days, seven days a week in an attempt to maximize use of the time available. Thus, in a good campaign, care is taken that the staff, the volunteers, and the candidate do not become fatigued to the point of feeling disenchanted with the campaign or disconnected from the constituents.

Money

Campaigns are costly. Expenses in a campaign can vary from $15,000 to $100,000 for a local city or county race to millions of dollars for a federal senatorial or presidential race. The higher the office or the larger the district, the greater the campaign costs. In addition, if volunteers are scarce, greater financial resources will be needed to hire or purchase the services necessary to successfully execute the campaign. Cash is the one resource flexible enough to meet any need that may arise. For example, if envelopes must be addressed and the campaign has a large number of volunteers to address them, the money saved can be used on advertising, but if the number of volunteers is limited, the campaign can hire outside help and use the vol-unteers for a more important task, such as canvassing.

Volunteers cannot help with certain tasks or may lack the skills to do so. For example, a U.S. senator cannot produce television advertising using volunteers alone. Office space, equipment, and other such necessities cannot always be donated or loaned to a campaign. In fact, if these items are provided by supporters, they are considered campaign contributions and must be reported to the election commission.

Both federal and state statutes are quite precise as to the categorization of in-kind and cash contributions, the permissible amounts of each, and the way in which disbursements are made throughout the campaign. These statutes place ceilings on total campaign contributions and on the amount and type of contribution that can be accepted from any one source.

On numerous occasions, very wealthy individuals have literally tried to buy themselves a legislative seat by using their financial resources to purchase advertising, supporters, and so forth. Often this has been to no avail. Although finances can compensate to some extent for a lack of volunteers, it is difficult to run a successful campaign without community support.

People

Although trite, it is nevertheless true that government in the United States is of the people and by the people. There is no way in our system of government to become an elected official without the help and support of people—both constituents and volunteers.

The people who work on a campaign are crucial not only to get the work done but also to keep up the image of the campaign. The emotional support, energy, and enthusiasm of volunteers who are also constituents often provide the best adver-tising possible, especially when it becomes evident that their efforts are contributing to the candidate's momentum and likelihood of success. For example, if 100 volunteers turned out to work on a rally, it would be clear that that many people support and believe in the candidate. The lower the level of the race, the more im-pressive a large turnout is because the support of 100 volunteers for a candidate in a county commissioner's race is much more impressive than the same turn-out would be for a U.S. Senate race.

Each campaign needs as many constituent volunteers as possible. Efforts have been made to "carpetbag" (to suddenly move into a district and run for office) not only the candidate but also the entire volunteer team. These efforts rarely succeed.

Campaign Management

A successful campaign not only requires time, people, and money, but also needs these resources early. Therefore, it is in the potential candidate's best interest to make an early decision to run, to find endorsers, and to recruit volunteers. Lining up volunteers, money, and other support early may deter some competitors and create a winning attitude for the candidate and often will induce others to jump on the bandwagon.

Essential to the operation of any campaign, no matter how compelling its theme or the candidate's personality, is an effective campaign plan. If the campaign theme is the message to be conveyed to voters, the campaign plan is the sequence of specific activities, all carefully budgeted, by which this message is to be conveyed.

Campaign management begins with a period of research. The necessary research includes a thorough assessment of the name recognition, physical appeal, background, and previous experience of both the prospective candidate and the opposition. It is important to know whether the candidate is effective in a debate situation or in front of television cameras. For example, President Obama is a master orator, whereas his 2008 opponent, Senator John MacCain, was better at person-to-person encounters.

Additional research must be done on the electorate to determine the demographics of the district. Is it young or old, middle class or poor? Also necessary is an assessment of the political climate to determine how many candidates will be in the race, whether it will pit an experienced politician against a newcomer, whether gender will be an issue, and what the voters are looking for. In lower-level races, this is done by talking with people in the community. At higher levels, comprehensive opinion polls are conducted. To offset any imbalance of time, money, or people, it is necessary to review the resources likely to be available to the candidate (Hamilton and Fauri, 2001).

Surprisingly, most campaign pollsters do not base their sample upon the population of all citizens of voting age. As is widely known, in the United States substantial numbers of eligible voters do not actually cast their ballots on election day.

Campaigns have learned through much hard experience that it is more efficient to concentrate their efforts on "likely voters" rather than to try to convince all eligible citizens that is it worth their while to vote. Accordingly, the first few questions on most survey instruments try to ascertain how likely it is that the citizen being questioned will actually vote. The interviewer will thank the unlikely voters and move on to other calls. As a result, campaign communications strategy is built around the interests of likely voters, and campaigns rarely make major efforts to attract votes among hard core nonvoters. (Atherton, date unknown)

Because campaigns require the performance of a variety of tasks, it is useful to recruit as many volunteers as possible with skills in interaction, finances, planning, graphic design, and other skills required to run a campaign. An accurate assessment of the volunteers' numbers, skills, and available time must be made at the outset of the campaign, and these resources must be continuously monitored throughout. This allows campaign managers to make the best use of talent and time and prevents volunteers from experiencing burnout or feeling underused.

Following the initial assessment, a campaign plan is developed to tie the resources to specific timed and budgeted programs that will be used to reach voters. If this is done before the campaign actually begins, usually there will be time for laying the groundwork and testing the assumptions of the campaign strategy. All of this occurs before the general public has really started to think about an election.

Campaigns seem to be a hodgepodge of activities, efforts, and loosely organized plans of action, but all successful campaigns actually are highly planned and thought out while still appearing to be spontaneous. When a campaign appears to be off track, volunteers may become frustrated if it does not switch to an emerging issue or a new challenge (Jansson, 1999). Campaign strategists must continuously review shifts in the political winds as the campaign progresses. However, they must be very careful not to change their plans with each political shift. The result of not sticking to a strategy could be a campaign that is wishy-washy and that does not address the main issues, thus failing to persuade the constituents.

In the 2008 presidential election, for example, the Democratic presidential candidate, Barack Obama, never abandoned the major issues of his campaign even after the nation's focus turned to the economy. Obama's main concerns were health care, education, global warming, the war in Iraq, and support for the middle class. As the world economy collapsed in the midst of the campaign, Obama used the economic crisis as a means to address his issues. The proposal to develop "green jobs" was an example of addressing the economy and global warming.

The Campaign Manager: Who Really Runs the Campaign?

Often it seems that the candidate is the one who is directing and running the campaign because, indeed, it is the candidate who is seeking public office. In reality, however, the campaign is run by the campaign manager, who has an advisory committee to help determine the direction in which the campaign is and should be going. The candidate usually is a member of the committee and has input into major decisions and the general direction of the campaign, but, in fact, the candidate has only one real function in a campaign: to meet with constituents and win their votes. The management of any campaign plan requires the staffing of at least the following positions: campaign manager, treasurer, volunteer coordinator, scheduler, and fund-raiser.

The demands on a candidate's time are so great that the candidate cannot be bothered with the day-to-day elements of the campaign: deciding what should be written on a postcard, who should receive thank-you notes, how a literature drop is to be organized and executed, and the like. But no campaign manager can persuade voters as effectively as the candidate. Thus, the candidate's time must be spent talking to undecided voters, not managing people who already are working on the campaign (Kleinkauf, 1982).

A campaign manager is essential to every campaign, regardless of its size. The manager is the administrative officer of the campaign. Because of the responsibilities accorded to the campaign manager, the candidate should have a long-standing relationship with the manager and a great deal of trust in him or her. Effective managerial skills alone are not enough.

All campaigns also must have a treasurer, someone to see that money is raised, that bills are paid, and that the campaign has a solid financial plan. Many governmental reports must be filed regarding the sources of contributions, the amount contributed by each, and the disbursement of campaign funds.

Higher-level campaigns have many kinds of advisors: people who assist with issues, speech writers, schedulers, and, in some situations, even wardrobe consultants. In lower-level campaigns, a volunteer or staff person may serve in several capacities, such as volunteer coordinator and scheduler.

Voter Contact

A candidate will have varying degrees of personal contact with voters. The ideal approach is to knock on the door of someone's home, talk to the person about the campaign, and ask for the constituent's support. To have the candidate telephone an individual and ask for support is only slightly less effective. Less effective means of contact are tactics such as sending a personal note. As in lobbying, the more effort and the more personal the touch, the more effective the pitch.

For decades there were only four basic channels that could be used to contact voters: in-person contact, telephone contact, mail contact, and media contact. Today, ever-expanding technology, has made available a greater variety of options for campaigns to get their message across to the voters. Some technical advances allow the campaign to customize a message and target specific voters. Along with the use of Internet social networking, the Obama campaign gathered email addresses and cell phone numbers for texting anyone who contacted the campaign or the website or attended a rally. The campaign sent emails and text messages on a consistent basis, with targeted messages, even after the election.

To repeat, the most effective way to solicit votes is for the candidate to meet one-on-one with individual voters. In lower-level races, more opportunities exist for individual contact with voters than during a presidential race, where it is impossible to shake hands or talk with all potential voters. However, a presidential candidate will "work the crowd," shaking as many hands as possible because, as bizarre as it may sound, the individuals with whom the candidate shakes hands will be more likely to vote for the candidate than those to whom the candidate presents only an issue statement. In addition, the image of personal interaction is seen by millions in newspaper pictures, on websites, and in news broadcasts.

In-person contact, telephone contact, mail contact, and electronic methods constitute direct contact with the individual voters. As stated previously, this type of direct, systematic, and personal contact with voters is the most effective campaign technique in existence, and voters continue to be most influenced by a personal meeting with the candidate. The second most influential method is when voters meet an enthusiastic and committed volunteer. Indirect methods, such as meetings with volunteers and campaign staff, staged rallies on behalf of the candidate, and media promotion (television, radio, mailers), will affect some voters but are aimed at a general level rather than an individual one. Least effective are media contact, and, in some cases, mail pieces. These are aimed at all voters and, therefore, are indirect methods. No matter what method is chosen, the contact program must carry the basic campaign theme with an emotional hook, and it must carry it attractively, consistently, and clearly.

Targeting

Targeting is an essential voter contact strategy. The first step in targeting is to identify people who can be persuaded to vote for the candidate. The second step is to determine the emotional hook that will motivate the voter to actually vote for the candidate. It is unfortunate but true that a large proportion of the people who are of age to vote are not registered to vote. Among those who are registered and will vote, three groups exist: (1) those who will vote for the candidate regardless of any campaign activity (that is, those who vote a party, ethnic, racial, gender, or single-issue [such as abortion] line); (2) those who, for the same reasons, will not vote for a candidate; and (3) those who have not made up their minds. It is toward this last group that a campaign will target its efforts.

The goal of targeting is to concentrate resources where they will be most effective. An effective campaign tries to employ strategies in precincts or with voters that will have the greatest payoff. To determine what message should be directed to certain groups of voters, campaigns rely on public opinion polls. The historical roots of political polling run deep. The first poll may have taken place when the senate divided the people of Athens into two sides of the city, the yea votes on the east and the nays on the west. But polling found its modern voice in the 1930s and 1940s, when George Gallup improved sampling procedures. Ever since—despite a few obvious disruptions, such as the infamous Dewey–Truman blunder—polls have been trusted fixtures in political campaigns (Selnow, 1994). However, with the 2000 presidential election, the trust in polling procedures was tainted by television coverage that called the state of Florida for Democrat Al Gore in the closest election since 1960. The television networks later that night retracted their prediction as it became evident that the Florida election was extremely close, and the outcome of the presidential race was left undecided for weeks.

Based on the difficulties and casualties of election night polling in 2000—which could have changed the outcome of the election—the television networks implemented widespread changes in both their election night coverage and their polling techniques and reporting.

To avoid another close call in 2004, the Bush campaign used micro-targeting by assembling information on millions of voters in swing states like Ohio and bombarded those people with messages they wanted to hear. They targeted people who vote often and were registered Democrats, but whom the Bush team thought they had a chance of persuading. It was especially effective in targeting African American voters in Ohio. Nationally, 8% of African Americans voted for Bush, but in Ohio he received 16% of the African American vote (Hoffman, 2008).

Clearly, the more information a candidate has about voters' fears, passions, preferences, and prejudices, the greater the success of targeting. Such information helps the campaign choose where to focus and what particular topics to avoid in particular areas. With this information, the campaign staff can determine where the candidate has the best opportunity to persuade voters, that is, where the undecided or independent voters are concentrated.

As we have pointed out, a candidate does not need every vote to win, only a majority of the votes cast. Consequently, the staff must also determine where they have the greatest potential to increase turnout among voters already committed to the candidate. Efforts to increase voter turnout consist of reminding registered voters about the election, sending them campaign-paid absentee voter registration ballot applications with their names and addresses already filled out, and offering such services as babysitting or transportation to and from the voting place if needed.

Issues

It is frequently said by those who have been involved in political campaigns that nobody really cares about issues. Sadly, there is a great deal of truth in this statement. Even in presidential elections, simplified issues and one-liners can be more effective in persuading people to vote for one candidate over another than the candidate's position on the major issues of the day. The candidate's party affiliation, gender, appearance, and religious or ethnic background also can persuade a voter to support a candidate, and often these factors are more persuasive than a review of the candidate's stance on the issues.

> In the campaign process, I found multifaceted skills necessary to social work to be an essential underpinning in my campaign effort. To be frank, all campaigns, no matter how well run or well organized, can be described as going between various states of chaos. The campaign is a dynamic process which must be susceptible to changes from day to day and minute to minute. People who are involved in the

campaign process must be able to reorder and regroup quickly to meet changing circumstances and diverse demands. Being able to work within a constantly changing arena, like any good social worker, enabled me to keep the necessary momentum during the campaign process.

By organizing various grassroots organizations to assist in the nuts-and-bolts organizing of the campaign, one maintains close contact with the concerns of the community. This kind of contact with the needs of the community is essential for effective governing. Many people who serve in elected positions lose simply because they lose touch with the electorate. As long as one can maintain contact with various community groups, you will manage to keep abreast and informed of their concerns.

Edolphus "Ed" Towns, MSW
U.S. Representative (New York)

The United States is made up of a very diverse population. In this country, there are people from every ethnic background, every country, every conceivable occupation, belief, and culture. Although this diversity poses fewer problems in lower-level races, it still has some effect on election outcomes. In order to obtain the required 51 percent of the votes, candidates attempt to take a neutral stance on as many issues as their ethics allow. On the issue of abortion, for example, some candidates have stated that they are personally against abortion but would allow a woman the right to determine what is done to her body.

Political action committees and special interest groups will want to know how a candidate stands on certain issues and will base their support or opposition on this information. The public and campaign volunteers can become very frustrated with a candidate who takes a hard stance on certain issues, which can be as devastating to the campaign as refusing to take any position at all. Also, a candidate who takes one position when talking to one group and a totally opposite position when meeting with another can cause more damage to a campaign than a candidate who takes a tough stance or no stance at all. But in the last analysis, voters who decide the outcome of elections do not vote on the basis of issues; they vote after they size up the personal characteristics of the candidates (Bannon, 2005).

Because candidates tend to avoid taking positions, especially on difficult issues, the election of a sympathetic candidate does not eliminate the need for post-election lobbying and monitoring.

Political Action Committees

U.S. Senator Debbie Stabenow, MSW, has stated, "It is easier to spend a few months and some money electing the right people than to spend years and a lot of money trying to get the wrong people to do the right things" (personal communication). That is the basic concept behind political action committees (PACs).

Running for office can be expensive, especially on a state or national level. Individuals running for higher offices will utilize PACs more than local-level candidates. However, all campaigns need to know about PACs. This section is included to give a short overview to familiarize social workers on the design and purpose of PACs.

A PAC is organized to raise funds, offer financial support to candidates, and to urge the PAC membership as well as the general public to support candidates endorsed by the parent organization. To meet state and federal regulations, PACs must be independently organized and funded. Special interest groups (business, labor, professional associations, corporate employees) coordinate and systematize efforts to support candidates who are sympathetic to their particular group's special interest. The parent organization assumes that receiving assistance from a PAC may lead a potential legislator to be increasingly supportive of the PAC's positions in the future (Abrams and Goldstein, 1982).

The National Association of Social Workers and most of the state chapters have PACs called PACE (Political Action for Candidate Election). PACE may seem self-serving because they endorse candidates that support the profession; however, the candidates that receive PACE endorsement have to some degree the core value of the profession, a commitment to social justice.

People who are most critical of PACs say they are organized to purchase votes from candidates. In reality, there are important reasons for a PAC's existence: (1) to provide information about candidates and issues to members and (2) to better use resources. PACs, help individuals keep abreast of the positions represented by various congressional, state, and local candidates, thus enabling them to determine how the election of each of these candidates may affect the special interest group.

Further, a PAC can alleviate the indecision that may arise when one attempts to determine how best to use one's own resources (time, skills, money) on behalf of a candidate. A candidate is far more likely to remember the contribution of a group whose endorsement represents approval of one's policies than a number of smaller contributions from several constituents. Furthermore, unlike most individuals, a PAC usually endorses and contributes to many candidates, so its potential influence extends to a much larger segment of the total legislative body than does that of one individual.

After a PAC has gathered and reviewed data from candidates in a particular race, the members must decide not only whom to endorse but also how. There are several ways in which an endorsement can be made.

1. The PAC can endorse the candidate by stating that the membership organization (e.g., NASW) recommends that social workers vote for that candidate. This is the simplest endorsement.
2. Services and support can be offered, including mailing and telephone lists. Candidates are aware that the endorsement alone will not guarantee membership votes, but mailing lists and telephone numbers facilitate the candidate's ability to reach PAC members and to gain their support and labor.

3. A PAC can recruit and assign volunteers from its membership to assist candidates, thereby increasing the effect of the endorsement. PACE has found this to be most effective because candidates have discovered that social workers have excellent campaign skills. Social workers listen well, are organized, are trained to take a broad perspective, and can work well with a variety of individuals (Wolk, 1981).
4. The most important form of support is financial support, which allows the candidate to mold the campaign to the community.

There is some unease in some quarters about the influence of PACs and the legal side-stepping of limits placed on candidates of donations received, etc. It seems that there is no will among the former presidents, senators, and congressmen to change a system that they have benefited from. So, PACs will continue to be part of the political landscape. PACs have proliferated and are contributing substantial dollars to political campaigns. Thus, social workers should be concerned that poor people and people who are in difficult circumstances and do not make campaign contributions be represented. The increased use of the Internet to obtain large numbers of small donations may cause some movement, or at least talk about moving away from taking money from PACs. Nevertheless, candidates and the NASW will have to continue to understand and use political action committees for the time being.

Social Workers and Campaigns

Innumerable skills carry over easily from social work practice to campaigning, the most obvious being communication skills. Social workers are trained to meet people, listen to their problems, and help them find solutions. They know how to manage hostility, how to reach out to shy and quiet people, and how to deal with groups as well as with individuals (Kleinkauf, 1982). Caseloads, lack of time, and lack of familiarity with political campaigns are reasons why social workers do not get involved in campaigns. Misinterpretation of the Hatch Act and state-level versions of the act, or fear of agency reprisal has kept many more social workers from involvement as well. Regardless of the setting in which a social worker is practicing, he or she has numerous useful skills that can be employed in a campaign. Ultimately, through election of sympathetic officials, the social worker's clientele will benefit.

The most important skills a social worker can contribute to a campaign are in the area of interpersonal relationships and listening skills. These can be used in many facets of a campaign, for example, in canvassing a neighborhood for support of the candidate or in working with campaign volunteers and with the candidate.

For most candidates, the entire campaign process is a challenge to their self-confidence, and they must recognize this in order to minimize defensiveness. The social worker's interpersonal skills can be valuable in offering support and reassurance when the candidate is faced with the discouragement that inevitably occurs as the campaign progresses. Just as a candidate needs support, campaign volunteers need reassurance and motivation, which social workers can provide.

Because social workers must deal daily with a multitude of problems and people, their experience can be particularly valuable to a campaign when positions on issues are being formulated. For example, one candidate was going to take a position, in response to public pressure, that all persons convicted of sexual abuse of children should receive a minimum ten-year prison sentence. Social workers with experience in this area pointed out that 70 percent of child sexual abuse occurs in the family, that the abuser usually is the father, that the mother usually is dependent on the abuser and would have to rely on governmental aid if separated from him, that the child involved would carry the guilt of having sent the father to jail, and that ten years of imprisonment would be quite costly to society. The candidate subsequently reversed his stand and instead supported a rehabilitation program designed to deal with the problem.

Because working effectively with individuals and groups is fundamental to social work practice, social workers will find their professional methods more useful in a political campaign than they might have expected (Salcido, 1984).

A few years ago, a social worker friend asked how to become involved in a political campaign. "Just call the campaign headquarters and tell them you want to volunteer," I said, noting they will be more than eager "to get you going in the campaign."

Bill said he was somewhat unsure what he could do. "I'm only a child protective services worker. Do you think I really can help the campaign? You know, those people are experienced in this kind of stuff."

Skills and roles natural to professional social work practice are also critical and relevant to political campaigns, be they local, regional, state, or national. The core skills of social work, what we can call "people skills," are also central in a political campaign: being able to quickly engage strangers (potential voters), communicate clearly, and listen to questions with understanding and empathy.

Management and planning skills that are part of social work practice, when combined with the professional understanding of people, places social workers in the unique position of being able to contribute in significant ways to electoral efforts: Campaign manager, volunteer coordinator, and research specialist are among those campaign functions and roles a social worker can easily fill.

As with Bill, the first step in working in a campaign is to volunteer. This can be done directly with the campaign or with your colleagues. The key is to get involved: Stuffing envelopes and campaign mailers, answering phones at campaign headquarters, canvassing potential voters, and putting up yard signs are among the many tasks social workers can do to help get the right people elected.

Organize other social workers to work one weekday night for the duration of a campaign effort; Tuesday night, for example, will be known as "social workers' night." The campaign staff and candidate will be very grateful, while recognizing and remembering your efforts. Be sure to have some campaign buttons made up for your volunteers that identify your group; a good button might say "Social workers for Smith" or "Social workers vote."

Organize a group of social workers to spend a Saturday putting the candidate's signs in yards. Start a phone bank, with the campaign's approval, and call other social workers to financially support your candidate. All campaigns need money; raise some funds by using your social work phone lists, for example, NASW unit membership, and ask each person to give $5 to the candidate. If you have 200 local members, that $5 becomes a $1,000 donation. Be assured the candidate will be extremely grateful to you and your social work friends.

Be creative in your ideas and efforts. Remember, every effort, every dollar helps in a campaign. Today, Bill is an active volunteer in his political party and is far removed from his first, tentative steps in electoral politics.

Ira Colby, Ph.D.
Dean, Graduate School of Social Work
University of Houston

What to Expect When Volunteering

A committed and enthusiastic volunteer who meets with voters is an important extension of the candidate. The effectiveness of such contacts far exceeds the influence of advertising and literature. Thus, the wealth of many campaigns is a function of the number of skilled, committed volunteers who are involved.

In some campaigns, nearly every task is performed by volunteers, especially when money is a scarce resource. Some volunteer assignments, in addition to campaign planning, canvassing, and policymaking, are as follows:

Addressing envelopes
Babysitting for voters or workers
Canvassing (both door to door and by telephone)
Clipping newspaper articles
Computer skills of any kind
Copying
Delivering news releases
Distributing advertising items at the polls
Doing research, writing, artwork, and the like
Driving voters to the polls
Getting out mailings
Leafleting or letter drops
Looking up telephone numbers
Making posters
Monitoring news programs
Organizing candidate coffees
Organizing fund-raising events
Preparing voter lists
Putting up signs
Recruiting additional volunteers
Running errands
Serving as messengers
Serving as poll watchers
Soliciting contributions

Often social workers who are just beginning campaign work feel frustrated when they are not allowed a great deal of input regarding issues and public concerns but instead are asked to do tasks such as those listed previously. They feel that their skills are not being used to the fullest, that they would rather use their expertise and skills in managing, consulting, and writing issue papers for the candidate. Indeed, a social worker may have these abilities and the ability to play that role in some campaigns. However, it is usually the campaign manager who has established a solid working relationship with the candidate that is essential to a successful campaign.

The best way for a social worker to be accorded more responsibility in a campaign is to become involved in it very early and to establish a good working relationship with the candidate. Nonetheless, regardless of when a social worker enters the campaign, one can make adequate use of other social work skills in conjunction with a variety of campaign tasks, most notably in dealing with people. Tasks may include making telephone calls in response to inquiries or personally contacting constituents. The core of a campaign is interaction with people, and who is better equipped for that than a social worker?

In reality, a campaign is a lot of hard work. It entails many long hours of tedious chores, such as those listed previously. Many volunteers become dismayed when they work on a campaign because they do so much tedious work, but if the campaign is in tune with the volunteers, they will be shown that what they are doing is an integral part of reaching the campaign's major goal—winning the election.

Social workers understand particularly well the need for balancing volunteer activities, work, and family. However, they must be aware of certain unique characteristics of a campaign in order to survive and be effective. The following are some problems that social workers may encounter within a campaign:

1. The political campaign organization, in contrast to a structured social work agency, is temporary and loosely organized and as such may not be responsive to the psychological and emotional needs of its workers (Salcido, 1984).
2. Conflicts in values and expectations often exist among the diverse groups and numerous individuals involved in a political campaign. For example, not all campaign workers (or even the candidate) may really care about human service issues.
3. Some of the political campaign's administrative and personnel problems, such as stress and uncertainty, are so common that they are considered intrinsic to campaign work and left untouched (Salcido, 1984).
4. There is always a lack of time to deal with individual constituent's problems.
5. The many clerical activities that must be performed during a campaign, such as stuffing envelopes, can be discouraging to campaign volunteers.
6. Lack of concern within the campaign about issues plus great concern about money can be discouraging to social work volunteers.

7. The pursuit of one goal, winning the election, leaves both the volunteers and some issues as a secondary concern.
8. Social workers may want the candidate to meet their colleagues, but the candidate, feeling this group is likely to give its support in any event, may consider such a trip a waste of limited resources that could be used to persuade undecided voters.

One benefit of working on a campaign, in addition to having the candidate's ear, is that the social worker will make a great many contacts in the legal, business, and commercial fields, as well as in other areas of the community. As a result of such contacts, social workers will often discover shared interests and concerns where none might have been thought to exist. A real estate agent, for example, may be supporting the social worker's candidate for the same reason as the social worker, namely, lack of adequate housing in the community. Such encounters can prove mutually enlightening. The real estate agent may gain insight into the need for low-cost housing, whereas the social worker may learn that an adequate supply of mortgage money at reasonable interest rates is needed for families to buy homes.

Almost all elected officials started in local elected positions like school boards and municipal governments. Often candidates for local election do everything from fund raising to door-to-door canvassing and campaign literature themselves. This is really grassroots social work at its best, building support one person, one street, and one group at a time. A social worker helping local-level candidates not only impacts the local community, but as elected officials are elected to a higher office, one's influence is also increased. Start early and start local.

Diane Marseglia, LCSW
Bucks County Commissioner, Pennsylvania

Postscript
Commissioner Marseglia ran six campaigns, losing three and winning three.

How to Volunteer for a Campaign

It might seem ridiculous to include a section on how to volunteer for a campaign, but all too often campaigns start quickly with a core group known to one another, and after a brief period, volunteer recruitment largely ceases. Later, the campaign becomes so hectic and confusing that volunteers feel lost and unsupported and drop out.

As previously mentioned, it is best to become involved in a campaign very early. In many instances, a good time to make one's interests known to a prospective candidate is January of an election year. Local party offices gener-ally are quite willing to assist volunteers in connecting with prospective candidates.

The best approach is to make yourself known to the candidate or the cam-paign manager and ask for an assignment. If one has the skills and the desire to do certain jobs on the campaign, that information should be made known. If your interest is not acknowledged, press again for some form of assignment. It must be remembered that, given the lack of time and the pressures of a campaign, volun-teers may fall through the cracks and not be adequately supported or thanked. A person wishing to volunteer often must persist long enough to make it clear that there really is a desire to help. Volunteers should indicate the number of hours and the level of commitment they are willing to give. In return, the volunteer should be given a clear description of what the job will entail and any deadlines that must be met.

Even if social workers feel their skills and abilities are not being used to the fullest, it is wise not to drop out of the campaign. Because of the pressure and the timing of any campaign, the campaign planning committee must be sure that vol-unteers are adequately dedicated to the campaign and that they can be trusted with major responsibilities. Given the highly sensitive nature of a campaign, the short time frame, and the amount of work involved, candidates must be careful in assigning responsibility. A key task left undone can badly damage the chances for achieving the campaign's goal.

Finally, it is important to publicize the fact that social workers are working on a particular campaign. Not only will elected officials know that you assisted in their victory but they and other legislators also will know that politically active social workers do exist. Such knowledge may lead the legislators involved to look more favorably on subsequent lobbying efforts by other members of the social work profession.

Conclusion

The campaign is probably the most confusing component of the political process, yet it is at the very heart of the system. Participation in a successful political campaign can enhance the effectiveness of subsequent lobbying and monitoring of government agencies and legislation. The campaign offers both excitement and tedious work, and the payoff to the individual social worker and to the profession is much greater than it appears on the surface.

Social workers must realize that their skills can be used in various segments of the political arena but are especially useful during a campaign. There is no greater satisfaction than knowing an elected representative has an understand-ing of and sympathy for the values exemplified by social work and will respond when a social worker wishes to address, endorse, or recommend a piece of legislation.

Social workers should run for public office, advocate before the legislature on policy and budget issues, and go to work in the legislative and executive branch agencies. The best way to have an impact on policy development is to be an active participant in the process.

David Knutson, Senior Research Analyst, House of Representatives
Children and Family Services Committee
Washington State Legislature
(Influencing State Policy, 1999)

All Social Work Is Political, So . . .

1. Review different campaign slogans, and determine for each what message the candidate is conveying. Surmise from a campaign slogan what positions you think the candidate would have on issues, and then check the position statements to determine whether your assumptions are accurate.

2. Contact the state NASW office and ask whether there are any social workers running for public offices.

3. Find out when the next election in your area will be held, when the filing date is for candidates, and what the requirements are to run.

4. Volunteer to work on a campaign. Determine what types and amount of influence you gain from the work you have done.

Suggested Readings

Brager, George A. 1968. "Advocacy and Political Behavior." *Social Work* 13 (April): 5–15.
Kleinkauf, Cecilia. 1982. "Running for Office: A Social Worker's Experience." In *Practical Politics: Social Work and Political Responsibility*, Maryann Mahaffey and John Hanks (eds.), pp. 181–194. Washington, DC: National Association of Social Workers.
Salcido, Ramon M. 1984. "Social Work Practice in Political Campaigns." *Social Work* 29 (March–April): 189–191.

References

Abrams, Harvey, and Sheldon Goldstein. 1982. "A State Chapter's Comprehensive Political Program." In *Practical Politics: Social Work and Political Responsibility*, Maryann Mahaffey and John W. Hanks (eds.), pp. 241–260. Washington, DC: National Association of Social Workers.
Atherton, Christopher. www.usembassy-israel.org.ilpublish/elections/arter.htm. Published date unknown. U.S. government public domain.
Bannon, Brad. 2005. "Campaign 101: Learning from Major Campaigns, Offers Insights into Running Local Elections" *Winning Campaigns Magazine*. Retrieved March 4, 2009 from http://www.completecampaigns.com/article.asp?articleid=90
Hamilton, David, and David Fauri. 2001. "Social Workers' Political Participation: Strengthening The Political Confidence of Social Work Students." *Journal of Social Work Education* 37 (2): 321–332.
Hoffman, Auren. August 25, 2008. "It Takes Tech to Elect a President." *Business Week Online* p. 6

Influencing State Policy. Fall 1999. "Student Projects." *Influence* 3.2: 10.

Jansson, Bruce S. 1999. *Becoming an Effective Policy Advocate.* Belmont, CA: Brooks/Cole.

Kleinkauf, Cecilia. 1982. "Running for Office: A Social Worker's Experience." In *Practical Politics: Social Work and Political Responsibility*, Maryann Mahaffey and John Hanks (eds.), pp. 181–194. Washington, DC: National Association of Social Workers.

Libby, Ronald T. 1999. *Eco-Wars: Political Campaigns and Social Movements. Power, Conflict, and Democracy.* New York: Columbia University Press.

Reisch, Michael. 1993. "The Social Worker in Politics as a Multi-Role Group Practitioner." In *Social Work with Groups: Expanding Networks*, Stanley Wenocur et al. (eds.), pp. 187–200. New York: Haworth Press.

Salcido, Ramon M. 1984. "Social Work Practice in Political Campaigns." *Social Work* 29 (March–April): 189–191.

Selnow, Gary W. 1994. *High-Tech Campaigns: Computer Technology in Political Communication.* Westport, CT: Praeger.

Wolk, James L. 1981. "Are Social Workers Politically Active?" *Social Work* 26 (July): 283–288.

11

Social Workers as Politicians

I am the first social worker in the United States Senate. Now I have a caseload of four million Marylanders! And though I am practicing in a different forum, those skills and values I learned as a community organizer in the streets of Baltimore are what make me an effective leader in the corridors of Congress.

—Barbara Mikulski*

At this point you are probability thinking: "Politician? I just want to be a social worker so I can help people." In the course of your career you will wonder—after helping a teenage mother find formula for her three-month-old child, or after helping a senior citizen pay for an emergency heating bill, or after informing a client that needed services are unavailable—how many other thousands of people may be facing the same problem. For this reason, the NASW Code of Ethics (section 6) states that the social worker's responsibility to the broader society includes political action. An obvious career choice that meets this mission is to seek political office. Clearly a social worker can multiply his or her efforts a hundredfold once elected to political office. Although few social workers consider a career as a social worker/politician, those that have taken such a career path have had far-reaching influence on the development and implementation of social policy.

The purpose of this chapter is to help budding social workers determine whether to consider a career as a social worker/politician. As your social work career progresses, we ask you to consider this career path. As you will read, social worker/politicians can have a tremendous impact on a large number of people. It must be remembered, however, that many aspects of political life are not discussed here because they are not necessarily unique to the social worker in political office.

*Barbara Mikulski is a U.S. senator (Maryland).

TABLE 11.1   *Social Workers in the 111th Congress*

Barbara A Mikulski, MSW, U.S. Senate, Maryland, Democrat
Deborah Ann Stabenow, MSW, U.S. Senate, Michigan, Democrat
Susan Davis, MSW, U.S. House of Representatives, California 49th District, Democrat
Barbara Lee, MSW, U.S. House of Representatives, California 9th District, Democrat
Ciro D. Rodriquez, MSW, U.S. House of Represenatives, Texas 28th District, Democrat
Edolphus "Ed" Towns, MSW, U.S. House of Representatives, New York 10th District,
Democrat

Source: National Association of Social Workers.

In the 111th Congress, the U.S. government spent billions of dollars on
human services, but only six social workers were members of the 535-person
Congress (Table 11.1). Although this is an increase from three social workers
in 1986, the number has remained constant through the last few election cycles.
Appropriations for human services represent a large proportion of state budgets.
The number of states with elected officials who are social workers has risen
steadily over the years. As of 2009, forty-three states and the District of Columbia
had at least one elected official from the social work field. Characteristics of these
social workers are illustrated in Tables 11.2, 11.3, and 11.4.

The material for this chapter was obtained from social workers who currently hold elected political office at the federal, state, and local levels. The data
were obtained from a questionnaire mailed in the summer of 1998 to 84 social
workers listed in the NASW publication *Social Workers Serving in Elected Office*
(1997). Questionnaires were sent to all social workers in Congress, state legislatures, and many local offices.

Questions were designed to determine unique successes and difficulties in
politics that could be attributed to a social work degree and background to holding political office. The questionnaire consisted of thirty questions: Seven gathered demographic data, such as age, gender, party affiliation, length of political

TABLE 11.2   *Social Workers in Elected Offices by Gender/Office, 2005*

	Women	Men	Total
U.S. Congress	5	1	6
State legislature	39	30	69
County/borough	21	9	30
City/municipal	32	12	44
School board	12	16	28
Total	109	68	177

Source: National Association of Social Workers. 2005. *Selected Characteristics of
Social Workers in Elected Offices.* Washington, DC: NASW. www.naswdc.org.
Copyright 2005, National Association of Social Workers, Inc.

TABLE 11.3 *Social Workers in Elected Offices by Race/Ethnicity/Office, 2005*

	African American	Asian American/ Pacific Islander	Caucasian	Hispanic/ Latino	Unknown
U.S. Congress	2		4	1	
State legislature	16	1	47	5	
County/borough	5		17	4	
City/municipal	7	4	33	3	1
School board	6	2	17	1	2
Total	36	7	118	13	3

Source: National Association of Social Workers. 2005. *Selected Characteristics of Social Workers in Elected Offices.* Washington, DC: NASW. www.naswdc.org. Copyright 2005, National Association of Social Workers, Inc.

TABLE 11.4 *Social Workers in Elected Offices by Credential/Office, 2005*

	BSW	MSW	DSW	Unknown
U.S. Congress		6		
State legislature	8	58	3	1
County/borough	4	22		4
City/municipal	5	37		1
School board		22	2	4
Total	17	145	5	10

Source: National Association of Social Worker. 2005. *Selected Characteristics of Social Workers in Elected Offices.* Washington, DC: NASW. www.naswdc.org. Copyright 2001, National Association of Social Workers, Inc.

service, and educational degrees; the remaining twenty-two questions were open ended and were intended to elicit information about the path to this political position. Topics included mentors, support from social workers, and any successes or problems these respondents experienced as politicians that were related to their social work training. These social worker/politicians were also asked to provide advice for other social workers who might be interested in running for elected office.

Respondent Characteristics

Of the eighty-four social worker/politicians to whom questionnaires were mailed, thirty-one returned completed surveys, a response rate of 37 percent. The majority of respondents were between forty-five and sixty-four years of age, and 80 percent were Democrats. An equal number of women and men responded. Among respondents, 93 percent held MSW degrees and 13 percent held both BSW and MSW degrees. Although the respondents' length of political experience ranged from two to twenty-eight years, 32 percent had held political positions for more than eleven years. Of the thirty-one respondents, one was in the U.S. Congress, twenty-five were in state legislatures, and five held elected positions at the local level.

Deciding to Run

Few individuals who attend a graduate or undergraduate program in social work intend to become politicians. Because few programs provide curriculum or field instruction about political skills and political office, the idea of running for office generally occurs later in a social worker's career and not directly as a result of social work education. In fact, there are reports that some social work programs hold that political preparation or political field placements might run counter to CSWE standards or public funding (Wolk, Pray, Weismiller, and Dempsey, 1996).

The social worker/politicians who responded came from varying backgrounds: clinical, administrative, and community organizing. The reasons that these social workers decided to run for office were wide ranging and likely representative of any candidate's decision: the availability of a vacant seat and previous political involvement in campaigns or in a political party. Several, however, described direct linkages between social work values and the desire to run. One legislator from North Dakota explained:

> Clients presented problems which were societally based, not client initiated, and it was frustrating to know that I was only applying Band-Aids. Professional social work education led me to the social work code of ethics which requires political involvement.

Eventually these social workers realized that more could be accomplished if they were actually in a political position, thus awakening in them the idea of running for office (Kleinkauf, 1982). Interestingly, all initially discounted the idea of running because they believed that a law degree was necessary for success.

Once awakened to the idea of running for office, many floundered while seeking guidance about how to begin. Because there are no formal means of obtaining such training, social workers who wish to enter the political arena need the benefit of informal support and guidance. When asked where they found this support, 77 percent said that they had had a mentor. The majority of the mentors were politicians; four were social workers. One of the political mentors was described as a community organizer, and another became a social worker after the candidate achieved election. Most of these social worker/politicians have mentored others. Quite obviously there are fewer opportunities to be mentored by a social worker/politician, but the social worker candidate benefits greatly from assistance from someone who knows the political scene, shares similar values, and is supportive.

Several problems are unique to social workers who wish to establish a political career.

1. The agencies in which social workers are employed are often reluctant to support the worker's candidacy for political office, citing "politics" as the reason. Private agencies fear alienating any of their sources of community support. This is particularly true for agencies that rely on community funding. Nor do agency executives want to offend board members who may hold views other than the candidate's on major campaign issues. In state-funded agencies, difficulties arise from state Hatch Acts, which often prohibit this type of employee political activity.

2. Agencies usually do not have the flexibility to allow social workers time to campaign. Attorneys in private practice may be able to reduce workloads during a campaign, unlike social workers, who generally are in full-time staff positions. Social workers in this situation may be forced to take a leave of absence without pay or to resign in order to campaign. This action can create extreme financial difficulties because social workers usually are paid less than other professionals.

3. The limitation of personal financial resources, already strained by the necessity of a leave of absence, will restrict the amount of money available to finance a first-time campaign. All of the respondents noted that funding for a first-time campaign must come from the candidate's own resources.

4. Compared with other professions, the social worker/politician has a limited ability to garner campaign support. Attorneys, for example, often can obtain support from their clients, who frequently represent a potentially powerful group of contacts. Social workers, however, cannot ethically use their clients, nor do their clients traditionally have influence or the resources likely to assist one in obtaining an office.

Although this list of obstacles is unique to social workers who run for political office, none of our respondents perceived the obstacles as monumental. They did, however, emphasize the need to convince a potential social worker/politician that the goal of political office is worth the effort necessary to overcome these obstacles.

Once a social worker decides to run for office, he or she must be doubly able: determined but also able to withstand losing. This fact was pointed out by all who had lost an election. Every social worker mentioned the need for determination. Many indicated that difficulty arose because of their belief in a life that balances work and family—a value the social work profession also advocates. This problem, which will be discussed later, also occurred while respondents were in office.

Building a Constituent Base

Financial support and volunteer efforts are the key elements in a campaign and, later, for success in office. These indispensable resources are particularly important to social worker/politicians. If money is limited, volunteers become even more important to counterbalance this deficit. Although campaign costs varied, volunteer time, skills, and ideological support were of significant importance to all interviewed.

Although the number of supporters is important, the amount of power these contributors have in terms of income, education, or status is also important. That is, to be elected and to remain in office, the candidate must be connected to a broad spectrum of people. Relating only to selected segments of the population, such as social workers, the poor, or African Americans, can easily lead to "labeling" and potential stigmatization. Furthermore, a broad constituent base enhances credibility.

It is well to remember, therefore, that many political issues may fall outside the scope of social work concerns. A social worker/politician must be able to assess ideologies other than those associated with social work. One of the politicians interviewed found himself in the middle of a community conflict between environmentalists and industrial developers over development of a shopping mall. The social work profession obviously does not have a position on such an issue; the social worker/politician formulated his position after assessing his constituents' opinions on this issue.

Given the small numbers in the population who are social workers and the relatively low priority that social workers give to political action, reliance on social workers as a constituent base is unwise, limiting, and potentially harmful to an aspiring social worker/politician. Building bridges to other professions and professional associations, such as lawyers, teachers, and psychologists, is essential for getting elected (Keith-Lucas, 1975). This is not to suggest that social workers creating a constituent base for a campaign should refrain from asking other social workers for support. Only 16 percent of the survey respondents did not ask other social workers for either financial or volunteer support; of the 84 percent who did ask, many received some type of support.

Social workers may view themselves as being ideologically opposed to many of their constituents—perhaps blue-collar workers, on the one hand, and the upper class on the other. As guardians of the "underdogs," social workers too often have taken a simplistic view of organized labor or the privileged elite as their opponents on social issues. It would be wise to view these groups (and others) as potential collaborators; what is in the best interest of the social work client often coincides with the best interest of the general community. Not only is this approach important for getting elected but generally it is also the only way a politician can be elected.

The economic crisis of 2008–2009, with corporate bailouts, high unemployment, and home foreclosures, could well unite organized labor, social workers, and corporate CEOs to seek solutions that benefit all, that is, solutions that provide incentives to employers to create jobs that also benefit the environment, national infrastructure, and other social issues. Certainly, labor unions and the social work profession have common objectives with respect to this goal.

Although the background of the survey respondents was varied, many had participated in community organizing, civic activities, political staff positions, or campaign work. These experiences likely enabled them to use their knowledge and connections to develop a constituent base. Three respondents had been assistants to state or national legislators; among the others were a borough president, a district leader, a precinct captain, the chair of a city political party, and a delegate to a national political convention; and three had served in community leadership roles (a planning and zoning commission, a community development commission, and a housing authority commission). These activities plus their social work positions provided many opportunities to establish linkages, gain experience, and build constituent bases.

Building or expanding a constituent base should not be attempted solely on the basis of the candidate's position on key issues. In the tradition of grassroots organizing, soliciting input on individual and community needs and on the relative importance of community problems is an excellent method for identifying and involving potential supporters.

Campaigning

A central question that immediately confronts the social worker who decides to run for elective office is whether to publicize a social work background or minimize it in the campaign. Although 95 percent of respondents acknowledged their social work backgrounds, their perception of its utility in their campaigns was mixed: Thirty-three percent noted that it helped, 39 percent did not think it made a difference, and 20 percent believed it hurt them. Those who described their social work background as helping their campaigns included comments such as these:

> Yes, it helped. People saw a strong fighter willing to do anything for the community. (New York legislator)

> Yes, I think it helped because people felt that I could identify with their problems because of my training and background. (U.S. congressman)

> Yes, I think it helped people trust me (they didn't trust lawyers or real estate developers). (California county official)

> Yes, I believe it was helpful as I stressed social work ethics and values of confidentiality, neutrality, service to others. (Arkansas local official)

> Yes, [it] helped show an ability to empathize and relate to people's problems. (Maryland legislator)

> Yes, people know social workers are compassionate and knowledgeable. (Kentucky legislator)

Depending on one's view, those who described using social work identification in their campaigns as hurting the campaign noted:

> Some opposition painted me as promoting dependency. (Illinois legislator)

> I was labeled as a tax-and-spend champion of social programs. (California legislator)

One U.S. congressman effectively used his MSW credentials and social work experience in a race against an attorney, convincing the voters that he had "people" experience, whereas his opponent had only "legal" experience. However, a state representative who chose to emphasize her social work background was unfavorably labeled as a "welfare queen." Despite this labeling, this social worker/politician won this race and eventually was elected to the state senate and is now a U.S. senator. And one Texas state legislator quipped, "My opponent accused me of being a 'liberal social worker from New York City,' but I won! I used my social worker organizing skills to organize my campaign and emphasized health and human service issues." One's decision is probably influenced by the demographic, political, and ideological characteristics of the total constituency, as well as by the campaign's major issues and the opponent's tactics. For example, if raising welfare allowances, which would raise taxes, is a volatile issue in a wealthy district, flaunting an MSW may not improve popularity. However, if legislation is pending to reimburse inhome care of the elderly (Medicaid waiver) and the district is an aged or aging one, a social work platform may be highly attractive.

The question is not whether the social worker/politician should deny the social work identity but whether the longerterm benefit of election to office warrants emphasizing or minimizing it. As one of the interviewees mentioned, "One should always tell the truth—but not always the entire truth." Related to this dilemma is a second question: Should one always adopt a position consistent with one's social work background, or a position reflecting that of the constituent majority, should it differ from the candidate's own? In a Catholic neighborhood, an avid pro-choice stance is unlikely to win votes. This is not to suggest that one's social work training be forgotten but that the candidate temporarily might need to subjugate it to the immediate goal of gaining office.

In addition to such concerns as one's position on the issues, there is also the matter of campaign skills. Where did these social worker/politicians acquire their campaign skills? Many noted that they acquired them from their mentors, by working on various campaigns and attending campaign training seminars, and from their social work education. The skills most necessary for success, according to the respondents, are varied.

1. The "people" skills of listening, responding, persuading, and caring are of primary importance. Historically, these are the core generic skills for social work. Regardless of their area of specialization, all social worker/politicians interviewed noted the importance of these skills to politicians and emphasized that they had been acquired during their social work education. If there is something new for the social worker/politician to learn, it is how to transfer these skills to nonclients (constituents) and to larger groups.
2. Political skills, such as linking, brokering, and advocacy, also part of generic social work training, are invaluable on the campaign trail, where proof may be acquired of the candidate's ability to deliver for the constituency. Again, the social worker may need only to transfer these skills from case (individual) to class (constituent) brokering and advocacy.

3. Other important political skills include the abilities to consider alternative solutions to problems and to attempt to achieve consensus during a campaign. A demonstrated capacity to seek multiple solutions to a problem may lead voters to view the candidate as flexible, open to compromise, and creative. Achieving consensus requires skills in group process, conflict resolution, and persuasion: All of these characteristics are essential to success in both political life and social work practice. Several social worker/politicians did note one deficit in social work training: the omission of strategies and skills for dealing with confrontation.

4. Negotiation and mediation are prime political skills that are not incompatible with social work practice. Clinicians negotiate daily with clients to arrive at clinical contracts regarding problem assessment, diagnosis, and treatment. Although political negotiations may seem more underhanded and less open than negotiations to establish contracts with clients in treatment, the negotiation and mediation skills used are the same, and both are necessary for the achievement of mutually agreeable and beneficial ends.

Realities of Office

Like members of the general public, social workers often have misconceptions about the benefits and costs of holding political office. Therefore, we asked our respondents about the realities of being an elected representative. These questions covered changes in the office holder's economic and social status after being elected and the effect on family life. Some openended questions about the difficulties, problems, and benefits were included.

Holding a political office received mixed reviews from the respondents, all of whom enjoyed their jobs but reported problems as well as benefits. An obvious benefit is the power to influence decisions. One social worker said what he liked most about his job was power. An elected representative not only has a vote in policy decisions but also has access to the media and can thereby attempt to increase public awareness of social problems.

A social worker/politician can also sensitize other legislators to human needs. For example, one respondent related a story about transportation tickets that were being provided in large quantities for use by the county's commissioners. The majority of the commissioners wanted to use them as political chips. The social worker on the commission, however, demonstrated that senior citizens were in need of free transportation and convinced the other legislators that use of the tickets by senior citizens could be both a sound social policy and good political practice because senior citizens are dependable voters.

> It is not unusual for a political candidate with a social services background to believe that s(he) possesses some special insight into the problems the constituency faces. Nor is it unusual for that successfully elected candidate to feel that the election was a public referendum confirming [his or her] worldview and the implications that view has toward solving societal problems.

Imagine the rude awakening the newly elected official receives when fellow elected officials (possessing the same egocentric delusional beliefs) do not share the same vision of education, local community, county, state, or national issues. Having served a decade on a local board of education and on a town council, I admit to having suffered from this political hubris. In the spirit of helping others avoid the trauma of this reality, I believe there are five laws all aspiring legislators need to learn:

1. New politicians need to learn how to count. Unless your vision for change has the necessary votes for passage, it will fail. Humor aside, this is a profound insight for most new legislators.
2. The United States is not a democracy. The majority does not rule. Rather, this is a representative form of government in which legislators have been chosen to exercise their best judgment. Exercising one's best judgment does not mean following the polls or the crowd in attendance the night of the public meeting.
3. There are no good decisions. Every time policymakers vote they choose from a set of proposals that will harm someone's interests. Hopefully, as an elected official you will choose the least harmful proposal to implement. To illustrate, to protect the spotted owl will increase unemployment in the lumber industry, to save funding for the Center on Substance Abuse Prevention may mean transferring funds from the Safe and Drug-Free Schools budget in the Department of Education, and to relax air pollution standards in order to increase industry profits will increase the incidence of lung disease and increase the pollution of the environment.

   Further, consider this situation. The necessary votes to dramatically change welfare programs are there. As a lawmaker, you do not support the act, but you do not have the ability to stop its passage. In exchange for your support and that of your colleagues, the majority of other lawmakers are willing to increase child care support provisions, not punish adolescent mothers and their infants, and provide greater flexibility in administering the program. Do you now support a bill you truly dislike? Not an easy decision, is it? In short, every choice entails a loss.
4. Politics is the art of the possible, not the ideal. The phrase *checks and balances* is most often used to describe the process of our government. To achieve the passage of a budget, an ordinance, or a law requires that numerous bodies concur. To reach the necessary majority often means compromising the original language in the motion. For the elected representative, it may mean exchanging support on another issue that is important to a fellow elected member. The business of government, because of this inclusionary process, is messy. Still, no other system as respectful of the rights of others has evolved.
5. Remember most, that "good" politicians increase the possibilities. Representative government means that all constituents have the opportunity to provide input into the legislative process. To avoid the paralysis that would otherwise accompany this reality, politicians must be willing to negotiate and willing to find ground upon which a majority can stand.

Thomas P. Gullotta, MSW
Former Member of the Glastonbury Board of Education
and Vice Chairman of the Glastonbury Town Council
Glastonbury, Connecticut

One difficulty noted by the respondents is the need at times to compromise social work values for political necessity. Such a compromise was described by a state representative who had been working unsuccessfully to change the juvenile code. During a past legislative session, a bill was introduced, with the urging of the Sheriffs' Association, that would have imposed limits on the incarceration of juveniles. The Sheriffs' Association's motive was to reduce costs and overcrowding in the jails. The social worker/politician's motive was to prevent the jailing of juveniles. The social worker/politician supported the bill because the solution, although not ideal, was a great improvement over existing practice.

According to our respondents, some of the difficulties of being a social worker/politician were these:

> Valuing the basic worth of all individuals and believing that all folks should be treated equally fly in the face of current beliefs and attitudes. (Kansas legislator)

> Social work values can lead us to pursuing our ideals in an inflexible way, leading us to win battles and lose wars. (Michigan legislator)

Two constant problems for all politicians are keeping current on social issues and responding to the continual demands and problems of constituents. An overwhelming majority of respondents indicated that they had little difficulty in these areas, for which they credited their social work training. Many remarked on their success in this area in comparison to that of politicians who are not social workers.

> Some may think that lawyers would have an advantage in the legislative arena. That is true. Although lawyers may be better able to decipher and discuss "the law," that doesn't make them better at politics. You see, politics really has more to do with service to people than with the letter of the law or with the type of bill enacted.
>
> Before you get to the point of bill proposals, floor debates, or legislative language, you have to understand the needs of the people. It is in being able to understand the needs of the people and translate those expressed and inchoate needs into bills and laws which will serve the people. If you can't communicate and have open exchanges with the people, you will never know what they want. Social workers have the ability to communicate and to create an atmosphere where others can communicate.
>
> *Edolphus "Ed" Towns, MSW*
> *U.S. Representative (New York)*

Before running for office, some respondents believed that a law degree was necessary for political success. As Ruth Messinger, MSW, former Manhattan borough president, stated, "People should not think that you have to study law in order to go into politics." In fact, 87 percent of the survey respondents said that they would still obtain a social work degree. When asked whether they would have pursued the same career path, many said yes, and many wished that they had started the political portion earlier. When asked whether social workers could be effective in other political areas, respondents agreed that social workers need to be involved in all areas of political involvement but said that "social workers in elected office are the most influential." Many shared this sentiment expressed by an Alabama legislator: "We bring a unique vision, knowledge, and understanding to the social issues" (personal communication).

One of the myths dispelled by the respondents was that economic status is greatly improved after election to office. The reader may be skeptical, as were the authors; however, when the expenses of the campaign and of maintaining an office are deducted, one's net worth seldom increases. The general public may feel that politicians are overpaid, but in reality, social work administrators receive salaries comparable to politicians. Politicians must attend fund-raising events in return for support received during the campaign and must join many organizations to expand their constituent bases. These additional expenditures often offset any salary increase. Also, social workers, unlike attorneys, cannot anticipate an increase in paying clients after leaving political office. Improving one's short- or long-term economic status is not likely to be an incentive for a social worker contemplating this career choice.

However, politics does offer the prospect of high social status, in clear contrast to the relatively low status accorded social workers. Thus, although improved economic status may not be an incentive or reward for the potential social worker/politician, improved social status may be. Seventy-five percent of the respondents reported enhanced social status as a result of contacts and invitations received once they were in office. Despite the public's apparent distrust of politicians, they are, in fact, regarded as community leaders and persons of influence and power.

On the surface, political life appears glamorous, and indeed it may be, but in reality, there are many nonglamorous aspects. The respondents confirmed that the job requires hard work and long hours. The hours invested in political life, particularly during the campaign, strain the social worker/politician's personal life. Public exposure and scrutiny intensifies this strain. Furthermore, the demands to attend social events, glamorous or not, should be met, and constraints on family activities must be accommodated. One respondent noted that her family could not participate in any federally funded project, thus prohibiting her child from using the public swimming pool.

Although these strains are not unique to social worker/politicians, they are particularly relevant to them because of the profession's emphasis on interpersonal relationships. We did not investigate the effect of such stress on family and marital relationships; however, it is evident from the survey responses that a spouse or partner must be committed to this career choice for it to succeed. However, as an Iowa legislator mentioned, "It's the same stress of any job you take seriously and have passion about—too little time to accomplish all you would like to" (personal communication). A number of alternatives to holding elected political office also offer an opportunity to define social problems and initiate appropriate solutions. Two of the most common roles that offer such an opportunity are legislative aide and administrative appointee.

Recommendations

We asked our respondents to advise social workers interested in pursuing a political career. Their recommendations to individual social workers included the following:

1. Pay your dues. Obtain experience in precinct politics, campaigning for another candidate, and so on.
2. Be willing to ask for financial and personal support, and don't be modest about your qualifications. As an Iowa legislator commented, "To be in political office, you have to do what your mother told you not to do: beg for money and brag about yourself."
3. Be comfortable with ideological conflict and confrontation, though compromise and political savvy should be exercised.

   > Social workers are trained to build consensus and are concerned with group process . . . but the political process involves being part of difficult decisions where there are winners and losers. (Colorado legislator)

4. Be cautious about taking exaggerated liberal positions, and be aware that acting in the best interest of the client or the community may require some short-term compromise of social work ideals and values in order to achieve longer-term societal reform.

   > Be willing to work hard, to stand up for your values and beliefs, but don't be dogmatic . . . keep listening. (New Hampshire legislator)

Our respondents also offered some advice concerning social work education and organization:

1. Social work education should include content on political and legislative processes from an action-oriented perspective, not only a historical, descriptive approach. Content on class advocacy, a highly valued social work ideal, should be reintroduced into all courses.
2. The policy course should include experiential and skill-based assignments and should be designed for both graduate and undergraduate students.
3. Field practicum experiences for all students should include political activities, and specialized placements should be available so students can experience working on an elected official's staff, lobbying during state legislative sessions, and policy development for public and nonprofit organizations.
4. Social work organizations should become more politically active and aware. They should promote political advocacy as a legitimate professional role. Client data, which may be useful in supporting or opposing legislation, should be obtained.
5. Social work organizations must investigate most closely the legal and regulatory constraints on political activity and organizational members in order to dispel myths about these obstacles.

Conclusion

It is clear from our research that social worker/politicians recognize a congruence between political and social work skills. The vast majority of those questioned, whether they came from a clinical or a community organization background, were positive about the appropriateness and logic of social work education and training as a basis for political life.

The social worker/politicians who responded to the survey described the rewards of this career choice:

> [Politics is] an excellent arena to make our views known and win passage of important legislation. (Idaho legislator)

> The reward I have received . . . is to know that I have had a meaningful and positive impact on the lives of others and upon my community. (Utah legislator)

> You can have greater influence at the policy level than you ever can helping people one at a time. (Oregon legislator)

> Too many decisions are made affecting the clients we serve to leave it only to non–social workers. So few come with our background, and there are many who just don't grasp the approach of problem solving or understand human behavior. (Maine legislator)

Although the pitfalls and difficulties of political office were recognized, almost all of the respondents indicated that they wished to continue in politics and probably would do so. Although social work schools and professional organizations could initiate programs to facilitate this career choice for more social workers, the final choice, of course, rests with the individual.

> Probably the most obvious asset a social worker has as a politician is the ability to listen reflectively and express empathy with constituents. Combining our constituents' issues with our knowledge of the person in their environment makes social workers uniquely qualified to advocate for change.
>
> *Diane Marseglia, LCSW*
> *Bucks County Commissioner,*
> *Pennsylvania*

Despite the respondents' differences in timing, previous experience, and choice of first political activity, the common and recurring recommendation they gave to potential social worker/politicians is that the only absolute prerequisite for success is to get involved. Further, the evidence is conclusive that there is no reason for social workers to expect their entry into politics to be anything but successful.

> On the night I won election to the United States Senate, I gave a speech in which I thanked everyone in the room. And then I looked directly into the camera and said, "Gee, Dad, I know you're watching. I'm sorry you can't be here, but I love you, and I thank you for everything you've done for me."

You see, my father was in a nursing home in the final stages of Alzheimer's disease. He could not be with me that night because of his illness.

I had gone through quite a learning experience. I went from Congresswoman Mikulski—knowing about Alzheimer's from briefing memos, hearings, and even touring great facilities like Johns Hopkins—to Barbara Mikulski, daughter, coping with the disease in my own family.

As our family went through this, I became determined to take our personal situation and our personal tragedy and turn it into positive action. I vowed I would not only learn about it, but I would know it, I would feel it, and would do something about it.

As a social worker and a feminist, I believe you make the personal political. That is, you take the personal experiences that you live through, in terms of day-to-day experiences, and then extrapolate them into national policy.

When my father became so ill that we needed to put him into a nursing home, I discovered the issue of "spend down." The cruel rules of our government became very apparent. Those regulations required that you "spend down" all of your assets to the meager sum of $3,000 before the government would step in and help.

Essentially, those rules penalized the good guys, the families who had saved all their lives for retirement, because it put them in the same situation as the spendthrifts, those who spent all their money on round-the-world cruises or gambling trips to Atlantic City.

No one should have to deal with the fact that after a lifetime of building lives together, saying they were one family, one name, one bankbook, one checkbook, that, because the rules administered by a social service agency say so, suddenly it becomes "his money" and "her money."

My family was fortunate; we had strong bonds and a strong faith. But it wasn't just my family. The people I would talk to every Sunday at the nursing home all told of how they went from being middle class to being pauperized.

My proudest accomplishment as a United States senator was getting legislation passed that lessened the burden of "spend down." My spousal anti-impoverishment bill restored the good-guy bonus and lets couples keep more of their assets when one of them faces prolonged nursing home care.

If that had been the only change I ever made in my political career, I would still know that I had helped hundreds of people live better, more secure lives.

Barbara Mikulski, MSW
U.S. Senator (Maryland)

I was first elected to the Michigan House of Representatives in 1979. I was aware that the Michigan Friend of the Court system, the arm of the court that handles issues related to children and divorce, was not working well, especially for the children, and needed reform. After discussions with my colleagues in the House of Representatives, I found that none of them wanted to touch the issue. I was told by seasoned legislators that, indeed, it was a law that needed to be rewritten, but it was too emotional an issue since it related to divorce, custody, visitation, and child care payments. Although it was a law that had not been rewritten since it was passed in 1919, and despite the fact that a lot of constituents complained that child support was not being paid and visitation orders were not being honored, it was viewed as a political loser. There seemed to be no way of bringing consensus from what appeared to be opposing factions of mothers, fathers, attorneys, and judges. Furthermore, the most important and most harmed group in this issue, and the group which had no political power, was the children.

It needed to be done, so I decided to test my social work skills. To start, I used a basic principle of the profession. I began by determining where the client groups were, with a process of hearings, just to listen to what people had to say about the system. I spent hours listening to people talk about their particular problem. After that, I put together a very large task force of all the interested groups and spent even more time listening to people. At moments the emotions were extreme. For example, one father, trying to make a point, started banging his shoe on the table telling me: "You can't understand this because you haven't been through the system." There was so much emotion and so many viewpoints and issues that the process took many months. My staff became frustrated with the process of letting people verbalize their complaints. The staff kept telling me that we were not doing anything or getting anywhere.

I knew the need for ventilation, and I discovered that there were common patterns and common problems. Finally, all agreed that the system was not working. This agreement was the common ground on which to build. The task force started listing issues which we had been hearing and started to get more specific and more practical. We began to hone in on exactly what could be done and on some specific solutions.

Because of my social work background as a caseworker, I was knowledgeable about families and had a holistic perspective. I also had one basic question that I kept in the forefront as we went through this process: "What is in the best interest of the children?" It wasn't the children's fault that their parents were divorced; they still have the right to be cared for financially, the right to a relationship with and the emotional support of both parents. The goal of this reform had to be to protect and foster their interests.

It was important to have a multi-issue package developed to gain the necessary votes to make it a law. If I brought a package to the legislators that strengthened only child support enforcement, it would have been viewed as an anti-noncustodial bill. On a practical level, I was aware that most noncustodial parents are fathers, that most legislators are men, and that some of these male legislators pay child support. Consequently, such a single-issue approach would not gain the necessary support.

However, it was clear that custodial parents needed child care payments to be made in the best interest of the children. So we included a process to increase the rate of payment. On the other side, noncustodial parents wanted to be assured of visitation and had provided examples of the withholding of visitation, which is also not in the best interest of children. Thus, we included penalties, including jail, for withholding visitation.

Another vocal constituency in this issue was the judges, who disliked these cases because they were asked to make decisions on custody and other issues that they felt unqualified to make. They wanted it out of the judicial system. Therefore, another part of this proposed legislation included a system of automatic administrative enforcement and mediation to work out as many problems as possible before a judge became involved.

However, ironically, at first the attorneys didn't want automatic enforcement and mediation because that meant that people didn't have to hire an attorney every time a problem occurred. However, these concerns looked too self-serving for them to oppose the new changes on these grounds. A compromise was struck, allowing attorneys to do mediation as well as others.

It took two years of work, but in 1982 a package of bills to reform the Friends of the Court system became law. These changes have placed Michigan in the number one position for collecting child support in the country. Michigan was also the first state with specific enforcement requirements for visitation.

I now have quite a reputation among my colleagues for being able to bring together diverse and competing groups to reach a solution.

Debbie Stabenow, MSW
U.S. Senator (Michigan)

Postscript
Various pieces of the Michigan law were adopted by the federal government under the Reagan administration in 1984. Other states around the country are using the Michigan model and either have pilot projects or have implemented similar legislation. Ms. Stabenow, who received her MSW from Michigan State University, has received national recognition for her work on the Michigan Friends of the Court reform legislation.

All Social Work Is Political, So . . .

1. Ask an elected official if you can "shadow" her or him for a day to learn more about what it is like to hold office. Describe the experience.

2. Examine the local positions in your community to which officials are elected, and determine which would be the most viable one for a social worker to hold. Note the reasons for your choice.

3. Attend a city or county council session to determine whether you would have the expertise to deal with the issues on the agenda. If not, what education, training, or experience would you need?

4. Work on a candidate's campaign. Analyze the tasks necessary for thorough organization and running of a campaign.

Suggested Readings

National Association of Social Workers. "Why Social Workers Should Run For Office." www.socialworkers.org/pace/why_run.asp.

Mathews, Gary. 1982. "Social Workers and Political Influence." *Social Service Review* 56 (December): 616–628.

Ribicoff, Abraham. 1962. "Politics and Social Workers." *Social Work* 7 (April): 3–6.

Thursz, Daniel. 1975. "Social Action as a Professional Responsibility and Political Participation." In *Participation in Politics*, J. Roland Pennock and John W. Chapman (eds.), pp. 27–34. New York: Lieber-Atherton.

References

Keith-Lucas, Alan. 1975. "An Alliance for Power." *Social Work* 21 (March): 93–97.

Kleinkauf, Cecilia. 1982. "Running for Office: A Social Worker's Experience." In *Practical Politics: Social Work and Political Responsibility*, Maryann Mahaffey and John Hanks (eds.), pp. 181–194. Washington, DC: National Association of Social Workers.

National Association of Social Workers. 1999. *Code of Ethics*. Washington, DC: NASW Press.

———. 2005. *Social Workers Serving in Elected Office: Political Action for Candidate Endorsement*. Washington, DC: NASW.

———. 2005. *Selected Characteristics of Social Workers in Elected Offices: Political Action for Candidate Endorsement*. Washington, DC: NASW. www.naswdc.org.

Wolk, James, Jackie E. Pray, Toby Weismiller, and David Dempsey. 1996. "Political Practica: Educating Social Work Students for Policymaking." *Journal of Social Work Education* 32 (1): 91–100.

12

Your Time Is Now!

No one is the master of any craft in a day. A craft is mastered through the fine tuning of skills with experience over a lifetime. Since politics is of and for the people, social work provides an admirable apprenticeship for politics.

—Karen S. Haynes and James S. Mickelson

By now, you may be asking yourself, "Where do I start? Should I write a letter to my representative, or should I run for office? Can I really have an impact?" We asked similar questions ourselves, as has everyone who has entered the political field. We know through our own experiences that a social worker who becomes involved in the political arena will find many opportunities and challenges.

In fact, a study indicated that the strongest predictors of political participation by social workers were related to efficacy—the ability to produce the desired effect (Hamilton and Fauri, 2001). This reinforces our premise: We must include these skills in both generic and specialized programs, at both BSW and MSW levels, and beyond just a minor mention in policy courses. The greater the skill development, the greater the exposure, the more likely that the political intervention will have some or all of the desired effect. And if this study is generalizable, then the likelihood that social workers will engage more in political activity increases as those activities are experienced as obtaining the desired outcome. We also know that social workers themselves must remove the barriers to becoming involved. Therefore, we end this book with some words of encouragement and advice.

Social workers are ideally equipped to deal with the problems of a nation. I cannot think of any educational underpinning better suited to a career in government and politics than social work. Whether you see the use of a background and training in social work as a helpful thing in the field of politics may well depend on how you see politics. The definition of politics that I understand holds that politics is merely the way we decide who gets what, when they get it, and how much they can expect. In essence, politics is a means through which resources in society are divided. There are few who know better about the disbursement of resources than social workers. We see the effects that the adequate and inadequate disbursement of resources has on the lives, health, and well-being of people every day.

Edolphus "Ed" Towns, MSW
U.S. Representative (New York)

Where to Start

Throughout this book, we have tried to provide answers to this question of where to begin. Assignments at the end of a chapter let you choose a comfortable level of involvement for you to get started. Suggested readings at the ends of chapters and a Glossary of Legislative Terms at the back of the book help you understand the language used in the political arena. Additionally, because we learned that social worker/politicians need mentoring and role models to learn the practice of social work in the political arena, throughout the book we have incorporated vignettes and quotations from such social work professionals. Remember, all have asked themselves the same question: "Where do I start?"

Here are some basics. Register to vote. Then vote! Get others to register and vote. Next, determine who represents you at all levels of government—federal, state, county, and city. Just Google "my elected officials" to obtain this information, or call the state or local departments that manage voter registration and elections. Now once you obtain the mailing addresses, phone numbers, and email addresses of your representatives, you are ready to do some advocacy.

Just Do It

The first time you do anything is the hardest. Every one of the social workers mentioned in this book who has affected change remembers how she or he got started. The most common recommendation is simply "Jump in." Travis Peterson, MSW, a private practitioner, put it this way: "I advise them all to jump in and learn and use their power and influence in the political arena, just as they would in other sectors, and to encourage their clients to use their power in the same way. I do that all the time with my clients" (personal communication).

Go to city hall or the state capitol and watch the process in action. Monitor the news on issues that federal, state, and local government bodies are addressing. Think about what they are *not* addressing. Send a letter stating your opinion on how your representatives should vote or how they could better address an issue (see Chapter 7). Find fellow social workers to team up with you on an issue and share what all of you have learned. Now you have started.

Such activity is the beginning of political intervention. We are not suggesting that you become a registered human service lobbyist, or run for political office, or even write your legislator once a week, although we hope some of you think about all those actions. Political activism takes an array of forms, and once incorporated, it becomes an integral part of our everyday professional selves. Regardless of the amount of experience a social worker has in the political arena, every time a new challenge is confronted, the same question will arise: "Where do I start?" This rule of thumb is no different from in clinical practice: the earlier the intervention, the greater the influence.

Laura Facas-Sullivan, a BSW student at Rutgers University–Newark, helped to plan and organize a conference to educate social work students and the community about their responsibility to influence state policy. The goal of the conference was to stress the importance of participating by voting and lobbying and providing attendees with practical information on impacting the legislative process. Active in local politics, she was able to recruit public officials and lobbyists for discussions on a range of issues including housing, managed care, mental health, disabilities, and women. The conference attracted over 100 people from New Jersey colleges as well as licensed social workers in the community and provided them with tools to influence policy decisions at the state and local levels.

Kristine Bickham, Shelli Schade, Linda Townsend, and Terri Ellis, University of Texas at Arlington MSW students, chose to oppose the passage of state legislation that would prohibit homosexuals from adopting children or serving as foster parents, and would remove foster children already placed with parents who were found to be gay or bisexual. By participating in Texas Social Work Student Day, they were able to educate legislators about the negative impact the proposed legislation would have on foster care and adoption. They were also able to point out the dangerous precedent of setting the stage for further discriminatory legislation.

Jennifer Hentowski, a Grand Valley State University MSW student, chose to fight passage of state legislation that would permanently expel from all state public schools any student who had assaulted someone while on school property. She met with school personnel, her state representative and numerous juvenile and court officials in order to educate them about the bills and their implications. She also met with community members to discuss the positive and negative aspects of the legislation.

Source: "Student Projects: State Policy Plus Two Entries." *Influence* 3 (2): 4–5, 1999. www.statepolicy.org. Used by permission.

A combined University of Missouri–St. Louis and Washington University effort led MSW field instructor Betsy Slosar and MSW students Elizabeth Corman and Susan Luke on a three-year effort to obtain successful passage of an Individual Development Account (IDA) bill in the 1999 session of the Missouri legislature. IDA's provide up to a three-to-one match for clients' personal saving for long-term investment strategies such as post-secondary education, home ownership, and micro businesses. The students did research, recruited sponsors, drafted and redrafted the bill, monitored the progress of the bill, and mobilized support. One student said: "The experience of lobbying was priceless. It dramatically improved my public speaking, my understanding of power, and my ability to think analytically."

A group of five George Mason University BSW students collaborated to lobby for the successful passage of Item 381 of the House of Delegates' Bill 30 in the Spring, 2000, session of the Virginia General Assembly. Juan Alhucema, Kelly Downey, Karla Fife, Sarah Peidl, and Laura Winston supported Item 381 because it provided a 10 percent increase for the Virginia TANF program. No increases had been given for 15 years. The students contacted the patron of the bill, involved the university community and friends and family, wrote a flyer, and hand delivered a signed letter to each member of the conference committee. Thirty-four thousand families were affected. Students learned about the lobbying process, working as a group, and that "we are the ones who will advocate for those who cannot, mobilizing the voices and concerns of our neighbors."

Source: "Student Projects: State Policy Plus Three Entries." *Influence* 4 (2): 1–2, 2000. www.statepolicy.org. Used by permission.

Do It Early

Just as early intervention is always more effective in work with individual clients, the same is true in the political arena: The earlier the intervention, the greater the impact. This rule has been mentioned in different ways throughout the book, whether it is working on a campaign when the candidate is just deciding to run or providing data and policy suggestions when a legislator is beginning to formulate the concept of a bill to be introduced. The concept of this rule may be clear; however, the execution is more difficult. Social workers have to keep in touch with those in the know and be ready to act quickly when opportunities arise. Clearly, this means having skills in developing trusting relationships and providing assistance when asked. Another related principle that we have emphasized is that no one else is better suited than social workers to get involved early. This principle leads us to the next rule.

People Influence People

Another rule to remember is that people influence people. You may be ready to disagree with this statement and argue that data, personal life experiences, heart-rending stories, and numbers influence legislators. Although that is true, these alone don't persuade.

People influence people through understanding each other's backgrounds and motivations, by listening carefully to concerns and objections, and by observing nonverbal cues and trying to understand the reason someone is angry or upset.

Who is better equipped than the social worker to influence other people? Social workers understand and embrace people from all walks of life. Social workers are experts—highly trained experts—in the areas of interpersonal relationships, observation and communication skills, and multiculturalism.

Stop thinking of "them"—your legislator, your delegation—as powerful and of yourself as weak. Start thinking of yourself as tough and powerful and "them" as weak, and you will have a very different perspective. Imagine how weak and ineffective legislators would seem if they were the direct line workers with these multiproblem families, trying to create self-esteem, find resources, and instill hope where there is none.

You Can Make a Difference

Do not become cynical about the "unsolvables"—poverty, physical abuse, chemical dependency. Rather, take those finely tuned skills of diagnosis, assessment, and goal setting, and begin where your job is doable—with people. Don't be overwhelmed. Many examples show how a few people can make a difference.

> One social work advocate, the executive of a two-person child advocacy organization, was concerned about the block grants that the 105th Congress was proposing. Congress was moving fast. How could one person make a difference in this process? The social worker began to ask questions, then collected data on how much the state would receive if block grants were funded on the basis of former allocation levels instead of the number of children in the state. The result was that children in his state would really suffer. This two-person organization held a press conference to propose a child population parity formula. The idea was well accepted by the media and others supported the issue. In a few days the social worker received a call from the press secretary of the U.S. House of Representatives Ways and Means chair, requesting more information. Several weeks later, the Ways and Means Committee set aside $100 million to top off the funding levels for the "fastest-growing states." Not yet ideal, but the children that the social worker was advocating for benefitted.

Know that you are one of the good guys. This story is often told by one of the best advocates we have met, Nancy Amidei:

> A good advocate is like those two good guys in the old cowboy movies, stuck up on a hill all by themselves. They're hopelessly outnumbered, and they don't stand a chance because down in the valley there is a horde of bad guys. These bad guys are mean and ugly, and they are riding hard toward the hill. So what do the good guys do? One of them gets behind a rock, gets a couple of stones, and starts making a lot of noise. The other one gets a big stick and starts whipping up a big cloud of dust. Pretty soon the bad guys down in the valley hear all that noise and rumbling; they see the huge cloud of dust and think, "Oh, no, they've got us outnumbered," and they turn around and run. Even if there are only two of you, one of you should get out there and make as much noise as you can while the other whips up the biggest possible cloud of dust. That's how our side is going to win.

Social work skills are of great value in political work. Remember always that there are times you will win and times you will lose. Whether it is a vote on the floor of your statehouse or a candidate's election, never get discouraged when you lose or become overconfident when you win.

If a student is interested in eventually running for elected office, my advice would be to work in the political sector first. There are a growing number of elected officials whose constituent services are run by social workers. These are perfect places for social work students to have a field placement or to use as an entry-level position to enter the political arena. Such practice as doing constituent work, public policy work, or working in a government agency can be a real strength when you run for office some day. The experience of suddenly being a candidate and being expected to know something about 132 issues is really hard to duplicate unless you spend some time in and around government. My point is that a legislative staff person to an elected official ends up with an extraordinary range of information that's useful in actually running for office.

Ruth Messinger, MSW
Former Manhattan Borough President

Advocacy Is Not for Wimps

To be candid, advocacy is not for wimps. You cannot bring about change if you are worried about your opponents' feelings. This statement may seem frivolous, but we have encountered social workers who worry more about "rocking the boat" or blocking communications than they do about the people who are suffering because of bad public policy. You must, of course, use your skills to your advantage; nevertheless, you must also remember that advocacy means countering the status quo and, consequently, you will have opponents. If you don't, then real change is not being proposed. Like it or not, the rules of the game have been set. You may be able to change these rules as your efforts in the political arena increase but not without entering the game as it is played today. Be comfortable with not always being liked or with perceptions that you are always angry; that's okay.

Social workers are trained to be open to others' thoughts and feelings and to be accepting of differences. We often go out of our way not to hurt or insult others or to block communication. This sensitivity, of course, is valued among our colleagues as well. We mention this because, when social workers enter the political arena, we need to remember the rules of the game and that the goal is to win. Compromise and win–win solutions are always desirable; however, bringing about change causes not only anxiety but also loss for someone, regardless of the overall social benefit. Social workers must have a thicker skin in this arena than in all the other areas of practice. Furthermore, change is difficult to bring about; successes, although pleasant, are few and far more incremental than one would hope.

Social workers need to learn to play the game of politics. Dennis Jones, MSW, former commissioner of the Texas Department of Mental Health and Mental Retardation, put it this way:

There is the stereotyped perception among many, especially social workers, that if one becomes involved in the political arena, you have compromised; ipso facto, you have dirtied your hands. They say, "Gee, that's politics, and politics is tainted." I see the needs of our clients and say, " 'Tain't enough." (personal communication)

Sometimes, strategies and approaches may seem like game playing or manipulation. There is one overriding rule in politics: Play to win. In short, if you don't, the opposition will. Social workers are the good guys, and the good guys should win.

The following is an example of playing to win. Dr. Ira Colby, former director of the School of Social Work at the University of Central Florida (now dean of the Graduate School of Social Work, University of Houston) set out to win at a public hearing. This is what happened:

The Florida House of Representatives Committee on Health and Human Services scheduled a public hearing on a controversial social service bill. In previous years, opposition groups had successfully defeated similar legislation. Once again, opponents lined up to lead a fierce attack. The bill's supporters included the Florida Chapter of NASW as well as a number of statewide social work affinity groups. The primary opponents included a conservative antigovernment group.

As required by public law, the room location and time of the hearing were announced a minimum of one day before the hearing. The room comfortably held about 100 people, and a lectern where people were to offer testimony was centered before a raised semicircular panel behind which the committee members sat.

Recognizing the importance of the first hearing, the proponents organized a simple two-step strategy. First, social workers wrote letters and telephoned the committee members' offices the week preceding the hearing. The goal was for each committee member to receive a minimum of fifty contacts.

The second stage involved recruiting 200 supporters to attend the hearing. Social workers from across the state traveled to the capitol to lend their support to the bill. In an organizational meeting the morning of the committee hearing, supporters were organized into small groups of five to eight people to visit each committee member and ask them to support the bill.

To bring visible recognition to the bill, supporters wore a blue and gold button, colors similar to Blockbuster Video Store that research shows to be the most recognizable, pleasing, and memorable colors, with a slogan relating to the bill. Supporters were cautioned not to frown or to make faces or disparaging remarks during the hearing but to act professional and cordial at all times. Finally, they were asked to personally thank the committee members when the meeting concluded and to follow up with a brief letter after they returned home.

Supporters were asked to arrive about one hour before the hearing time and occupy critical seats in the front row as well as the end seats on each row. The goal was for the committee members to look out on a sea of supporters. In addition, by occupying the seats at both ends of each row, opponents called to testify would have to climb awkwardly over other people to get to the lectern.

When the supporters arrived, they found that the opposition lobbyist had reserved six seats in the front row. Very quickly, the remaining 100 seats were filled by the bill's supporters. When the hearing began, the bill's proponents were comfortably seated while the opponents were left to stand against the wall for the two-and-a-half-hour meeting.

The last speaker for the hearing, who had helped write the bill, recognized that those standing were opponents while those seated were supporters. During his testimony, he stated that a number of people had traveled from across the state to lend their support to the bill but were not going to speak. He asked for the committee chair's permission for these people to stand up and be recognized by the committee. When the chair consented, all those seated, except for the six in the front row, stood. From the committee's perspective, it seemed that nearly everyone in the packed room supported the bill! (Remember, the opponents who were standing had no place to sit at that point and now were engulfed by the supporters.) As the meeting ended, supporters swarmed to the front of the room and essentially cut off the opponents' access to the committee members. Following the hearing, the bill's chief sponsor noted this was the best-organized hearing he had experienced in his many years as a legislator.

The lesson to be learned here is that success in the legislative process requires much more than a rational approach. Basic community organization skills are equally if not more important than the actual testimony. Nevertheless, some might see such tactics as game playing. We have said before, and it bears repeating, that we need to do whatever it takes to win.

During the 105th Congress there were numerous attempts to muffle social workers. These activities became known as the Istook Amendments. U.S. Representative Ernest Istook (R-Oklahoma) was the spokesperson for the conservative right. The approach was quite slick. The conservatives attempted to limit the activities of nonprofit advocacy organizations by reducing the amount they could spend on lobbying from 20 percent to 5 percent of their contributions. The rule applied to agencies that received federal dollars or collaborated with others that received federal dollars. The amendments did not completely prohibit nonprofits from lobbying, so social workers could not say that their constitutional right to free speech had been infringed. Representative Istook stated that these amendments would keep social service agencies from using federal dollars to lobby. The truth is that it has always been illegal to use federal money to lobby, but because his statement made it sound as if federal monies were being used to lobby, Representative Istook gained public support. The amendments were attached to the most unlikely bills at the last minute so that the opposition would not have time to fight them. Such efforts were warded off only because of continuous monitoring. This story points out that even though we may not like the game, we have no choice but to play hardball.

Speak Out

There is something that an individual social worker can do to affect other people's attitudes. Speak out whenever and wherever misinformation or stereotyping takes place. Feel empowered, and know that you know the facts, the truth. You will find more opportunities than you expected to get your message across. One easy trick to use in elevators, buses, and restrooms is to find someone you know and begin, "Hey, did you see what the Senate Human Resources Committee did yesterday?" Your friends may wonder why you are doing this to them, why you are putting them through this in front of all of these people. This friend/colleague hopefully, will say, "No, what did they do?" "They did something yesterday that could affect every working family in America, and I bet most people don't even know it." By now, the rest of the people in the elevator (train, bus) are listening attentively (Amidei, 1992).

Do it in checkout lines. When you overhear people talking—like two women talking about those lousy welfare mothers who had left their young kids at home alone—interrupt them and say, "Do you know what the cost of day care is? Do you know any jobs where you can bring your three-year-old?" Give them something to think about.

You can do it at professional meetings of all kinds. For example, at a school district meeting, educators were talking about an experimental school built for public housing students with a few new academic ideas and some high-tech stuff, making a point that this would surely "get these families off welfare." A good advocate cannot sit quietly. Educate them about the complexity of these families' problems and the variety of interventions beyond academic that are necessary.

You want to be an advocate? You want to speak up? You want to get people's attention? Do it anyplace. It doesn't make any difference where you speak out. Get the message across. An essential ingredient to political advocacy is disseminating information. We have a great deal of the real information, and information is a powerful tool. Once again, social workers are the highly trained experts, and others will be influenced by our information and opinions.

Just Say No

During a workshop that addressed shrinking budgets, the authors were astonished to hear a social worker present the "creative" idea that staff members should give up their Saturdays for staff meetings, without additional compensation, to allow them to handle even more cases. This presenter never discussed the question of the effects on the staff or the issue of burnout. There comes a time when it is better to say no than to do the job with insufficient resources.

Social workers need to learn that we don't have to "take it" when changes in policies or regulations jeopardize our practice, principles, or philosophy. **Just say no!** In privatized models, in budget reshaping and downsizing, we have too often abdicated our professional roles to volunteers, agreed to higher caseloads, or cut technology or professional development from our budgets. Social workers may have to give a little, but we must know when we are being asked to do too much. We must remember that it may be in the long-term best interest of our clients to refuse to do more with less.

Finally, and most important, keep a sense of humor. Politics can be erratic, crazy, perplexing, and discouraging as well as rewarding and stimulating. It is all right to take a rest, to find a new way of working, or to slip into the background for a while. As long as others are in need, however, it will never be all right to give up (Amidei, 1992).

Conclusion

We believe that the roots and essence of our profession compel us to enter the political arena; to do anything less would be an aberration of our historical mission and would place us in an indefensible position in the future. Social work will need to compete with many other interests in the public and legislative arenas.

We must compete effectively and consistently, developing the skills and using the technology necessary to support our advocacy efforts for our clients. We trust that this book will help you to be a more effective advocate. "When the combined efforts of both micro and macro practitioners focus on the needs of clients, social justice for all will be achieved" (Mickelson, 1995, p. 99).

If we have convinced you that all social work is political, we hope that you will also now believe that we have great power to intervene in the political arena. So here are a few last admonitions. Remember the power you have in knowledge and compassion; think about the power that comes with knowing that social work is both an avocation and a vocation; think about the power that comes from understanding that service on behalf of others is the very purpose of life and not something to be relegated to one's spare time.

Arm yourself with the power that comes from our commitment, which has held firm for more than a century to offer human dignity, nondiscrimination, equality, and social justice.

And when you are doing political social work and someone disparagingly calls you a "bleeding-heart liberal" or a "do-gooder," don't cringe and become apologetic. Stand tall and remind yourself that caring deeply and doing good are nothing of which to be ashamed. But also remember that caring deeply is not enough; taking your values, knowledge, and interactional skills into the political arena does require the abilities to challenge others' assumptions; explore alternative solutions; and arrive at clear, consistent, and defensible positions (Keller, Whittaker, and Burke, 2001).

If you are doing political social work and someone says, "You're just a social worker, what do you know about . . .?" don't stutter and become tongue-tied. Tell them, "I am a student in the only profession that te`aches systems thinking, that examines problems and issues from multiple, not single, perspectives—a profession that understands the synergism that derives from multidisciplinary analysis and a profession that has always valued collaborative rather than competitive practice."

If you are doing political social work and someone asks, "How do you know what works, you're not a researcher, you're just a social worker?" do not disparage research or quantitative analysis. Instead, say, "I have the same level of expertise as lawyers and medical doctors, an expertise that comes from a sound professional education and from informed practice."

If you are advocating and someone says, "What do social workers know about political action?" don't mutter something inaudible. Look them straight in the eye and reply loudly, "Politics is about interpersonal relations, group dynamics, mediation and negotiation, analyzing the person in an environment, and finding solutions to complex public problems. And that is exactly what social work is about!"

Finally, we hope that you are convinced that our country's basic values and beliefs and our professional code mean

- that democracy ensures the right to differing beliefs, views, and lifestyles
- that our founders rebelled against a government so powerful that it could ignore the rights of individuals
- that we value individual freedom and local control but realize the importance of vibrant and viable community projects and important protections for vulnerable people that are possible because of federal and state policies and funding
- that government is an ongoing process, not a one-shot, fix-it-by-Tuesday solution, and respectful dialogue, constant participation, and eternal vigilance are required to keep it working well
- that the profession of social work is obligated to move from case to cause in the pursuit of social justice

We hope that we have convinced you that it is social workers who can truly create more humane policies. It is social workers who understand both the fiscal and the human savings from prevention; who see the people, not only the statistics; who believe in rehabilitation, not only punishment; who are wise enough to understand that there are no simple and standard answers to most of today's complex problems. It is social workers who must continue to provide the connection between private troubles and public issues.

Leadership is a state of mind. It is not a position paper on every issue or an empty slogan. So how do we create a leadership role? First, really listen to people and the stories of their lives. We can't create an agenda out of conventional Washington analysis or think-tank memos; hear what people are saying—the innate wisdom of the neighborhoods. Second, have a defining economic and social purpose. You cannot be an effective leader with a void in the center that is filled with the latest polls and tidbits from media consultants. The purpose of leadership is to create an opportunity structure that helps people to help themselves, not with guarantees but with earned opportunities. Third, policies should attach consequences to behavior. We should reward hard work and honesty, and we have to assert the truth that there is a cost to pluralism. We do not live in a no-cost democracy. Fourth, we must hold to the habits of the heart, the great traditions of neighbor helping neighbor that built this country. And we have to be committed to helping people who have been left behind. Finally, we must empower people. We must always lead the way toward equality and human dignity.

Barbara Mikulski, MSW
U.S. Senator (Maryland)

Your Time is Now

Over the last three decades, the authors have had to deal with many political leaders who were less then supportive to human needs and services and with a profession that accepted political action slowly and reluctantly. We kept writing, teaching, and advocating in an effort to move the profession into the political arena to bring about real and lasting change. Short of Mr. Obama's being a professional social worker, we witnessed in the 2008 election change that we only dreamed of. This is a window of opportunity for us to pass the torch of affecting change to the new generation of social workers. Now is your time to take up the cause, to move the profession along, to use your political power to help others. *Your time is now!*

All Social Work Is Political, So . . .

1. On a note card, write a motivational statement about how social work advocates have made and can make a difference. Read it when things get difficult or frustrating or when others devalue your efforts.

2. Go to the website of Influencing State Policy (www.statepolicy.org) to see what things other students have done. Enter the next "Influencing State Policy contest."

3. Find a colleague who is interested in learning more about the political process. Attend meetings of a government body together; then divide up tasks to learn more about the process or an issue and share with each other what you have learned.

4. Write a brief position paper (no more than two pages) on an issue that is coming up before your state legislature or an issue that you think the legislature should address. Send the paper to your representative and to members of the appropriate committee to ask for their consideration in addressing this problem. Offer to meet with them or their aides to provide more information on the issue.

References

Amidei, Nancy. 1992. *So You Want to Make a Difference: Advocacy Is the Key,* 3rd ed. Washington, DC: Office of Management and Budget.

Gingerich, Wallace J., and Ronald Green. 1996. "Information Technology: How Social Work Is Going Digital." In *Future Issues for Social Work Practice,* Paul R. Raffoul and Aaron C. Mc-Neece (eds.), pp. 19–28. Boston, MA: Allyn & Bacon.

Hamilton, David, and David Fauri. 2001. "Social Workers/Political Participation: Strengthening the Political Confidence of Social Work Students." *Journal of Social Work Education* 37 (2): 321–332.

Influencing State Policy. Fall 1999. "Student Projects: State Policy Plus Two Entries." *Influence* 3.2: 4–5.

Influencing State Policy. 2000. "Student Projects: State Policy Plus Three Entries." *Influence* 4.2: 1–2.

Keller, Thomas E., James K. Whittaker, and Tracey K. Burke. 2001. "Student Debates in Policy Courses: Promoting Policy Practice Skills and Knowledge through Active Learning." *Journal of Social Work Education* 37 (2): 343–355.

Mickelson, James S. 1995. "Advocacy." In *Encyclopedia of Social Work,* 19th ed., pp. 95–100. Washington, DC: NASW.

Glossary of Legislative Terms

This glossary of legislative terms defines words and phrases frequently used in the legislative process. It is compiled from a variety of state and federal pamphlets.

Adjournment sine die. "Adjournment with a day." It marks the end of a legislative session because it does not set a time for reconvening.

Administrative bill. A bill proposed or favored by a governor.

Adoption. Approval or acceptance; usually applied to amendments or resolutions.

Agency bill. A bill proposed by an executive agency.

Aide. Legislative staff member, hired or appointed to perform clerical, technical, or official duties.

Amendment. Any alteration made or proposed to be made in a bill, motion, or clause thereof by adding, changing, substituting, or omitting.

Amendment, constitutional. Resolution passed by both houses that affects the Constitution; requires approval by voters at a general election. *See also* Referendum.

Appropriate. To allocate funds.

Appropriation. A legislative authorization of money in a specific amount for a specific purpose. Funds are allotted to the agencies by the budget agency after the appropriation is made by the general assembly.

Approved by governor. Signature of a governor on a bill passed by the legislature.

Assembly. The legislature, made up of a certain number of members; elected from districts apportioned on the basis of population.

Author. The member who introduces a bill in the house of origin. *See also* Sponsor.

Bill. Proposed law presented to the legislature for consideration.

Bill, emergency. A bill to take effect on signing by a governor or the president.

Bill, prefiled. Bills prepared and filed prior to the opening of a regular session.

Bill, vehicle. A bill that is introduced by title only. Because some legislation is complicated to write, for example, a school-aid distribution formula, it may not be ready to file by the filing deadline. The chairperson with responsibility for that measure files the bill under a very broad title to ensure its timely introduction.

Bill analysis. Brief summary of the purpose, content, and effect of a proposed measure.

Bill room. A room where bills may be studied. Other useful legislative material for reference purposes is also available in the bill room.

Bills, special order of. An order by the legislative body to consider and reconsider a matter that has been before the legislative body at one time.

Bloc. A group of legislators who have certain interests in common and who may vote together on matters affecting those interests (also called a caucus).

Budget. An estimate of the receipts and expenditures needed to carry out programs for a fiscal year.

Budget, executive. Suggested allocation of state money presented by the governor for consideration by the legislature.

Budget agency. An executive agency that prepares the budget document for the governor or the president.

Budget bill. A bill specifying the amounts approved by the general assembly for each program of state government.

Budget committee. A committee of legislators that acts in an advisory capacity to the budget agency between sessions of the general assembly (also called an appropriations committee).

Calendar (House).   A daily list, prepared by the speaker, of the bills eligible for second and third readings that day.

Calendar (Senate).   A daily list of all bills eligible for second or third readings that day.

Chair.   Presiding officer or chairperson.

Chamber.   Official hall for the meeting of a legislative body.

Clerk of the House.   The chief administrative officer elected by the members.

Code.   A systematic and complete compilation of the laws on a given subject. A code supersedes all prior acts on the subject.

Committee, ad hoc.   A committee appointed for some special purpose. The committee automatically dissolves on the completion of its specified task.

Committee chair.   A member appointed to function as the parliamentarian head of a standing or special committee in the consideration of matters assigned to such committee by the legislative body.

Committee of the whole.   A parliamentary device by which the entire membership of one house sits as a committee to consider legislation. Like other committees, it reports its recommendations to the house.

Companion bill.   Two or more bills dealing with related aspects of the same topic (also called a tie bar).

Concurrence.   Action by which one house agrees to a proposal or action that the other house has approved. A proposal may be amended, adopted, or returned to the other house for concurrence.

Concurrent resolution.   A statement of the attitude or feeling of the two houses not having the force of law.

Conference committee.   A bill may be passed by both houses but in differing forms. If the house of origin objects to the version passed by the second house, a special committee is appointed by the leadership of each house to reconcile the differences.

Constituent.   A citizen residing within the district of a legislator.

Constitutional amendment.   A change in the provisions of a constitution by modifying, deleting, or adding portions.

Constitutional majority.   A constitutional majority is a bare majority of all members of each house, not merely the majority of members voting on a given issue.

Contingency fund.   Money appropriated by the respective houses for incidental operating expenses.

Convene.   The meeting of the legislature daily, weekly, and at the beginning of a session as provided by the Constitution or law.

Convention, constitutional.   The assembling of delegates for the purpose of writing or revising a constitution.

Convention, joint.   The assembling of both houses of the legislature for a meeting.

Cosponsor.   One of two or more persons proposing any bill or resolution.

Day certain.   Adjournment with a specific day to reconvene.

Debate.   Discussion of a matter according to parliamentary rules.

Digest.   A brief summary of the contents of a bill, which must be attached to the bill before introduction.

Dissent.   Difference of opinion; also, to cast a negative vote.

District.   The division of the state represented by a legislator. These can be designated numerically or by geographical boundaries.

Division.   A method of voting.

Division of question.   Procedure to separate a matter to be voted on into two or more questions.

Do pass.   The affirmative recommendation made by a committee in sending a bill to the floor for additional action; "Do pass as amended" means that a committee recommends certain changes in a bill.

Effective date.   A law becomes binding either on a date specified in the law itself or, in the absence of such date, within a certain number of days specified by the Constitution or law.

Emergency clause.   A phrase added to a bill to make it effective immediately after passage and signing by the governor or president. Laws normally become effective after copies of the acts are distributed to the clerks of the circuit courts.

En bloc voting.   To consider in a mass or as a whole; for example, to adopt or reject a series of amendments by a single vote.

Enabling act.   A statute that makes it lawful to do something that otherwise would be illegal. In some states, the legislature enacts a law that becomes operative only on the adoption by the people of an amendment to the Constitution.

Engrossing.   A procedure for incorporating any amendments and checking the accuracy of a printed bill.

Ex officio.   Holding two offices, one of which is held by virtue or because of the first; for example, the lieutenant governor is also a member of the state senate.

Executive committee action.   The formal recommendation of a standing committee on any proposal referred to such committee for consideration.

Executive session.   A session excluding from the chamber all persons other than members and essential staff personnel.

First reading.   To read for the first of three times the bill or title for consideration.

Fiscal note.   States the estimated amount of increase or decrease in revenue or expenditures and the present and future fiscal implications of pending legislation.

Fiscal year.   An accounting period of one year.

Floor.   That portion of the assembly chamber reserved for members and officers of the legislature and other persons granted the privilege of the floor.

Gallery.   Balconies over the chamber from which visitors may view proceedings of the legislature.

Governor's proclamation.   A means by which the governor may call an extra or special session.

Grandfather clause.   Laws providing new or additional professional qualifications often contain a "grandfather clause" exempting persons presently practicing the affected profession from having to comply.

Hearing.   A session of a legislative committee at which witnesses present testimony on bills under consideration.

House.   The federal legislative body more commonly known as the House of Representatives; the lower house of the General Assembly.

House of origin.   The chamber in which a measure is first introduced is known as its house of origin. A bill is filed with either the clerk of the House or the secretary of the Senate, is numbered, and is assigned to a committee. One can determine from a bill's number its house of origin. Numbers given to legislation introduced in the House are preceded by HB (House bill).

Numbers assigned to Senate bills begin SB (Senate bill).

Immediate effect.   Legislative action to render a law effective at an earlier date than the normal course of events would allow. For example, "Takes effect upon" is usually written into the bill.

Introducer.   One who presents a matter for consideration. Cointroducers are those who subsequently sign a bill or resolution. The primary introducer is the first named of several introducers.

Introduction.   The formal presentation of a bill or resolution for consideration.

Journal.   An official chronological record of the action taken and proceedings of the respective houses.

Law.   A bill passed by both houses and signed by the governor or president. A bill also may become law if each house, by majority vote, overrides the governor's or president's veto.

Legislative study committee.   Frequently an ad hoc committee is established with membership selected by the leadership to work on a controversial subject between sessions in the hope that legislation acceptable to both houses can be developed.

Lobbyist.   A representative of a special interest who attends sessions of the legislature to influence legislation.

Majority leader.   A member of the house chosen by members of the majority party as their leader and floor spokesperson.

Majority party.   Party having the greater number of members in the legislature of either house.

Majority whip.   A member of the House or Senate designated to perform certain functions, usually of a partisan nature.

Members elect.   Members who are elected but who have not taken the oath of office or are not officially serving.

Members present.   Refers to those members who are actually present at a daily session.

Message from the Senate or House.   Official communication from the opposite house read into the official record.

Minority leader.   A member of the minority party designated to be the leader.

Minority party.   Party having the fewest members in the legislature or either house.

Minority report.   A report that reflects the thinking of the members not favoring the majority position on action on an issue.

Minority whip. A member of the legislature designated to perform certain functions, usually of a partisan nature.

Minutes. Accurate record in chronological order of the proceedings of a meeting.

Motion. Formal proposal offered by a member of a deliberative assembly.

Motion, main. A consideration of a bill is a main motion. Consideration of an amendment to that bill would be a subsidiary or secondary motion. Consideration of a bill may be postponed. Consideration of an amendment to that bill generally cannot be deferred to another day when the body is to continue its deliberations on the bill because the body in the meantime may dispose of the main questions.

Motion to reconsider. A move that places the question in the same status in which it was prior to the vote on the question.

Nondebatable. Subjects or motions that cannot be discussed or debated.

Officers. That portion of the legislative staff elected by the membership, for example, the Speaker of the House or the whip.

Out of order. Business that is not conducted under proper parliamentary rules and procedures.

Pair or pairing. An arrangement between two members of a house by which they agree to be recorded on opposite sides of an issue and to be absent when the vote is taken.

Parliament inquiry. Question posed to the chair for clarification of a point in the proceedings.

Party caucus. Each party convenes all its members to elect leaders and establish party positions on specific issues. Party discipline can be very strict, and on certain major issues individual legislators are discouraged from taking independent positions. The party leadership can exert strong influence.

Party leadership. Within the legislature, party leadership consists of the majority leader (in the House called the Speaker and in the Senate the president pro tempore), the minority leader, and their whips. They are elected by their respective caucuses.

Passage of bill. Favorable action on a measure before either house.

Per diem. Literally, "per day"; daily expense money rendered to legislators and personnel.

Petition. A formal request submitted by an individual or group of individuals to the legislature.

Plank. Statements on issues that form the foundation of a political party's platform.

Platform. The principles and policies of a political party.

Point of order. Calling attention to a breach of order or rules.

Postpone indefinitely. A means of disposing of an issue by not setting a date to reconsider the same.

Postpone to a day certain. To defer consideration to a definite later time or day.

Precedent. Interpretation of rulings by presiding officers on specific rules; also unwritten rules that are established by custom.

Prefile. List of all bills, amendments, and resolutions filed before a session convenes.

President of the Senate. By constitutional enactment, the lieutenant governor; title of the person who presides over the Senate (may vary by state).

President pro tempore. The majority floor leader in the Senate who presides in the absence of the president of the Senate.

Presiding officer. Person designated to preside at a legislative session.

Previous question. A motion to close debate and bring the pending question or questions to an immediate vote.

Procedures. Rules and traditional practices of the respective houses of the legislature.

Promulgation. A proclamation of a governor declaring that the acts of the general assembly have been distributed as required by law.

Proof of publication. A regulation requiring the journal to show that the legislature has determined that notice of intention to apply for passage of any local or special law was published in the affected community the required number of days prior to introduction of the proposed law.

Public acts. Enacted acts.

Public laws. Legislation enacted into law. A bill, as passed by both houses of the legislature, that has been enrolled, certified, approved by the governor, or passed over the governor's veto, and published.

Publication clause. Section incorporated in a bill to enable legislation to become effective on a specific date.

Question, privileged. Those questions that, according to rules or by consent of the assembly, shall have precedence.

Quorum. The number of members of a house who must be present for the body to conduct business.

Ratify. To approve and make valid.

Reading. Presentation of a bill before either house by the reading of the title; a stage in the enactment of a measure.

Reading, first. A bill is read aloud on the floor of the House or Senate by title only and is assigned to a committee by the Speaker of the House or the president of the Senate.

Reading, second. After a committee finishes its work on a measure, it may report it out of committee. Copies of the legislation are printed and distributed to all members of the appropriate house. At this juncture, called the second reading, debate takes place in the chamber and a bill can be amended, killed, or passed.

Reading, third. A bill is reprinted with second-reading changes incorporated. Its title is read for a third time. At this point a two-thirds majority is necessary to amend the bill. A final vote is taken, and the legislation either passes or fails.

Ready list. List of all proposed legislation reported out of committee and ready to be placed on the agenda.

Recall (a bill). Request by a house that the other house or the governor return a bill, usually for a corrective amendment.

Recede. Withdraw from an amendment or position on a matter.

Recess. Intermission in a daily session.

Recommit. To send back to committee for further investigation or to another committee.

Reconsideration. A motion that, when granted, gives rise to another vote annulling or reaffirming an action previously taken.

Record. By custom, members of a legislative body often request that the record show a statement or that it be recorded a certain way. These requests, if approved, are entered in the journal and are said to be "on the record."

Referendum. A vote at the polls for the purpose of allowing the wishes of the people on a subject to be expressed. A referendum may be held on any issue.

Referral. The sending or referring of a bill to committee.

Regular order of business. The established sequence of business set up for each legislative day.

Regulation. A rule or order of an agency promulgated under the authority of a statute passed by the legislature.

Rejection. An action that defeats a bill, motion, or other matter.

Repeal. A method by which legislative action is revoked or abrogated.

Representative. A member of the House of Representatives.

Rerefer. The reassignment of a bill or resolution to a committee.

Rescind. Annulment of an action previously taken.

Resolution. A document expressing the sentiment or intent of the legislature, governing the business of the legislature, or expressing recognition.

Resolution, joint. A form of legislation used to pose amendments. Joint resolutions do not become laws and do not require a signature by the governor.

Resolution, Senate or House. Same as a concurrent resolution except it is the expression of one house.

Revenue. Yield of taxes and other sources of income the state collects.

Revised code. Statutory laws of the state.

Roll call. The recording of the presence of members or the taking of a vote on a bill.

Roster. Booklet containing names of members, officers, employees, and a list of standing committees and districts of each house for the current session.

Rules. Regulating principles; methods of procedure.

Rules, joint. Rules governing the relationship and affecting matters between the two houses.

Rules, standing. Permanent rules adopted by each house for the duration of the session.

Rules, suspended. Temporarily setting aside the rules.

Rules, temporary. Practices usually adopted at the beginning of each session until standing rules are adopted, generally consisting of the standing rules of the preceding session.

Rules, waive. A procedural step used to forgo a rule in order to speed the process of enactment of a measure.

Second house. A house other than the house of origin.

Secretary of the Senate. A nonmember officer of the Senate elected or appointed by the members to serve as chief administrative officer.

Section.   A portion of the codes; sections are cited in each bill that propose to amend, create, or replace the same.

Segment.   A portion of a bill.

Select committee.   A special committee of legislators, members of the Senate, or members of the House.

Senate.   The upper house of the General Assembly, consisting of fifty members.

Seniority.   Recognition of prior legislative service, sometimes used in making committee assignments.

Session.   Period during which the legislature meets.

Session, daily.   Each day's meeting of a legislative body.

Session, extraordinary.   Special session called by and limited to matters specified by the governor.

Session, joint.   Meeting of the two houses together.

Session, regular.   The annual session at which all classes of legislation may be considered.

Simple resolution.   An expression of the sentiments of one house on matters related to that house. A simple resolution does not require action by the other house.

Sine die.   Adjournment without a day being set for reconvening. Final adjournment.

Speaker of the House.   The presiding officer of the House of Representatives, chosen by the members.

Speaker pro tempore.   Substitute presiding officer, taking the chair on request of the Speaker in his absence; elected by the body.

Special order.   Matter of business set for a special time and day.

Sponsor.   A member who agrees to introduce and support a bill in the second house after its passage by the house of origin. *See also* Author.

Standing committee.   Regular committees of the legislature set up to perform certain legislative functions.

State the question.   To place a question before a legislature for its consideration.

Statutory committee.   A committee created by statute.

Stopping the clock.   Practice of lengthening the hours of the legislative day, irrespective of the passing of the hours of the calendar day.

Strike out.   Delete language from a bill or resolution.

Stripping.   The entire contents of one bill may be deleted and a completely new measure inserted under the title of the old bill. It is a technique employed to resurrect a measure that may have died in committee.

Substitute.   An amendment that replaces an entire bill or resolution.

Sufficient seconds.   The support of the number of members required to make certain motions and procedures.

Supplemental appropriation.   Adjustment of funds allocated over the original allocation.

Table.   A means of disposing of a bill or other matter for an indefinite period of time.

Term.   Duration of office of an elected official.

Title.   Statement of the general subject of a bill.

Unanimous consent.   Usually requested to suspend rules for a specific purpose.

Unfinished.   Business that has been laid over from a previous day.

Uniform and model acts.   Legislation recommended by various national groups for passage in all or several states. Uniform acts are prepared by the Conference of Commissioners on Uniform State Laws and are intended to be adopted verbatim by the various states. Model acts are prepared by numerous organizations to serve as guides for state legislation and may be modified to suit each individual state.

Veto.   The president's or governor's disapproval of a bill passed by both houses of the General Assembly. The governor is allowed a set number of days to sign or veto a bill or allow it to become law without his signature. Bills vetoed during a session must be returned to the house of origin for reconsideration, and vetoes may be overridden by the vote of a constitutional majority in each house.

Veto override.   To pass a bill over the president's or governor's veto.

Voice vote.   Oral expression of the members when a question is submitted for their determination. Response is given by yeas and nays, and the presiding officer states the decision as to which side prevailed.

Vote.   Formal expression of the will or decision of the body.

Vote, division and rising.   To vote by a show of hands or by standing.

Vote, en bloc.   To dispose of several items, such as a series of amendments, by taking one vote.

Vote, record. A roll call vote in which members answer to their names and announce their votes yea or nay. Each vote is recorded in the journal.

Vote, roll call. Individual votes of members are recorded in the journal.

Whip. An elected member whose duty it is to keep the rest of the members informed as to the decisions of the leadership.

Withdraw a motion. To recall or remove a motion according to parliamentary procedure.

Without recommendation. A committee report that is neither favorable nor unfavorable.

Yeas and nays. Recorded vote of members on an issue.

Yield. The relinquishing of the floor to another member to speak or ask a question.

Index